Power Quotes

Power Quotes

For Life, Business, and Leadership

Danai Krokou

BEP BUSINESS EXPERT PRESS

Power Quotes: For Life, Business, and Leadership

First published in 2018 by
Business Expert Press, LLC
222 East 46th Street, New York, NY 10017
www.businessexpertpress.com

ISBN-13: 978-1-63157-749-9 (paperback)
ISBN-13: 978-1-63157-750-5 (e-book)

Business Expert Press Human Resource Management and Organizational Behavior Collection

Collection ISSN: 1946-5637 (print)
Collection ISSN: 1946-5645 (electronic)

Cover and interior design by Exeter Premedia Services Private Ltd., Chennai, India

First edition: 2018

10 9 8 7 6 5 4 3 2 1

Printed in the United States of America.

Yes. To all of you who dare and risk ....

Abstract

Would you fancy an intellectual vitamin mix that inspires and motivates you to greatness? Much has changed in the past decades. Genuine wisdom, though, has not. Because it never does. The quotes featured in this book are not your typical quotes. My aim through this book is to offer you the best bits of the best minds. Most of us lead busy, stressful lives that leave little space for daily introspection. I believe there is a quote for every situation or challenge life throws at us. Most of the statements you will find here are the distillation of the experience of a lifetime. Thousands of quotes were evaluated and arranged by subject based on their relevance, originality, motivational power, and depth of meaning. Language shapes behavior. Through your reading you will notice that certain quotes are a call to action while others an opportunity for contemplation. Throughout human history, great leaders have used the power of words to transform our emotions, to engage us in their causes, and to shape the course of History. *Power Quotes* span from Antiquity to the 21st century. These statements were thought, spoken, and written by people as unrelated as Alexander the Great, Confucius, Shakespeare, Leonardo Da Vinci, Dalai Lama, Aristotle, Machiavelli, Einstein, Oscar Wilde, Bill Gates, or Mother Teresa. The book is divided into three main sections. Each section is introduced by personal thoughts and theories on Life, Business, and Leadership. Theories I live and swear by. Theories that I have developed over the course of many years rich in life, study, travel, and business experience. *Power Quotes* have been a great source of inspiration for me and have helped change and shape my personal and professional life for the better. It is my hope that they will have a similar impact on yours.

Keywords

Bucephalus Complex, business, Corporate Fingerprint (CF), entrepreneurship, inspirational quotes, leadership, maxims, motivational quotes, leadership, Unique Personality Pairings (UPP), Unique Skill Pairings (USP), world philosophy

Contents

Most people are other people. Their thoughts are someone else's opinions, their life a mimicry, their passions a quotation.

—Oscar Wilde, *De Profundis*

A Word About Words

It has been said of Winston Churchill that he took the English language and sent it into battle. I believe this is exactly what you have the power to do with words too. You have the possibility to send them into battle against negative thoughts and wrong perspectives that sabotage your life and career goals. You can use them as a way to influence your worldviews, actions or mood of the moment. Words count. They are powerful vehicles that convey meanings, thoughts and emotions. It's through smart use that you can turn them into valuable tools. I have always regarded words as containers of creative power and I believe that it is up to us to decide what kind of power we want our words to carry. As Tom Stoppard said "Words are sacred. They deserve respect. If you get the right ones, in the right order, you can nudge the world a little."

Life and Business can look terrifying with the right (wrong) perspective. Would you fancy an intellectual vitamin mix that inspires and motivates you to greatness? This is the aim of these quotations. I am passionate about quotes. Quotes are records of the wisest, most memorable—and often—funniest things ever said. My aim through this book is to offer you the best bits of the best minds. I believe that if a book has one sentence, passage, main idea or core message with the power to change a person's life, this very bit alone justifies reading the whole book. From my earliest childhood I've developed a deep love for books, I spent countless hours of my life reading all sorts of books, from academic books to literature and self-development books. Books written in various languages by people who lived in different time periods and countries. I have always wished to read a book that would gather all the "aha" moments I went through many years of reading, all these sentences that had a great impact on my heart and mind. *Power Quotes* is precisely the sort of book that I've always wanted to enjoy as a reader in moments of major life transition. I found that it is in periods of change—like taking a flight to the other side of the planet to settle there, or starting a brand new business venture—that powerful quotes have influenced me the most.

The quotes featured in this book are not your typical quotes. I have only included the ones I can't live without. These statements ignite in me the desire to pause and reflect, the urge to make life-changing decisions, set goals and work towards achieving them. Thousands of quotes were evaluated based on their relevance to the main title, their originality, motivational power, their depth of meaning and also what I call "quotational gravity," that is, the weight and authority that the original author adds to a particular statement. For instance the statement "If I had known, I'd become a shoemaker" is nothing but a casual phrase that could come from the mouth of any person who took a wrong career turn. It gains a lot of weight though when you know that the person who spoke this phrase was Albert Einstein, when, in the beginning of his career, his theories received a lot of skepticism and rejection by a large part of the scientific community of the time.

Power Quotes is divided into three main sections: *Life, Business,* and *Leadership.* Each section includes various topics that are relevant to the main title. Some could argue that I should have included Leadership as a subtopic under the *Business* section but I regard *Leadership* as a major life skill, a skill that should not be solely limited to the workplace. You may also notice that some quotes and topics can be applied to all three sections. For instance *Learning* is a subtopic that I chose to place under the *Business* section, but is equally applicable to *Leadership* and *Business.* Each section is introduced with a few personal thoughts and theories on the subject. In the comments section you will discover my personal philosophy on leadership and career development. Theories I live and swear by.

I believe that variety can only bring more inspiration; to reflect complexity in *Life, Leadership* and *Business* I have purposely selected quotes which complement and very often contradict each other. By doing this, my intention is to take you on an emotional roller-coaster ride. I included various quotes in each section to create a mix of optimism, pessimism, humor and philosophy. I hope that instead of causing the reader confusion, such quotes will offer food for thought by helping you consider one same topic from different angles. You will be able to notice that different quotes on a same topic will cause mixed feelings and thoughts. Some will leave you rather confused while others will make you feel enthusiastic about a new idea or a brand new way of perceiving *Life* and *Business*. I encourage you to write down or simply underline the quotes that are most relevant to you—the ones that make you tick—and integrate them into your daily life. I have myself divided my favorite quotes into subsections to match various circumstances of my own life.

Statements that you will find in *Power Quotes* were collected from many sources. They date back to Antiquity and extend to the beginning of the 21st century. The words, thoughts and ideas that you will find in there originated in the minds and mouths of influential people of different nationality, culture, social class, religion, profession, and so on. Many quotes were originally uttered by historic figures, philosophers and politicians, while others by entrepreneurs, industry leaders and scientists. Some were written by writers, poets and artists. You will find quotes by people as unrelated to each other as Aristotle, Leonardo Da Vinci, Confucius, Shakespeare, Mahatma Gandhi, Machiavelli, Margaret Thatcher, Bill Gates or Alexander the Great. You will also find many statements by lesser known individuals, next door professionals, CEOs and people who make a big difference in their workplace and community. Studying the wisdom of the ages in a society that is being accused of bringing shallowness and dumbing-down to new heights is a vital step toward regaining ethical and intellectual standards.

Life often comes down to a chaotic mix of opposing ideas and systems of thought. It's an arena where differing perspectives and possible ways of being fight for supremacy. There is no instruction manual to life. There are a billion possible lives you can live. Every quote represents a life stance. I like to think of each quotation as a distinct line, an axis passing through a single point. There are an infinite number of lines that can pass through this point, each one of them pointing to a different direction. I invite you to see every topic as that single point and the lines passing through it as the thoughts and arguments that can be expressed about this topic. It's up to you how you will choose to engineer your life map. You plan your day in advance because you know well that "failing to plan is planning to fail". If it makes good sense to plan your daily actions why not plan your daily thoughts and emotions as well? That would be great, right? After all it is thoughts that guide actions. Fueling your actions with the right thoughts and statements can only add to your success in Life and Business. Incorporating *Power Quotes* in your everyday routine can only be beneficial.

As humans we are hardwired to observe patterns. It is more or less consciously that we scan daily life events in order to detect mechanisms and fundamental patterns we can use for survival and happiness. We are on the lookout for a better system, a better pattern that will allow us to lead more meaningful and prosperous lives. What I like about powerful inspirational statements is that they invite the reader to contemplate an alternative existence, a career they never thought before, a different life direction, a new challenging goal. Maintenance is required though. I believe motivation is a muscle. It doesn't happen by itself and it doesn't last long. You have to train, maintain and feed it daily or it will become atrophied. Likewise, I regard success less as a linear process leading to a goal and more like a muscle you develop gradually. You cannot succeed at some point in your career and just rest on your laurels. It is daily practice and training at being successful that guarantees long-term success in Business and Life.

The statements included here have been a source of reflection and inspiration for me. They have influenced my worldviews, shaken certain beliefs, stimulated my imagination, strengthened my willpower, and helped me overcome tough challenges in my own personal and professional life. I have been using many of these quotes as a daily vitamin to uplift my mood and enter into the most advantageous mood state depending on the specific situation I find myself in. Words are wonderful things. They are free though and can be misused. If used in a wrong way language can end up being pretty limiting, demoralizing, and often destructive. What makes *Power Quotes* effective is that the impact words have in our brain, emotions, habits, and decisions is not only immediate, but also *ongoing*. People tend to perceive words—especially spoken ones—as volatile and impermanent. Words do fly but not as far as you might think. If not used in a smart and conscious way they can turn into haunting bats. Optimum use of positively loaded language is necessary to uplift our mood and thus enable our brain to function at its best before it can serve the life goals each of us has set for themselves.

The strength of *Power Quotes* lies precisely on the *ongoing* power carried by *intentionally* spoken words. The impact of those words and thoughts that we, either consciously or unconsciously, keep repeating in our mouths and heads is unbelievably strong. The main aim of this book is to be a source of inspiration and a trigger for action in your daily life. In the pages that follow you will find powerful statements that will stimulate your brain and nourish your soul. These statements will hopefully motivate you to stand up and step forth, from where you stand currently to where you want to move next on various levels of your life. These quotes have helped change and shape my professional and personal life for the better. It is my hope that they will have a similar impact on yours.

Speeding up Your Emotional Metabolism

Words are multidimensional. They come in different forms, shapes and sizes. Some carry heavy meanings and a greater intensity while others are much "lighter." Words can be thought, spoken, heard, and written. They can be totally yours. They can be adapted and molded at wish to fit any situation and convey a message. Most importantly, they have the power to *ignite action*. What I find phenomenal about words is their ability to inspire us to rise above adversity and pursue goals. By the same token, if used in a wrong way, they can cause self-doubt, inhibit creativity, and sometimes even destroy careers and relationships. Are the thoughts you think and the words you speak bringing you closer to your life goals? Do the words you utter help you to better navigate life's challenges and achieve your professional goals? Or do they rather sabotage your career potential and life project?

Your mind is an incredibly elaborate engine. In the same way that your physical metabolism deals with hormonal imbalances and regulates your overall body weight through the thyroid gland, your mind is a system whose main function is to keep you sane and mentally balanced. How powerful your emotional metabolism is defines how successfully you process thoughts, eliminate toxic emotions and make decisions. The greatest advantage of a healthy and powerful emotional metabolism is its ability to bounce back to its optimum performance level after having reached bottom. Both success and failure are part of life adventure. The point is to learn to love your downs as much as you love your ups and regard them as a stepping stone, a valuable lesson and an essential part of your overall life experience. Before you can even put your emotional metabolism to work, it is necessary that you develop a much more basic skill: emotional hygiene.

Have you ever wondered why most people function below their actual potential? I believe poor emotional hygiene is the major reason. What do most of us know about emotional hygiene though? What do we know about our emotional health? Not much. Children learn to take care of their physical health and know how to brush their teeth three times a day and clean a cut before they can spell their name. As we grow older we dedicate more time and resources taking care of our car and house than the greatest asset we will ever possess: our mind. Physical health seems more important than our emotional health. However, we sustain psychological injuries more often than we do physical ones. Failure, rejection, guilt, loneliness, and loss are only a few emotional traumas many of us deal with on a daily basis. The thing about physical injuries is that they are too obvious to be ignored. Ignoring a broken leg is simply not an option. Likewise, emotional wounds, if not treated properly can impact your life in a very negative way in the long run.

A 100 years ago with the development of Psychoanalysis people started practicing emotional hygiene and–in just a matter of decades–with the combined efforts of medicine, life expectancy rose by more than 50 percent. Our lives can improve dramatically if we practice emotional hygiene in a regular manner. Words are a great vehicle for this. Can you imagine how the world would be if all of us were emotionally healthier? If there was less loneliness and less depression? If people knew how to stay unaffected by repeated failures? If they felt fulfilled and empowered to pursue their life and career goals? What is astonishing about practicing emotional hygiene is that, by changing your perception, you change the game. The life game. The business game.

Many studies have shown that the brain of an average individual produces no less than 70,000 thoughts in a day. The conscious mind controls only 5 percent of our daily thoughts, while the remaining 95 percent is controlled by the subconscious part. It is important to realize that something as intangible and volatile as thoughts and words can have tangible, biological effects. Emotion is a key factor in how your subconscious mind processes and stores information. The more emotionally charged the experience, the more impactful and long-lasting the memory will be. As a result, language needs to be inspiring, creative, uplifting, and generative to affect your nervous system in a positive and effective way and help propel you to success in *Life* and *Business*. It is through creating optimum *self-induced mood states* that you will be able to put language at your service and fully experience its power. The aim is to prime your mind for action; it is all about getting into a mood that encourages motivation and ignites the urge for action.

To better understand what I mean by this, imagine this works in the same way one would use naughty words to arouse sexually their partner, causing them to manifest the desired physical reaction. Or, in the way coaches use powerful words of encouragement to drive their athletes toward their optimum level of performance. In *Power Quotes* though, you have both roles to perform; you are the trainer and the trainee, all at the same time. First, it is by identifying those statements that make you tick the most and fit best your specific life experience, situation and goals then it is by integrating them into your life like some sort of personal mantra that you can find your gateway to instant mental self-arousal. People possess brains and lots of action potential that remains dormant thus limiting their chances of success and happiness in life. It is time to give your emotional metabolism a kick! It is a painless, equipment-free process. Just a few minutes of daily "me" time and the willingness to access a more advantageous mood state.

People tend to feel as strong as their last success and as weak as their last failure. Is this though the way things should be? Absolutely not. The problem is that every single day, all of us are exposed to an unhealthy amount of advertising and brand messages. Corporations keep exploring more subtle ways to penetrate our subconscious mind by applying elements of behavioral psychology in their marketing strategy and advertising campaigns. This is fine and great business for them but not for you. Your mind gets hijacked every single day without you even noticing. It requires, in fact, a superhuman ability and focus power to maintain ownership of your own mind. Don't allow anyone to hijack your mind and your mental health defense mechanisms. Sanity is not merely about "being normal," rather it is about being *aware* and in control of one's thoughts, words, and actions.

We all have a default set of beliefs and feelings that gets triggered whenever we encounter frustrations and setbacks. Are you aware of how your mind reacts to daily emotional challenges? Unfortunately, our minds are not the trustworthy friends we think they are. They are a rather moody friend who can be supportive for a while, then totally unpleasant the next moment. Studies have shown that when our self-esteem is low we are more vulnerable to stress, anxiety, a weak immune system, and low productivity. Rumination of negative thoughts is one of the most common and dangerous emotional habits. All of us do it. By changing your reaction to failure, by battling negative thinking you won't just heal your emotional wounds. By practicing emotional hygiene you lay the foundation for success in life and business. Most importantly, being in full possession of your thoughts and emotions will make you the master of your mind.

Power Quotes can be read in two ways: as an energy-boosting drink or as a remedy. You can read the book from start to finish like you would read most books. You can sit back, make yourself comfortable, and enjoy the thoughts of some of the world's most influential minds to reflect, boost your motivation and see life from various angles. It's a bit like having an energy drink as a way to instantly boost your energy levels. The book can also be read in another way, in which case the order you will choose to read each section or subtopic will be dictated by the needs or mood of the moment. Pretty much in the way you would take a paracetamol pill to treat a headache, you can choose a more targeted reading approach by selecting specific topics which are relevant to your situation at a given time. Say you feel down after a bad day at work, a breakup, an argument with a member of your team, when dealing with Sunday night blues or when facing life's greatest challenges like an illness or the loss of someone dear.

I found that the second way of reading *Power Quotes* has a more powerful impact on me than the first one. Don't listen to me though! Test both ways and choose the one that serves your needs best. When you finish reading a particular section you might either feel more confused or clearer about a specific topic or aspect affecting your life. Either way you choose to read it, *Power Quotes* will demand a small amount of homework from your side and mental presence. Although at the very beginning I was using quotes in a more self-centered way–aiming to cheer myself up when I was in a not-so-high mood, at the end of an exhausting week or when I needed to supercharge my motivation reserves before a challenging negotiation or a critical agreement–I later found that quotes must be passed around to people who need inspiration to overcome daily challenges and recover from life's misfortunes. I understood the real impact *Power Quotes* can have when I started posting them to friends when they needed them the most; after a major setback, during a serious health problem or in the aftermath of a painful breakup. It is all about looking at career challenges and life obstacles from a different perspective, so that you can transform your relationships, your team and workplace, and ultimately, your whole life.

Through your reading you will notice that certain quotes are a call to action while others an opportunity for contemplation. Whatever your reaction might be, I suggest that you let your thoughts run wild and let them take you where they will. Allow those who speak to your particular situation take deep root and manifest their hidden power. They will hopefully help clarify your life purpose, ignite a desire for action and the urge to achieve your life goals. It is possible that you have a different understanding of a same quote than another person. You may also find that reading a same quote again, when in a different mood, or at a later stage of your life, might lead your thoughts to a different direction. I believe that great quotes are timeless. The interpretation you make of them will fit your particular life context.

The aim of these quotes is to make you reflect on your own life situation. Words as beautiful and inspiring as they are won't help you unless *you* act. Their full potential cannot be experienced unless they affect your physical reality, that is, unless they transform you not only mentally but also on a physical and material level. Effectively putting words and thoughts into action will lead to a transformation of your physical surroundings, your daily reality and, hopefully, your overall life condition. The amount of attention you will give each one of them and the pace at which you read them, the time you take to pause and reflect quote after quote are all essential in turning these statements into executive orders. Make these quotes work for you!

Life

Life is too short to be small.

—Benjamin Disraeli

The Essence of Life

"Live as you were living already for the second time" Viktor Frankl, a 20th century Austrian medical doctor, psychiatrist and Holocaust survivor, famously said and I made of this quote one of my favorite statements on Life. There is nothing that expresses better my personal philosophy on how life should be lived than this great quote, which invites us to imagine that the present is past, and that the past may yet be amended. Perceiving life from this angle confronts us with life's *finiteness* in general and ultimately brings up the question of the *finality* of our own concrete life. Your life goal is yours to set. It is sad to see that so many people instead of regarding themselves as taskmasters of their own life actually behave as if their lives were a task, almost a chore assigned to them. Does your life goal revolve around your professional growth, career ambitions, and personal development? Is it about being an agent of positive change within your family or wider community? It is up to you to define what the finality, your very *raison d'être* is.

Michel de Montaigne, one of the most influential writers of the French Renaissance, said that *"we are entirely made up of bits and pieces, woven together so diversely and so shapelessly that each one of them pulls its own way at every moment."* This is not only a very accurate definition of the human condition but also a great definition about the complexity and contradictions of life itself. Life is about survival. No big news here. In his 1946 book, *Man's Search for Meaning*, Viktor Frankl shares his experience as one of the few survivors of Nazi extermination camps. Many prisoners who desperately hoped to survive finally died, most of them in the gas chambers and many from disease. Unlike other Holocaust survivors though, Frankl didn't write that book with the aim to share the suffering and horror he went through. Rather than describing his experience as a prisoner in Auschwitz, the hardships he faced, and how all these prisoners died, he focused on *why anyone survived at all*. He describes how those prisoners who had lost all hope and finally gave up on life were inevitably the first to die. They died more from lack of hope and a reason to live than from a lack of medicine and proper food. By contrast, Frankl managed to keep himself alive thanks to his mental strength. It was through summoning up images and thoughts of his wife and family and the prospect of seeing them again that he managed to survive 3 years in the camps. During the same period he set a major goal: to return to university after the war and teach his students the lessons he learned from his camp experience. Most importantly, his experience reinforced what was already his main life philosophy: life is not a quest for pleasure, as Freud taught, nor a quest for power, as Alfred Adler, a fellow Austrian psychotherapist believed, but rather a *quest for meaning*.

Frankl thus believed that the greatest task of any individual is to find *meaning* in their life. He identified three main sources of meaning: work (which consists in doing something substantial), love (caring for another person or the community), and courage (the quality of mind and spirit that enables a person to face adversity) during hard times. He regarded suffering as something *meaningless*. He also believed that people are the ones who attribute meaning to their suffering by the way they choose to respond to it. Frankl's most enduring insight is one that many of us have experienced in various life circumstances: forces beyond one's control can take away everything, except *one* thing: your freedom to choose how you will react to that situation. Frankl would have argued that people are never left with nothing as long as they are in control of their mind, as long as they retain the freedom to choose how they will respond when confronted with adversity. Because life, from birth to death, involves a great deal of challenges that most people need to deal with on a daily basis, finding meaning in life when confronted with hardship is not only possible but also favorable to self-discovery.

Knowing that the meaning we choose to attribute to things and circumstances is what makes life's challenges bearable—sometimes even exciting—is one of the most useful mind tools you can ever possess. The very belief that a person's mental stamina can raise them above their outward fate can be applied in the context of every aspect of Life and Business. The influence of the New Age movement in recent decades has led people to try to *find themselves* through introspection. While this can present certain advantages I believe that true meaning is to be discovered in the outside world; being human always points to something external to oneself. A purposeful, active existence renders life meaningful and the more people focus on a meaningful, purposeful life, the better they become in adding value to their community, workplace and family.

People want to make sense out of their lives. To quote Nietzsche: "He who has a 'why' to live for can bear almost any 'how.'" To live fully, one needs to live in a meaningful way. Whatever adds meaning to your life automatically adds value to it. Leading a life of meaning means leading a life of purpose. Finding a purpose in life is, however, virtually impossible unless you have found meaning first. Always remember that the meaning of life varies based on the challenges and changes that take place at different stages of your life but it never ceases to be.

Power Quotes is neither teaching nor preaching. The aim of these quotes is far removed from moral exhortation. These statements will hopefully help widen your vision field so that the whole spectrum of potential life meanings and possibilities becomes conscious and visible to you. Defining *your* finality is the first and most important step toward setting a life or career goal and working to achieve it. An important thing to keep in mind is that you don't have to marry your life goals, neither should you think that the meaning you choose to give your life at a given time must remain static. In other words, it is often through changing circumstances and unwelcome challenges that you will find yourself questioned by life. In search of a concrete meaning, do not lose perspective, for the meaning of life varies from person to person and from one life stage to the next. At the end of the day, life is an adventure where each one of us decides their level of involvement. The strongest our sense of purpose, the more engaging the journey becomes. Life flows. Make sure you are not left behind.

Life Quotes

The purpose of life is a life of purpose.

—Robin Sharma

He not busy being born is busy dying.

—Bob Dylan

Most of us spend our lives as if we had another one in the bank.

—Ben Irwin

Life is a process of becoming, a combination of states we have to go through. Where people fail is that they wish to elect a state and remain in it. This is a kind of death.

—Anaïs Nin

What to do with your one life? The same thing you would do if you had two lives, and this were the second.

—Robert Brault

One's only real life is the life one never leads.

—Oscar Wilde

When you were born, you cried and the world rejoiced. Live your life in such a manner that when you die the world cries and you rejoice.

—Indian Saying

Many people take no care of their money till they come nearly to the end of it, and others do just the same with their time.

—Johann Wolfgang von Goethe

The proper function of man is to live, not to exist. I shall not waste my days in trying to prolong them.

—Jack London

We are always getting ready to live but never living.

—Ralph Waldo Emerson

Life is made up of sobs, sniffles, and smiles, with sniffles predominating.
—O. Henry, The Gifts of the Magi

The art of living lies less in eliminating our troubles than in growing with them.
—Bernard M. Baruch

Things happen in life that make us question our faith when perhaps they ought to make us question our life.
—Robert Brault

Here I am trying to live, or rather, I am trying to teach the death within me how to live.
—Jean Cocteau

A simple definition of life: The chance you've been waiting for.
—Robert Brault

How we spend our days is, of course, how we spend our lives.
—Annie Dillard

I think of life itself now as a wonderful play that I've written for myself, and so my purpose is to have the utmost fun playing my part.
—Shirley MacLaine

But in the end one needs more courage to live than to kill himself.
—Albert Camus, a Happy Death

I don't want to get to the end of my life and find that I lived just the length of it. I want to have lived the width of it as well.
—Diane Ackerman

There are but three events in a man's life: birth, life, and death. He is not conscious of being born, he dies in pain, and he forgets to live.
—Jean de la Bruyère

For a long time it had seemed to me that life was about to begin—real life. But there was always some obstacle in the way. Something to be got through first, some unfinished business, time still to be served, a debt to be paid. Then life would begin. At last it dawned on me that these obstacles were my life.

—Fr. Alfred D'Souza

You live longer once you realize that any time spent being unhappy is wasted.

—Ruth E. Renkl

Men for the sake of getting a living forget to live.

—Margaret Fuller

When one has a great deal to put into it, a day has a hundred pockets.
—Friedrich Nietzsche, Human, All Too Human

Fear not that life shall come to an end, but rather fear that it shall never have a beginning.

—John Henry Cardinal Newman

But I am greedy for life. I do too much of everything all the time. Suddenly one day my heart will fail. The Iron Crab will get me as it got my father. But I am not afraid of The Crab. At least I shall have died from an honorable disease. Perhaps they will put on my tombstone "This Man Died from Living Too Much."
—Ian Fleming, From Russia with Love

Our repugnance to death increases in proportion to our consciousness of having lived in vain.
—William Hazlitt, On the Love of Life, 1815

If life has those moments—ecstasies of health, youth and peace...— treasure them.

—Byron Caldwell Smith, letter to Kate Stephens

The fear of death follows from the fear of life. A man who lives fully is prepared to die at any time.

—Author unknown

Live as you will wish to have lived when you are dying.
—Christian Furchtegott Gellert

If you believe in forever, then life is just a one-night stand.
—Righteous Brothers, "Rock & Roll Heaven"

Life is change.
—Heraclitus of Ephesus

Life is a series of tasks that you absolutely must get done before they don't matter anymore.
—Robert Brault

Is there life before death?
—Author Unknown

May you live all the days of your life.
—Jonathan Swift

You don't get to choose how you're going to die. Or when. You can only decide how you're going to live. Now.
—Joan Baez

Life, if well lived, is long enough.
—Seneca, De Ira

Who well lives, long lives; for this age of ours should not be numbered by years, days, and hours.
—Guillaume de Salluste Du Bartas, Divine Weeks and Works, 1578

Don't ever save anything for a special occasion. Being alive is the special occasion.
—Author Unknown

Life is not a problem to be solved but a mystery to be lived.
—Thomas Merton

Addiction

Addictions started out like magical poets, pocket monsters. They did extraordinary tricks, showed you things you hadn't seen, were fun. But came through some gradual, dire alchemy, to make decisions for you. Eventually, they were making your most crucial life decisions. And they were…less intelligent than goldfish. William Gibson

Addiction is the only prison where the locks are on the inside.??

Addictions do come in handy sometimes: at least you have to get out of bed for them.

—Martin Amis

Adversity

Tough times never last. Tough people do.

—Author Unknown

Problems are not stop signs. They are guidelines.

—Robert Schuller

Don't let a bad day make you feel like you have a bad life.

—Author Unknown

The only thing that's the end of the world is the end of the world.
—President Barack Obama, farewell press conference,
January 18, 2017

Problems are only opportunities with thorns on them.

—Hugh Miller, Snow on the Wind

You will never truly know yourself or the strength of your relationships until both have been tested by adversity.

—J.K. Rowling

In prosperity our friends know us. In adversity we know our friends.

—John Churton Collins

The gem cannot be polished without friction nor man without trials.

—Confucius

If you are irritated by every rub, how will you be polished?

—Rumi

Ask not for a lighter burden, but for broader shoulders.

—Jewish Proverb

Bad is never good until worse happens.

—Danish Proverb

Problems are the price you pay for progress.

—Branch Rickey

Pain is weakness leaving the body.

—United States Marine Corps

The distinguishing mark of true adventures is that it is often no fun at all while they are actually happening.

—Kim Stanley Robinson

Adventure is just bad planning.

—Roald Amundsen

An inconvenience is only an adventure wrongly considered; an adventure is only an inconvenience rightly considered.

—G.K. Chesterton

Look back at your life. It's always the hardest times that made you who you are.

—Casey Neistat

The keenest sorrow is to recognize ourselves as the sole cause of all our adversities.

—Sophocles

Fortune knocks but once, but misfortune has much more patience.

—Author Unknown

A problem is a chance for you to do your best.

—Duke Ellington

Scars are tattoos with better stories.

—From a Toyota advertisement in Sports Illustrated magazine

Every flower must grow through dirt.

—Proverb

At times, challenges hit with the force of a roaring, rushing waterfall. The true test, however, is whether you can put your arms up and enjoy the feel of the water.

—Aviva Kaufman

Pain is sometimes the cost of a meaningful existence. I can handle that.

—Jeb Dickerson

Damaged people are dangerous. They know they can survive.

—Josephine Hart

Adversity has the effect of eliciting talents which, in prosperous circumstances, would have lain dormant.

—Horace

Just as we develop our physical muscles through overcoming opposition – such as lifting weights – we develop our character muscles by overcoming challenges and adversity.

—Stephen Covey

…once the storm is over you won' remember how you made it through, how you managed to survive. You won't even be sure, in fact, whether the storm is really over. But one thing is certain. When you come out

of the storm you won't be the same person who walked in. That what this storm's all about.

—Haruki Murakami, Kafka on the Shore

Sometimes you have to breakdown before you can breakthrough.

—Marilyn Ferguson (1938–2008)

Problems are messages.

—Shakti Gawain

Never was anything great achieved without danger.

—Niccolo Machiavelli

Adversity is like a strong wind. It tears away from us all but the things that cannot be torn, so that we see ourselves as we really are.

—Arthur Golden, Memoirs of a Geisha

Every problem has in it the seeds of its own solution. If you don't have any problems, you don't get any seeds.

—Norman Vincent Peale

We have no right to ask when sorrow comes "Why did this happen to me?" unless we ask the same question for every moment of happiness that comes our way.

—Author Unknown

We acquire the strength we have overcome.

—Ralph Waldo Emerson

Adversity is the first path to truth.

—Lord Byron

A man is insensible to the relish of prosperity 'til he has tasted adversity.

—Sa'di

There are two things that one must get used to or one will find life unendurable: the damages of time and injustices of men.
—Sébastien-Roch Nicolas

Sleep, riches, and health to be truly enjoyed must be interrupted.
—Johann Paul Friedrich Richter, Flower, Fruit, and Thorn

There is in every true woman's heart a spark of heavenly fire, which lies dormant in the broad daylight of prosperity; but which kindles up, and beams and blazes in the dark hour of adversity.
—Washington Irving, The Sketch Book, 1820

Adversity has the same effect on a man that severe training has on the pugilist: it reduces him to his fighting weight.
—Josh Billings

Turn your wounds into wisdom.
—Oprah Winfrey

To have become a deeper man is the privilege of those who have suffered.
—Oscar Wilde

He who has a 'why' to live can bear almost any 'how'.
—Friedrich Nietzsche

Birds sing after a storm; why shouldn't people feel as free to delight in whatever remains to them?
—Rose F. Kennedy

Suffering is above, not below. And everyone thinks that suffering is below. And everyone wants to rise.
—Antonio Porchia, Voces, 1943, translated from Spanish by W.S. Merwin

As long as you keep getting born, it's alright to die some times.

—Orson Scott Card

Smooth seas do not make skillful sailors.

—African Proverb

May you get what you wish for.

—Old Chinese Curse

Body and mind, like man and wife, do not always agree to die together.

—Charles Caleb Colton

We must embrace pain and burn it as fuel for our journey.

—Kenji Miyazawa

Use your enemy's arrows for firewood.

—Matshona Dhliwayo

It just wouldn't be a picnic without the ants.

—Author Unknown

The Lord gives us friends to push us to our potential—and enemies to push us beyond it.

—Robert Brault

A problem is a chance for you to do your best.

—Duke Ellington

Prosperity is not without many fears and distastes, and adversity is not without comforts and hopes.

—Francis Bacon

Everybody ought to do at least two things each day that he hates to do, just for practice.

—William James

Scars remind us where we've been—they don't have to dictate where we're going.

—Jeff

And thus the heart will break, yet brokenly live on.

—Lord Byron

Criminal Minds.

—Davis, Rick Dunkle, and Oanh Ly

When you're feeling your worst, that's when you get to know yourself the best.

—Leslie Grossman

It is foolish to tear one's hair in grief, as though sorrow would be made less by baldness.

—Cicero

Poverty, Frost, Famine, Rain, Disease, are the beadles and guardsmen that hold us to Common Sense.

—Ralph Waldo Emerson

Age

When I grow up I want to be a little boy.

—Joseph Heller

Old age isn't so bad when you consider the alternative.

—Maurice Chevalier

Age is something that doesn't matter unless you are a cheese.

—Luis Bunuel

You can live to be 100 if you give up all the things that make you want to live to be 100.

—Woody Allen

Very few people do anything creative after the age of 35. The reason is that very few people do anything creative before the age of 35.

—Joel Hildebrand

When I was ten I read fairy tales in secret. Now that I am 50 I read them openly. When I became a man I put away childish things, including the fear of childishness.

—C.S. Lewis

The years between 50 and 70 are the hardest. You are always being asked to do things and yet you are not decrepit enough to turn them down.

—T.S. Eliot

Inside every older woman is a young girl wondering what the hell happened?.

—Cora Harvey Armstrong

Anger

I feel an army in my fist.

—Friedrich Schiller

Speak when you are angry and you will make the best speech you will ever regret.

—Ambrose Bierce

Anger is short-lived madness.

—Horace

It is wise to direct your anger towards problems—not people, to focus your energies on answers—not excuses.

—William Arthur Ward

Anger is the only thing to put off till tomorrow.

—Czech proverb

If a small thing has the power to make you angry, does that not indicate something about your size?

—Sydney J. Harris

Whatever is begun in anger ends in shame.

—Benjamin Franklin

You will not be punished for your anger, you will be punished by your anger.

—Buddha

Anger and worry are the most unprofitable conditions known to man. They are like thieves that steal precious time and energy from life. Anger is a highway robber and worry is a sneak thief.

—Horace Fletcher, Menticulture, 1895

How much more grievous are the consequences of anger than the causes of it.

—Marcus Aurelius

He who angers you conquers you.

—Elizabeth Kenny

Resentment is like taking poison and waiting for the other person to die.

—Malachy McCourt

Not the fastest horse can catch a word spoken in anger.

—Chinese Proverb

Count up the days in which you have not been angry. I used to get angry every day, then every other day, then every three or four days.

If you manage not to be angry for as long as thirty days offer a sacrifice to the Gods.

—Epictetus, Greek philosopher

Holding on to anger is like grasping a hot coal with the intent of throwing it at someone else; you are the one who gets burned.

—Buddha

For every minute you are angry, you lose sixty seconds of happiness.

—Author Unknown

Resentment is an extremely bitter diet, and eventually poisonous. I have no desire to make my own toxins.

—Neil Kinnock

Anger is an acid that can do more harm to the vessel in which it is stored than to anything on which it is poured.

—Baptist Beacon

If you kick a stone in anger, you'll hurt your own foot.

—Korean Proverb

Before you give someone a piece of your mind, make sure you can get by with what is left.

—Author Unknown

Do not teach your children never to be angry; teach them how to be angry.

—Lyman Abbott

All of the evil passions are traceable to one of two roots. Anger is the root of all the aggressive passions. Worry is the root of all the cowardly passions.... It is not necessary to engage in battle the small army of lesser passions if you concentrate your efforts against anger and worry, for they are all children of these parents.

—Horace Fletcher, Menticulture, 1895

If you are patient in a moment of anger, you will escape one hundred days of sorrow.

—Chinese proverb

I don't have to attend every argument I'm invited to.

—Author unknown

Anything done in anger can be done better without it.

—Dallas Willard

Never strike your wife—even with a flower.

—Hindu Proverb

Be Yourself

The life of every man is a diary in which he means to write one story, and writes another.

—James Matthew Barrie

Always be a first-rate version of yourself, instead of a second-rate version of somebody else.

—Judy Garland

You were born an original.—Don't die a copy.

—John Mason

We are so accustomed to disguise ourselves to others that in the end we become disguised to ourselves.

—François VI de la Rochefoucault

We are what we pretend to be, so we must be careful about what we pretend to be.

—Kurt Vonnegut

There is just one life for each of us: our own.

—Euripides

It is better to be hated for what you are than to be loved for something you are not.

—Andre Gide

An unfulfilled vocation drains the color from a man's entire existence.
—Honoré de Balzac, Scènes de la vie Parisienne

Man is least himself when he talks in his own person. Give him a mask, and he will tell you the truth.

—Oscar Wilde

How many cares one loses when one decides not to be something but to be someone.

—Gabrielle "Coco" Chanel

We all wear masks, and the time comes when we cannot remove them without removing some of our own skin.
—André Berthiaume, Contretemps

What I am is good enough if I would only be it openly.

—Carl Rogers

Almost every man wastes part of his life in attempts to display qualities which he does not possess, and to gain applause which he cannot keep.
—Samuel Johnson, The Rambler, 1750

Hateful to me as the gates of Hades is that man who hides one thing in his heart and speaks another.

—Homer

Originality is... a by-product of sincerity.

—Marianne Moore

Never be bullied into silence. Never allow yourself to be made a victim. Accept no one's definition of your life; define yourself.
—Harvey Fierstein

Your time is limited, so don't waste it living someone else's life.

—Steve Jobs

When one is pretending the entire body revolts.

—Anaïs Nin

Be what you are. This is the first step toward becoming better than you are.

—Julius Charles Hare

Be who you are and say what you feel because those who mind don't matter and those who matter don't mind!

—Author unknown

It is the chiefest point of happiness that a man is willing to be what he is.

—Desiderius Erasmus

Most of our faults are more pardonable than the means we use to conceal them.

—François de la Rochefoucault

When you dance to your own rhythm,
Life taps its toes to your beat.

—Terri Guillemets

Rabbi Zusya said that on the Day of Judgment, God would ask him, not why he had not been Moses, but why he had not been Zusya.

—Walter Kaufmann

Body

Our arms start from the back because they were once wings.

—Martha Graham

*Our own physical body possesses a wisdom which we who inhabit the
body lack. We give it orders which make no sense.*

—Henry Miller

Our bodies are apt to be our autobiographies.

—Frank Gillette Burgess

Sometimes your body is smarter than you are.

—Author Unknown

*The body is a big sagacity, a plurality with one sense, a war and a
peace, a flock and a shepherd.*

—Friedrich Nietzsche

*There is an Indian proverb that says that everyone is a house with four
rooms, a physical, a mental, an emotional and a spiritual. Most of us
tend to live in one room most of the time but, unless we go into every
room every day, even if only to keep it aired, we are not a complete
person.*

—Rumer Godden, A House with Four Rooms

*I have ceased to question stars and books; I have begun to listen to the
teaching my blood whispers to me.*

—Herman Hesse

Take care of your body. It's the only place you have to live.

—Jim Rohn

The way he treats his body, you'd think he was renting.

—Robert Brault

*Emotion always has its roots in the unconscious and manifests itself
in the body.*

—Irene Claremont de Castillejo

Man is an intelligence in servitude to his organs.

—Aldous Huxley

I'm emotions and bones held together by skin and reality.

—Terri Guillemets

The dumbest kidney is smarter than the smartest nephrologist.

—Unknown physician

The body is not a permanent dwelling, but a sort of inn which is to be left behind when one perceives that one is a burden to the host.

—Seneca

There is a wisdom in the body that is older and more reliable than clocks and calendars.

—John Harold Johnson

We have a pharmacy inside us that is absolutely exquisite. It makes the right medicine, for the precise time, for the right target organ—with no side effects.

—Deepak Chopra

Hormones, vitamines, stimulants and depressives are oils upon the creaky machinery of life. Principal item, however, is the machinery.

—Martin H. Fischer (1879–1962)

The trouble with having a body is that people know it's where you hang out and you don't get any privacy.

—Robert Brault

Many people can listen to their cat more intelligently than they can listen to their own despised body. Because they attend to their pet in a cherishing way, it returns their love. Their body, however, may have to let out an earth-shattering scream in order to be heard at all.

—Marion Woodman

What spirit is so empty and blind, that it cannot recognize the fact that the foot is nobler than the shoe, and skin more beautiful that the garment with which it is clothed?

—Michelangelo

The Church says: The body is a sin.
Science says: The body is a machine.
Advertising says: The body is a business.
The body says: I am a fiesta.

—Eduardo Galeano

Our body is a machine for living. It is geared towards it; it is its nature. Let life go on in it unhindered and let it defend itself; it will be more effective than if you paralyze it by encumbering it with remedies.

—Leo Tolstoy

Good for the body is the work of the body, good for the soul the work of the soul, and good for either the work of the other.

—Henry David Thoreau

Massage is the only form of physical pleasure to which nature forgot to attach consequences.

—Robert Brault

Some patients I see are actually draining into their bodies the diseased thoughts of their minds.

—Zacharty Bercovitz

Varicose veins are the result of an improper selection of grandparents.
—William Osler

Your cells are as depressed as you are, and your cells are as happy and frisky as you are.

—Abraham–Hicks

My entire approach to my body and to fitness in general had been based on the concept of deficit. I thought of aerobics classes and how I had panted my way through movements just to give myself smaller thighs, pumping iron to shape my narrow back, dieting to lower my fat level. I had always approached my body as if it were a problem needing to be solved.... This attitude was not really different from the notion of original sin, forever reaching for an ideal we are constitutionally incapable of attaining. But here I was, truly broken now, weak, emaciated, yet in front of me this teacher was saying that just by the virtue of my being, I was complete. I always had been. The only thing I needed to do was honor that.

—Samantha Dunn, "Brick by Brick"

So long as we are in conflict with our body, we cannot find peace of mind.

—Georg Feuerstein

Attention to the human body brings healing and regeneration. Through awareness of the body we remember who we really are.

—Jack Kornfield

Abdicate, v.: to give up all hope of ever having a flat stomach.

—Author Unknown

Why do we pay for psychotherapy when massages cost half as much?

—Jason Love

But one thing, at least, is certain, that no system can be satisfactory, much less successful, which does not provide for the healthy training of the whole being of the child, dividing and distinguishing mental and bodily exercise if it will, but at the same time co-ordinating them in due relations to each other...

—E. Warre, 1884

The ear tends to be lazy, craves the familiar, and is shocked by the unexpected: the eye, on the other hand, tends to be impatient, craves the novel and is bored by repetition.

—W.H. Auden, The Dyer's Hand

Few of us have lost our minds, but most of us have long ago lost our bodies.

—Ken Wilbur

Most psychologists treat the mind as disembodied, a phenomenon with little or no connection to the physical body. Conversely physicians treat the body with no regard to the mind or the emotions. But the body and mind are not separate, and we cannot treat one without the other.

—Candace Pert

Your body is a temple but only if you treat it as one.

—Terri Guillemets

Books

The man who doesn't read has no advantage over the man who can't read.

—Author unknown

Books are a uniquely portable magic.

—Stephen King

Great novels are always a little more intelligent than their authors.

—Milan Kundera

Books are immortal sons deifying their sires.

—Plato

Miss a meal if you have to but don't miss a book.

—Jim Rohn

When you re-read a classic you do not see in the book more than you did before. You see more in you than there was before.

—Clifton Fadiman

A good book has no ending.

—R.D. Cumming

Reading is to the mind what exercise is to the body.

—Richard Steele

Women and books should be looked at daily.

—Dutch Proverb

"Tell me what you read and I'll tell you who you are" is true enough, but I'd know you better if you told me what you reread.

—François Mauriac

A book should serve as an ax for the frozen sea within us.

—Franz Kafka

Never judge a book by its movie.

—J.W. Eagan

Assimilate ubiquitously. Doublethink. To deliberately believe in lies, while knowing they're false...Examples of this in everyday life: "oh, I need to be pretty to be happy. I need surgery to be pretty. I need to be thin, famous, fashionable...This is a marketing holocaust. Twenty-four hours a day for the rest of our lives, these powers hard at work dumbing us to death. So to defend ourselves, and fight against assimilating this dullness into our thought processes, we must learn to read. To stimulate our own imagination, to cultivate our own consciousness, our own belief systems. We all need skills to defend, to preserve, our own minds."

—Henry Barthes

The wise man reads both books and life itself.

—Lin Yutang

To read a book for the first time is to make an acquaintance with a new friend; to read it for a second time is to meet an old one.

—Chinese Saying

There is a great deal of difference between an eager man who wants to read a book and a tired man who wants a book to read.

—G.K. Chesterton

A book is like a garden carried in the pocket.

—Chinese Proverb

To acquire the habit of reading is to construct for yourself a refuge from almost all the miseries of life.

—W. Somerset Maugham

To read without reflecting is like eating without digesting.

—Edmund Burke

Reading—the best state yet to keep absolute loneliness at bay.

—William Styron

Good friends, good books and a sleepy conscience: this is the ideal life.

—Mark Twain

It is what you read when you don't have to that determines what you will be when you can't help it.

—Oscar Wilde

Books are the bees which carry the quickening pollen from one mind to another.

—James Russell Lowell

That is a good book which is opened with expectation and closed with profit.

—Amos Bronson Alcott

A writer only begins a book, it is the reader who completes it; for the reader takes up where the writer left off as new thoughts stir within him.

—David Harris Russell (1906–1965),
Children Learn to Read, 1949

What the candystore was to other kids, the bookstore was to me. The library was my vacation.

—Terri Guillemets, "Young bookworm," 1998

I don't think any good book is based on factual experience. Bad books are about things the writer knew before he wrote them.

—Carlos Fuentes

Fiction reveals truths that reality obscures.

—Jessamyn West

Some books are undeservedly forgotten but none are undeservedly remembered.

—W.H. Auden

Don't just read the easy stuff. You may be entertained by it, but you will never grow from it.

—Jim Rohn

How many a man has dated a new era in his life from the reading of a book.

—Henry David Thoreau, Walden

The worst thing about new books is that they keep us from reading the old ones.

—Joseph Joubert

Outside of a dog, a book is a man's best friend. Inside of a dog, it's too dark to read.

—Groucho Marx

To sit alone in the lamplight with a book spread out before you, and hold intimate converse with men of unseen generations—such is a pleasure beyond compare.

—Kenko Yoshida

A good book should leave you... slightly exhausted at the end. You live several lives while reading it.

—William Styron, interview, Writers at Work, 1958

We read in bed because reading is halfway between life and dreaming, our own consciousness in someone else's mind.

—Anna Quindlen, How Reading Changed My Life, 1998

If there's a book you really want to read but it hasn't been written yet, then you must write it.

—Toni Morrison

My test of a good novel is dreading to begin the last chapter.

—Thomas Helm

Books let us into their souls and lay open to us the secrets of our own.

—William Hazlitt

You know you've read a good book when you turn the last page and feel a little as if you have lost a friend.

—Paul Sweeney

Books serve to show a man that those original thoughts of his aren't very new after all.

—Abraham Lincoln

There are more truths in a good book than its author meant to put into it.

—Marie Dubsky

Sometimes, looking at the many books I have at home, I feel I shall die before I come to the end of them, yet I cannot resist the temptation of buying new books. Whenever I walk into a bookstore and find a book on one of my hobbies... I say to myself, "What a pity I can't buy that book, for I already have a copy at home."

—Jorge Luis Borges

I'm old-fashioned and think that reading books is the most glorious pastime that humankind has yet devised.

—Wisława Szymborska

I suggest that the only books that influence us are those for which we are ready, and which have gone a little farther down our particular path than we have yet got ourselves.

—E.M. Forster, Two Cheers for Democracy, 1951

This will never be a civilized country until we expend more money for books than we do for chewing gum.

—Elbert Hubbard

Reading means borrowing.

—Georg Christoph Lichtenberg

I divide all readers into two classes; those who read to remember and those who read to forget.

—William Lyon Phelps

From every book invisible threads reach out to other books; and as the mind comes to use and control those threads the whole panorama of the world's life, past and present, becomes constantly more varied and interesting, while at the same time the mind's own powers of reflection and judgment are exercised and strengthened.

—Helen E. Haines

Book lovers never go to bed alone.

—Author unknown

When you reread a classic you do not see more in the book than you did before; you see more in you than was there before.

—Clifton Fadiman

A book that is shut is but a block.

—Thomas Fuller

I find it necessary to confine my purchases strictly to books. My me! Yes, strictly to books.

—Munson Havens, Old Valentines:
A Love Story, 1914

There are worse crimes than burning books. One of them is not reading them.

—Joseph Brodsky

Books are good company, in sad times and happy times, for books are people—people who have managed to stay alive by hiding between the covers of a book.

—E.B. White

There is a temperate zone in the mind, between luxurious indolence and exacting work; and it is to this region, just between laziness and labor, that summer reading belongs.

—Henry Ward Beecher

When a new book is published, read an old one.

—Samuel Rogers

From my point of view, a book is a literary prescription put up for the benefit of someone who needs it.

—S.M. Crothers

There are many persons pretending to have a refined literary taste, who seldom read any books but those which are fashionable...

—Charles Lanman

Sometimes, you read a book and it fills you with this weird evangelical zeal, and you become convinced that the shattered world will never be put back together unless and until all living humans read the book. And then there are books... which you can't tell people about, books so special and rare and yours that advertising your affection feels like a betrayal. It wasn't even that the book was so good or anything; it was just that the author... seemed to understand me in weird and impossible ways.

—John Green

He fed his spirit with the bread of books.

—Edwin Markham

A book is a garden, an orchard, a storehouse, a party, a company by the way, a counsellor, a multitude of counsellors.

—Henry Ward Beecher

There is reading, and there is reading. Reading as a means to an end, for information, to cultivate oneself; reading as an end in itself, a process, a compulsion.

—Sven Birkerts

Having your book turned into a movie is like seeing your oxen turned into bouillon cubes.

—John LeCarre

He who lends a book is an idiot. He who returns the book is more of an idiot.

—Arabic proverb

Never lend books; no one ever returns them. The only books I have in my library are books other people have lent me.

—Anatole France

One of the advantages of reading books is that you get to play with someone else's imaginary friends, at all hours of the night.

—Dr. SunWolf

Books, too, begin like the week—with a day of rest in memory of their creation. The preface is their Sunday.

—Walter Benjamin

Knowledge is of two kinds. We know a subject ourselves, or we know where we can find information upon it. When we inquire into any subject, the first thing we have to do is to know what books have treated of it. This leads us to look at catalogues, and the backs of books in libraries.

—Samuel Johnson, 1775, quoted by James Boswell in The Life of Samuel Johnson

The best of a book is not the thought which it contains, but the thought which it suggests.

—Oliver Wendell Holmes

Books are a hard-bound drug with no danger of an overdose. I am the happy victim of books.

—Karl Lagerfeld

One of the joys of reading is the ability to plug into the shared wisdom of mankind.

—Ishmael Reed

Some books are to be tasted, others to be swallowed, and some few to be chewed and digested.

—Francis Bacon

I would never read a book if it were possible for me to talk half an hour with the man who wrote it.

—Woodrow Wilson

It often requires more courage to read some books than it does to fight a battle.

—Sutton Elbert Griggs

The time to read is any time: no apparatus, no appointment of time and place, is necessary. It is the only art which can be practiced at any hour of the day or night, whenever the time and inclination comes, that is your time for reading; in joy or sorrow, health or illness.

—Holbrook Jackson

Boredom

Men grow tired of sleep, love, singing and dancing sooner than of war.
—Homer, Iliad

Boredom: the desire for desires.

—Leo Tolstoy

Boredom flourishes when you feel safe. It's a symptom of security.
—Eugene Ionesco

Is not life a hundred times too short for us to bore ourselves?
—Friedrich Nietzsche

Boredom is the feeling that everything is a waste of time; serenity, that nothing is.

—Thomas Szasz

Boredom is rage spread thin.

—Paul Tillich

We have a world of pleasures to win but nothing to lose but boredom.
—Raoul Vaneigem

Boredom is the feeling that everything is a waste of time; serenity, that nothing is.

—Thomas Szasz

A man can stand almost anything except a succession of ordinary days.
—Attributed to Goethe, by Huebsch

I am never bored anywhere: being bored is an insult to oneself.
—Jules Renard

Ennui has made more gamblers than avarice, more drunkards than thirst, and perhaps as many suicides as despair.

—C.C. Colton

Punctuality is the virtue of the bored.

—Evelyn Waugh

Boredom is a sickness the cure for which is work; pleasure is only a palliative.

—Le Duc de Lévis

The cure for boredom is curiosity. There is no cure for curiosity.
—Dorothy Parker

When I bore people at a party they think it is their fault.
—Henry Kissinger

Earth's nothing more than a rotating ball of boredom.
—Star Trek: Deep Space Nin

When I get really bored, I like to drive downtown and get a great parking spot, then sit in my car and count how many people ask me if I'm leaving.
—Steven Wright

Carpe Diem

Every man dies. Not every man really lives.

—Braveheart

Each moment is a place you've never been.

—Mark Strand

Either you run the day or the day runs you.

—Jim Rohn

Enjoy yourself. It's later than you think.

—Chinese Proverb

Life is not lost by dying; life is lost minute by minute, day by dragging day, in all the thousand small uncaring ways.

—Stephen Vincent Benet

The important thing is not how many years in your life but how much life in your years.

—Edward J. Stieglitz

Live every day as if it were going to be your last; for one day you're sure to be right.

—Anonymous Author

I still find each day too short for all the thoughts I want to think, all the walks I want to take, all the books I want to read and all the friends I want to see.

—John Burroughs

Go for it now. The future is promised to no one.

—Wayne Dyer

Spend the afternoon. You can't take it with you.

—Annie Dillard

A man that is young in years may be old in hours, if he has lost no time.

—Francis Bacon

I'm less interested in why we're here. I'm wholly devoted to while we're here.

—Erika Harris

Do not take life too seriously. You will never get out of it alive.

—Elbert Hubbard

There are a million ways to waste a day, but not even a single way to get one back.

—Tom DeMarco and Timothy Lister

Why must conversions always come so late? Why do people always apologize to corpses?

—David Brin

Consumerism

He who buys what he does not need steals from himself.

—Author Unknown

The hardest thing is to take less when you can get more.

—Kin Hubbard

Earth provides enough to satisfy every man's need, but not every man's greed.

—Mohandas K. Gandhi, quoted in E.F. Schumacher,
Small Is Beautiful

You have succeeded in life when all you really want is only what you really need.

—Vernon Howard

There will presently be no room in the world for things; it will be filled up with the advertisements of things.

—William Dean Howells

The only reason a great many American families don't own an elephant is that they have never been offered an elephant for a dollar down and easy weekly payments.

—Mad Magazine

You can never get enough of what you don't need to make you happy.

—Eric Hoffer

Who covets more, is evermore a slave.

—Robert Herrick

Do not trouble yourself much to get new things, whether clothes or friends.... Sell your clothes and keep your thoughts.

—Henry David Thoreau

To perceive Christmas through its wrappings becomes more difficult with every year.

—E.B. White

Stuffocation: being overwhelmed by the stuff one has bought or accumulated.

—Author Unknown

The secret of happiness is to admire without desiring.

—Francis H. Bradley

The gap in our economy is between what we have and what we think we ought to have—and that is a moral problem, not an economic one.

—Paul Heyne

Be glad that you're greedy; the national economy would collapse if you weren't.

—Mignon McLaughlin

We realize we can't have everything, and so begins the mad scramble to have everything else.

—Robert Brault

There must be more to life than having everything!

—Maurice Sendak

What a unique treasure are the things we have learned to live without, for no thief can take them from us.

—Robert Brault

Be content with what you have, rejoice in the way things are. When you realize there is nothing lacking, the whole world belongs to you.

—Lao Tzu

We don't need to increase our goods nearly as much as we need to scale down our wants. Not wanting something is as good as possessing it.

—Donald Horban

Somebody has to teach Americans that we don't always have to have something newer, better every year. Or in the case of our upside-down economic system, every quarter.... Somewhere along the way we bought into this insane idea that everything always has to get bigger, especially sales. Having a really good year and then just repeating it—not good enough. In corporate America, the stock market is the tail that wags the dog. Growth, growth, holy growth, is the only thing that ever matters. Better than last quarter, beat expectations, eat more hamburgers...

—Bill Maher, "New Rule: Growth At Any Cost," Real Time (HBO), September 23, 2016

Death

He who doesn't fear death dies only once.

—Giovanni Falcone

Death is beautiful when seen to be a law, and not an accident—It is as common as life.

—Henry David Thoreau

While I thought that I was learning how to live, I have been learning how to die.

—Leonardo Da Vinci

No one knows whether death is really the greatest blessing a man can have, but they fear it is the greatest curse, as if they knew well.

—Plato

And they die an equal death—the idler and the man of mighty deeds.

—Homer, Iliad

The idea is to die young as late as possible.

—Ashley Montagu

Some people are so afraid to die that they never begin to live.

—Henry Van Dyke

There's nothing certain in a man's life except this: That he must lose it.

—Aeschylus, Agamemnon

The goal of all life is death.

—Sigmund Freud

Life is a great surprise. I do not see why death should not be an even greater one.

—Vladimir Nabokov

Is there anyone so foolish, even though he is young, as to feel absolutely sure that he will be alive when evening comes?

—Cicero

A man does not die of love or his liver or even of old age; he dies of being a man.

—Percival Arland Ussher

When we fear death, we are letting him wrap his bony hands around our necks during the best times of our lives, choking us with imaginary threats and preventing us from breathing from pure air of now.

—Terri Guillemets

For three days after death, hair and fingernails grow but phone calls taper off.

—Johnny Carson

Death never takes the wise man by surprise; He is always ready to go.

—Jean de La Fontaine

All say: 'how hard it is that we have to die' – a strange complaint to come from the mouths of people who have had to live.

—Mark Twain

People do not die for us immediately, but remain bathed in a sort of aura of life which bears no relation to true immortality but through which they continue to occupy our thoughts in the same way as when they were alive. It is as though they were traveling abroad.

—Marcel Proust

Everybody has got to die, but I've always believed an exception would be made in my case.

—William Saroyan

Death is not warden of life, not thief, nor enemy—but Life's most equal partner.

—Terri Guillemets

From my rotting body, flowers shall grow and I am in them and that is eternity.

—Edvard Munch

I shall not die of a cold. I shall die of having lived.

—Willa Cather

We never bury the dead, son. We take them with us. It's the price of living.

—Mark Goffman and Jose Molina

Death is a delightful hiding place for weary men.

—Herodotus

A man's dying is more the survivors' affair than his own.

—Thomas Mann, The Magic Mountain

Death is for many of us the gate of hell; but we are inside on the way out, not outside on the way in.

—George Bernard Shaw

Death is not the greatest loss in life. The greatest loss is what dies inside us while we live.

—Norman Cousins

Death is not poison but merely life's final remedy.

—Terri Guillemets

The day which we fear as our last is but the birthday of eternity.

—Seneca

Death is patiently making my mask as I sleep. Each morning I awake to discover in the corners of my eyes the small tears of his wax.

—Philip Dow

Death may be the greatest of all human blessings.

—Socrates

Death bumps into life many times as just a passerby.

—Terri Guillemets

In any man who dies there dies with him, his first snow and kiss and fight. Not people die but worlds die in them.

—Yevgeny Yevtushenko

To die proudly when it is no longer possible to live proudly. Death of one's own free choice, death at the proper time, with a clear head and with joyfulness, consummated in the midst of children and witnesses: so that an actual leave-taking is possible while he who is leaving is still there.

—Friedrich Nietzsche, Expeditions of an Untimely Man

Dying man needs to die, as a sleepy man needs to sleep, and there comes a time when it is wrong, as well as useless, to resist.

—Stewart Alsop

To the psychotherapist an old man who cannot bid farewell to life appears as feeble and sickly as a young man who is unable to embrace it.

—C.G. Jung

Old persons are sometimes as unwilling to die as tired-out children are to say good night and go to bed.

—Joseph Sheridan Le Fanu

God made death so we'd know when to stop.

—Steven Stiles

As a well-spent day brings happy sleep, so a life well used brings happy death.

—Leonardo da Vinci

I intend to live forever. So far, so good.

—Steven Wright

Happy the man who dies before he prays for death.

—Publilius Syrus

Desire

If men could regard the events of their own lives with more open minds they would frequently discover that they did not really desire the things they failed to obtain.

—André Maurois

Desire is the very essence of man.

—Baruch Spinoza

Suffering is caused by desire.

—Buddha

Man is the only animal whose desires increase as they are fed; the only animal that is never satisfied.

—Henry George

The desire engendered in the male glands is a hundred times more difficult to control than the desire bred in the female glands. All girls who limit their actions to arousing desire and then defending their honor should be horsewhipped.

—Marlene Dietrich

If you don't get what you want, it's a sign that you did not seriously want it, or that you tried to bargain over the price.

—Rudyard Kipling

Dreams

Dreams are today's answers to tomorrow's questions.

—Edgar Cayce

If your dreams do not scare you, they are not big enough.

—Ellen Jonson Sirleaf

I dream my painting and then paint my dream.

—Vincent Van Gogh

All men dream but not equally. Those who dream by night in the dusty recesses of their minds, wake in the day to find that it was vanity: but the dreamers of the day are dangerous man, for they may act their dream with open eyes, to make it possible.

—T.E. Lawrence

Dreaming permits each one of us to be quietly and safely insane every night of our lives.

—Charles William Dement

The best reason for having dreams is that in dreams no reasons are necessary.

—Ashleigh Brilliant

Dreams say what they mean, but they don't say it in daytime language.

—Gail Godwin

Dreaming is an act of pure imagination, attesting in all men a creative power, which if it were available in waking, would make every man a Dante or Shakespeare.

—H.F. Hedge

Some colors exist in dreams that are not present in the waking spectrum.

—Terri Guillemets

We are not only less reasonable and less decent in our dreams... we are also more intelligent, wiser and capable of better judgment when we are asleep than when we are awake.

—Erich Fromm

Only in our dreams are we free, the rest of the time we need wages.

—Terry Pratchett

I have dreamed in my life dreams that have stayed with me ever after, and changed my ideas; they have gone through me, like wine through water, and altered the color of my mind.

—Emily Brontë

Those who have compared our life to a dream were right.... We sleeping wake, and waking sleep.

—Michel de Montaigne

Education

To teach is to learn.

—Japanese Proverb

The problem it is not people being uneducated. The problem is that they are just educated enough to believe what they've been taught and not educated enough to question what they've been taught.

—Author Unknown

A teacher is one who makes himself progressively unnecessary.

—Thomas Carruthers

Education is an ornament in prosperity and a refuge in adversity.

—Aristotle

The whole purpose of education is to turn mirrors into windows. Education has produced a vast population able to read but unable to distinguish what is worth reading.

—G.M. Trevelyan

The one real object of education is to have a man in the condition of continually asking questions.

—Mandell Creighton

Exams and grades are temporary, but education is permanent.

—Author Unknown

What will matter is not what you learned but what you taught.

—Michael Josephson

Too often we give children answers to remember rather than problems to solve.

—Roger Lewin

Every time you stop a school, you will have to build a jail. What you gain at one end you lose at the other. It's like feeding a dog on his own tail. It won't fatten the dog.

—Mark Twain, 1900

Education is not preparation for life; education is life itself.

—John Dewey

You cannot teach a man anything, you can only help him find I within himself.

—Galileo Galilei

No man who worships education has got the best out of education.... Without a gentle contempt for education no man's education is complete.

—G.K. Chesterton

Educating the mind without educating the heart is no education at all.

—Aristotle

When you know better, you do better.

—Maya Angelou

The great difficulty in education is to get experience out of ideas.

—George Santayana

It is a thousand times better to have common sense without education than to have education without common sense.

—Robert G. Ingersoll

The tragedy of education is played in two scenes—incompetent pupils facing competent teachers and incompetent teachers facing competent pupils.

—Martin H. Fischer (1879–1962)

Education spoils you for actual work. The more you know the more you think somebody owes you a living.

—Will Rogers

My parents told me: "Finish your dinner. People in China and India are starving." I tell my daughters: "Finish your homework. People in India and China are starving for your job."

—Thomas L. Friedman

I prefer the company of peasants because they have not been educated sufficiently to reason incorrectly.

—Michel de Montaigne

They say that we are better educated than our parents' generation. What they mean is that we go to school longer. It is not the same thing.

—Richard Yates

Nations have recently been led to borrow billions for war; no nation has ever borrowed largely for education. Probably, no nation is rich enough to pay for both war and civilization. We must make our choice; we cannot have both.

—Abraham Flexner

Who knows the difference between education and training? For those of you with daughters, would you rather have them take sex education or sex training? Need I say more?

—Dennis Rubin

Education should be exercise; it has become massage.

—Martin H. Fischer

Real education must ultimately be limited to men who INSIST on knowing, the rest is mere sheep-herding.

—Ezra Pound

There is nothing so stupid as the educated man if you get him off the thing he was educated in.

—Will Rogers

Education is learning what you didn't know you didn't know.

—George Boas

Education would be much more effective if its purpose was to ensure that by the time they leave school every boy and girl should know how much they do not know, and be imbued with a lifelong desire to know it.

—William Haley

You send your child to the schoolmaster, but it's the schoolboys who educate him.

—Ralph Waldo Emerson

The modern world belongs to the half-educated, a rather difficult class, because they do not realize how little they know.

—William R. Inge

Why should society feel responsible only for the education of children, and not for the education of all adults of every age?

—Erich Fromm

To me education is a leading out of what is already there in the pupil's soul. To Miss Mackay it is a putting in of something that is not there, and that is not what I call education. I call it intrusion.

—Muriel Spark

Much education today is monumentally ineffective. All too often we are giving young people cut flowers when we should be teaching them to grow their own plants.

—John W. Gardner

A good teacher must know the rules; a good pupil, the exceptions.

—Martin H

We are students of words: we are shut up in schools, and colleges, and recitation-rooms, for ten or fifteen years, and come out at last with a bag of wind, a memory of words, and do not know a thing.

—Ralph Waldo Emerson

Emotions

The walls we build around us to keep sadness out also keeps out the joy.

—Jim Rohn

It is within the experience of everyone that when pleasure and pain reach a certain intensity they are indistinguishable.

—Arnold Bennett

Too much emotion is like none at all.

—Du Mu

Feelings are much like waves, we can't stop them from coming but we can choose which one to surf.

—Jonatan Mårtensson

Feelings are just visitors, let the come and go.

—Mooji

Sometimes we can't let go of the pain because we think it's the one thing holding us together.

—Terri Guillemets

We might be the master of our thoughts, still we are the slaves of or emotions.

—Author Unknown

The finest emotion of which we are capable is the mystic emotion.
—Albert Einstein

Your intellect may be confused, but your emotions will never lie to you.

—Roger Ebert

Sadness is almost never anything but a form of fatigue.
—Andre Gide

People cry not because they are weak but because they have been strong for too long.

—Author Unknown

The purpose of thinking is to so arrange the world in our minds that we can apply emotion effectively. In the end, it is emotion that makes the choices and decisions.
—Edward De Bono

If you don't manage your emotions, then your emotions will manage you.

—Deborah Rozman

When dealing with people, remember you are not dealing with creatures of logic, but creatures of emotion.
—Dale Carnegie

Guilt is always hungry—don't let it consume you.
—Terri Guillemets

Faith

I don't believe in hope. Hope is a beggar. Hope walks through the fire. Faith leaps over it.

—Jim Carrey

Faith is spiritualized imagination.

—Henry Ward Beecher

Faithless is he that says farewell when the road darkens.

—J.R.R. Tolkien

In faith there is enough light for those who want to believe and enough shadows to blind those who don't.

—Blaise Pascal

Faith is much better than belief. Belief is when someone else does the thinking.

—R. Buckminster Fuller

Faith is reason grown courageous.

—Sherwood Eddy

Faith is the bird that sings when the dawn is still dark.

—Rabindranath Tagore

To me faith means not worrying.

—John Dewey

Faith is believing in things when common sense tells you not to.

—George Seaton

There is nothing more perplexing in life than to know at what point you should surrender your intellect to your faith.

—Margot Asquith

Every tomorrow has two handles. We can take hold of it by the handle of anxiety, or by the handle of faith.

—Author Unknown

Faith... must be enforced by reason.... When faith becomes blind it dies.

—Mahatma Gandhi

Faith enables persons to be persons because it lets God be God.

—Carter Lindberg

Faith is not about everything turning out okay, faith is about being okay no matter how things turn out.

—Author Unknown

Of course I doubt. I do not practice a certainty. I practice a faith.

—Robert Brault

Faith is taking the first step even when you don't see the whole staircase.

—Martin Luther King, Jr.

Faith and prayer are the vitamins of the soul; man cannot live in health without them.

—Mahalia Jackson

The opposite of faith isn't doubt. It's certainty.

—Author Unknown

Fear

Aversion is a form of bondage. We are tied to what we hate or fear. That is why, in our lives, the same problem, the same danger or difficulty, will present itself over and over again in various prospects, as long as we continue to resist or run away from it instead of examining it and solving it.

—Patañjali

Nothing in life is to be feared. It is only to be understood.

—Marie Curie

Fear: False Evidence Appearing Real.

—Author Unknown

To lead is difficult when you're a follower of fear.

—T.A. Sachs

Keep your fears to yourself but share your courage with others.

—Robert Louis Stevenson

There are several good protections against temptation, but the surest is cowardice.

—Mark Twain

There are only two forces that unite men – fear and interest.

—Napoleon Bonaparte

Fear is a darkroom where negatives develop.

—Usman B. Asif

He who fears to suffer, suffers from fear.

—French Proverb

Decide that you want it more than you are afraid of it.

—Bill Cosby

A cat bitten once by a snake dreads even rope.

—Arab Proverb

I prefer my people to be loyal out of fear rather than conviction. Convictions can change, but fear remains.

—Josef Stalin

There is a time to take counsel of your fears, and there is a time to never listen to any fear.

—George S. Patton

If a man harbors any sort of fear, it makes him landlord to a ghost.

—Lloyd Douglas

Fear is the lengthened shadow of ignorance.

—Arnold Glasow

You can discover what your enemy fears most by observing the means he uses to frighten you.

—Eric Hoffer

There is much in the world to make us afraid. There is much more in our faith to make us unafraid.

—Frederick W. Cropp

Fear is the highest fence.

—Dudley Nichols

I have learned over the years that when one's mind is made up, this diminishes fear.

—Rosa Parks

Fear makes the wolf bigger than he is.

—German Proverb

You are the one giving fear a leg to stand on.

—Dodinsky

Feed your faith and your fears will starve to death.

—Author Unknown

The way you overcome shyness is to become so wrapped up in something that you forget to be afraid.

—Lady Bird Johnson

I must not fear. Fear is the mind-killer. Fear is the little-death that brings total obliteration. I will face my fear. I will permit it to pass over me and through me. And when it has gone past I will turn the inner eye to see its path. Where the fear has gone there will be nothing. Only I will remain.

—Frank Herbert (1920–1986), Dune

The only thing we have to fear is fear itself.

—Franklin D. Roosevelt

A life lived in fear is a life half lived.

—Spanish proverb

Freedom

Most people will give up an acre of freedom for a closet of security.

—Dr. Idel Dreimer

Nothing is more difficult, and therefore more precious, than to be able to decide.

—Napoleon Bonaparte

A man's worst difficulties begin when he is able to do as he likes.

—T.X. Huxley

Freedom is never free.

—Author Unknown

It is true that liberty is precious; so precious that it must be carefully rationed.

—Lenin

Those who deny freedom to others deserve it not for themselves.

—Abraham Lincoln

Complete possession is proved only by giving. All you are unable to give possesses you.

—Andre Gide

Freedom is the right to be wrong, not the right to do wrong.

—John Diefenbaker

Everyone appears to be noticing only the statue's torch and not the manacles on her ankles.

—Roger L. Green

All mankind is divided as it is always has been into slaves and free-men. Whoever has less than two-thirds of his day for himself is a slave, be he a statesman, a merchant, an official or a scholar.

—Friedrich Nietzsche

My definition of a free society is a society where it is safe to be unpopular.

—Adlai Stevenson

Freedom means choosing your burden.

—Hephzibah Menuhin

The most important kind of freedom is to be what you really are.

—Jim Morrison

Liberty doesn't work as well in practice as it does in speeches.

—Will Rogers

We feel free when we escape—even if it be but from the frying pan into the fire.

—Eric Hoffer

Freedom is that instant between when someone tells you to do something and when you decide how to respond.

—Jeffrey Borenstein

We must be free not because we claim freedom, but because we practice it.

—William Faulkner

No man can put a chain about the ankle of his fellow man without at last finding the other end fastened about his own neck.

—Frederick Douglass, speech, Civil Rights Mass Meeting, Washington, D.C., 1883

Power is duty; freedom is responsibility.

—Marie Dubsky, Freifrau von Ebner-Eschenbach (1830–1916), translated by Mrs Annis Lee Wister, 1882

We are free, truly free, when we don't need to rent our arms to anybody in order to be able to lift a piece of bread to our mouths.

—Ricardo Flores Magon, speech, May 31, 1914

If liberty means anything at all, it means the right to tell people what they do not want to hear.

—George Orwell

If you want total security, go to prison. There you're fed, clothed, given medical care and so on. The only thing lacking... is freedom.

—Dwight D. Eisenhower

Gambling

Gambling: The sure way of getting nothing from something.

—Wilson Mizner

Money won is twice as sweet as money earned.

—From the movie The Color of Money

In a bet there is a fool and a thief.

—Proverb

The safest way to double your money is to fold it over once and put it in your pocket.

—Kin Hubbard

No wife can endure a gambling husband, unless he is a steady winner.
—Thomas Robert Dewar

The better the gambler, the worse the man.

—Publilius Syrus

The urge to gamble is so universal and its practice is so pleasurable, that I assume it must be evil.

—Heywood Broun

A gambler is nothing but a man who makes his living out of hope.
—William Bolitho

You cannot beat a roulette table unless you steal money from it.
—Albert Einstein

Lottery: A tax on people who are bad at math.
—Author Unknown

The house doesn't beat the player. It just gives him the opportunity to beat himself.

—Nick Dandalos

At the gambling table, there are no fathers and sons.
—Chinese Proverb

A racehorse is an animal that can take several thousand people for a ride at the same time.

—Author Unknown

Happiness

The happiest people don't have the best of everything, they just make the best of everything.

—Author Unknown

Happiness is a form of courage.

—Holbrook Jackson

When a man has lost all happiness, he's not alive. Call him a breathing corpse.

—Sophocles

Happiness is the settling of the soul into its most appropriate spot.

—Aristotle

Hell is empty and all the devils are here.

—William Shakespeare

Nothing prevents happiness like the memory of happiness.

—André Gide, L'Immoraliste

Happiness is an inside job.
If you want to live a happy life, tie it to goals, not people or objects.

—Author Unknown

Happiness is beneficial for the body but it is grief that develops the powers of the mind.

—Marcel Proust

Don't put the key to happiness in someone else's pocket.

—Author Unknown

Even if happiness forgets you a little bit, never completely forget about it.

—Jacques Prévert

Man is fond of counting his troubles, but he does not count his joys. If he counted them up as he ought to, he would see that every lot has enough happiness provided for it.

—Fyodor Dostoevsky

We are happy when for everything inside us there is a corresponding something outside us.

—W.B. Yeats

Happiness is an occasional brief glance into how simple it all can be.

—Robert Brault

You need to learn to be happy by nature, because you'll seldom have the chance to be happy by circumstance.

—Lavetta Sue Wegman

Happiness consists more in conveniences of pleasure that occur every day than in great pieces of good fortune that happen but seldom.

—Benjamin Franklin

We are no longer happy so soon as we wish to be happier.

—Walter Savage Landor

The essence of philosophy is that a man should so live that his happiness shall depend as little as possible on external things.

—Epictetus

When neither their property nor their honor is touched, the majority of men live content.

—Niccolo Machiavelli

We have no more right to consume happiness without producing it than to consume wealth without producing it.

—George Bernard Shaw

To be without some of the things you want is an indispensable part of happiness.

—Bertrand Russell

I don't think most people want to be unhappy. It's just something they've gotten good at.

—Robert Brault

Happiness is not a goal. It is a by-product.

—Eleanor Roosevelt

I hope everybody could get rich and famous and have everything they ever dreamed of, so they will know that is not the answer.

—Jim Carrey

Don't confuse fun with fulfillment, or pleasure with happiness.

—Michael Josephson

I never ask God to give me anything; I only ask him to put me where things are.

—Mexican Proverb

Certain people think they will feel good if certain things happen…the trick is: you have to feel good for no reason.

—Richard Bandler

The foolish man seeks happiness in the distance; the wise grows it under his feet.

—James Openheim

It's pretty hard to tell what does bring happiness. Poverty and wealth have both failed.

—Frank McKinney "Kin" Hubbard

A man's as miserable as he thinks he is.

—Seneca

Be happy, and a reason will come along.

—Robert Brault

Happiness is not a goal; it is a by-product.

—Eleanor Roosevelt

I go about looking at horses and cattle. They eat grass, make love, work when they have to, bear their young. I am sick with envy of them.

—Sherwood Anderson

People don't notice whether it's winter or summer when they're happy.

—Anton Chekhov

All persons carry with them some means of happiness.

—James Lendall Basford

A great obstacle to happiness is to expect too much happiness.

—Bernard de Fontenelle

A full heart has room for everything and an empty heart has room for nothing.

—Antonio Porchia, Voces, 1943, translated from Spanish by W.S. Merwin

Indeed, man wishes to be happy even when he so lives as to make happiness impossible.

—St. Augustine

There is no cosmetic for beauty like happiness.

—Lady Blessington

To be obliged to beg our daily happiness from others bespeaks a more lamentable poverty than that of him who begs his daily bread.

—Charles Caleb Colton

But what is happiness except the simple harmony between a man and the life he leads?

—Albert Camus

Some pursue happiness, others create it.

—Author Unknown

Happiness makes up in height for what it lacks in length.

—Robert Frost

Happiness often sneaks in through a door you didn't know you left open.

—John Barrymore

If only we'd stop trying to be happy we could have a pretty good time.

—Edith Wharton

Happiness is a well-balanced combination of love, labour, and luck.

—Mary Wilson Little

Most folks are about as happy as they make up their minds to be.

—Abraham Lincoln

Find a place where there's joy, and the joy will burn out the pain.

—Joseph Campbell

Those who can laugh without cause have either found the true meaning of happiness or have gone stark raving mad.

—Norm Papernick

There are some days when I think I'm going to die from an overdose of satisfaction.

—Salvador Dali

If there were in the world today any large number of people who desired their own happiness more than they desired the unhappiness of others, we could have a paradise in a few years.

—Bertrand Russell

Joy is a net of love by which you can catch souls.

—Mother Teresa

You will never be happy if you continue to search for what happiness consists of. You will never live if you are looking for the meaning of life.

—Albert Camus

Happiness is usually attributed by adults to children, and by children to adults.

—Thomas Szasz

One joy scatters a hundred griefs.

—Chinese Proverb

Real happiness is cheap enough, yet how dearly we pay for its counterfeit.
—Hosea Ballou

Unhappiness is not knowing what we want and killing ourselves to get it.

—Don Herold

There are two things to aim at in life: first, to get what you want; and after that, to enjoy it. Only the wisest of mankind achieve the second.
—Logan Pearsall

The world is full of people looking for spectacular happiness while they snub contentment.

—Doug Larson

Happiness is a by-product of an effort to make someone else happy.
—Gretta Brooker Palmer

Happy is the man who can endure the highest and lowest fortune. He who has endured such vicissitudes with equanimity has deprived misfortune of its power.

—Seneca

Joy is not in things; it is in us.

—Richard Wagner

If you want to be happy, be.

—Leo Tolstoy

Don't put the key to happiness in someone else's pocket.

—Author Unknown

Even if happiness forgets you a little bit, never completely forget about it.

—Jacques Prévert

Happiness is when what you think, what you say, and what you do are in harmony.

—Mahatma Gandhi

Happiness is never stopping to think if you are.

—Palmer Sondreal

Most people would rather be certain they're miserable, than risk being happy.

—Robert Anthony

The best way to cheer yourself up is to try to cheer somebody else up.

—Mark Twain, 1896

If only we'd stop trying to be happy we could have a pretty good time.

—Edith Wharton

Happiness is excitement that has found a settling down place. But there is always a little corner that keeps flapping around.

—E.L. Konigsburg

Nobody really cares if you're miserable, so you might as well be happy.

—Cynthia Nelms

Happiness is always a by-product. It is probably a matter of temperament, and for anything I know it may be glandular. But it is not something that can be demanded from life, and if you are not happy you had better stop worrying about it and see what treasures you can pluck from your own brand of unhappiness.

—Robertson Davies

Those who can laugh without cause have either found the true meaning of happiness or have gone stark raving mad.

—Norm Papernick

All persons carry with them some means of happiness.

—James Lendall Basford (1845–1915), Sparks from the Philosopher's Stone, 1882

I don't think you can feel a sense of entitlement and still be happy. Happiness always comes from feeling that you've been blessed.

—Robert Brault, rbrault.blogspot.com

Man is fond of counting his troubles, but he does not count his joys. If he counted them up as he ought to, he would see that every lot has enough happiness provided for it.

—Fyodor Dostoevsky

Happiness is not something you postpone for the future. It's something you design for the present.

—Jim Rohn

What a wonderful life I've had! I only wish I'd realized it sooner.

—Colette

The foolish man seeks happiness in the distance; the wise grows it under his feet.

—James Openheim

Happiness often sneaks in through a door you didn't know you left open.

—John Barrymore

"Well," said Pooh, "what I like best," and then he had to stop and think. Because although Eating Honey was a very good thing to do, there was a moment just before you began to eat it which was better than when you actually were, but he didn't know what it was called.

—A.A. Milne

People take different roads seeking fulfillment and happiness. Just because they're not on your road doesn't mean they've gotten lost.

—H. Jackson Brown

It's pretty hard to tell what does bring happiness. Poverty and wealth have both failed.

—Frank McKinney "Kin" Hubbard

Happiness and sadness run parallel to each other. When one takes a rest, the other one tends to take up the slack.

—Hazelmarie Elliott ("Mattie")

We have no more right to consume happiness without producing it than to consume wealth without producing it.

—George Bernard Shaw

Happiness: an agreeable sensation arising from contemplating the misery of another.

—Ambrose Bierce

Three grand essentials to happiness in this life are something to do, something to love, and something to hope for.

—Joseph Addison

Often people attempt to live their lives backwards; they try to have more things, or more money, in order to do more of what they want, so they will be happier. The way it actually works is the reverse. You must first be who you really are, then do what you need to do, in order to have what you want.

—Margaret Young

If you are not happy here and now, you never will be.

—Taisen Deshimaru

People take different roads seeking fulfillment and happiness. Just because they're not on your road doesn't mean they've gotten lost.

—H. Jackson Brown

There is no way to happiness—happiness is the way.

—Thich Nhat Hanh

There can be no happiness if the things we believe in are different from the things we do.

—Freya Stark, The Journey's Echo

The best way for a person to have happy thoughts is to count his blessings and not his cash.

—Author Unknown

Happiness is the interval between periods of unhappiness.

—Don Marquis

To be happy, we must not be too concerned with others.

—Albert Camus

We are seldom happy with what we now have, but would go to pieces if we lost any part of it.

—Mignon McLaughlin

Happiness is the feeling you're feeling when you want to keep feeling it.

—Author Unknown

Most of us believe in trying to make other people happy only if they can be happy in ways which we approve.

—Robert S. Lynd

The greatest happiness you can have is knowing that you do not necessarily require happiness.

—William Saroyan

Be happy. It's one way of being wise.

—Colette

Sometimes we don't find the thing that will make us happy because we can't give up the thing that was supposed to.

—Robert Brault

Learn how to be happy with what you have while you pursue all that you want.

—Jim Rohn

Honesty

Speak the truth but leave immediately afterwards.

—Slovenian Proverb

People who are brutally honest get more satisfaction out of the brutality than out of the honesty.

—Richard J. Needham

Honesty is a very expensive gift. Don't expect it from cheap people.

—Warren Buffett

Worse than telling a lie is spending the rest of your life staying true to a lie.

—Robert Brault

A lie gets halfway around the world before the truth has a chance to put its pants on.

—Winston Churchill

The most exhausting thing in life is being insincere.

—Anne Morrow Lindbergh

Honesty doesn't always pay, but dishonesty always costs.
—Michael Josephson

A truth that's told with bad intent
Beats all the lies you can invent.
—William Blake (1757–1827), "Auguries of Innocence"

The least initial deviation from the truth is multiplied later a thousandfold.
—Aristotle

If you tell the truth you don't have to remember anything.
—Mark Twain, 1894

The truth needs so little rehearsal.
—Barbara Kingsolver, Animal Dreams

A half-truth is a whole lie.
—Yiddish Proverb

A lie has speed, but truth has endurance.
—Edgar J. Mohn

Every lie is two lies—the lie we tell others and the lie we tell ourselves to justify it.
—Robert Brault

The most dangerous untruths are truths moderately distorted.
—Georg Christoph Lichtenberg

Man is least himself when he talks in his own person. Give him a mask, and he will tell you the truth.
—Oscar Wilde

With lies you may get ahead in the world—but you can never go back.
—Russian Proverb

When you stretch the truth, watch out for the snapback.

—Bill Copeland

A lie may take care of the present, but it has no future.

—Author Unknown

Worse than telling a lie is spending the rest of your life staying true to a lie.

—Robert Brault

Always telling the truth is no doubt better than always lying, although equally pathological.

—Robert Brault

If falsehood, like truth, had but one face, we would be more on equal terms. For we would consider the contrary of what the liar said to be certain. But the opposite of truth has a hundred thousand faces and an infinite field.

—Michel Eyquem de Montaigne

A lie is just the truth waiting to be itself.

—Terri Guillemets

Am I lying to you if I tell you the same lie I tell myself?

—Robert Brault

If we were all given by magic the power to read each other's thoughts, I suppose the first effect would be to dissolve all friendships.

—Bertrand Russell

Truth is such a rare thing, it is delightful to tell it.

—Emily Dickinson

Reality is bad enough. Why should I tell the truth?

—Patrick Sky

Society can exist only on the basis that there is some amount of polished lying and that no one says exactly what he thinks.

—Lin Yutang

If we were all given by magic the power to read each other's thoughts, I suppose the first effect would be to dissolve all friendships.

—Bertrand Russell

A little inaccuracy sometimes saves tons of explanation.

—Saki

It takes two to lie. One to lie and one to listen.

—Homer Simpson, The Simpsons

As important in a trusting relationship as the truths you share are the lies you never have to tell.

—Robert Brault

Someday a computer will give a wrong answer to spare someone's feelings, and man will have invented artificial intelligence.

—Robert Brault

Humankind

In each generation the human mind in every man reverts to its starting-point; each new man is a primitive man.

—Alexandre Vinet

Man—a being in search of meaning.

—Plato

There are too many people, and too few human beings.

—Robert Zend

Man is harder than rock and more fragile than an egg.

—Yugoslav Proverb

One man is equivalent to all creation. One man is the world in miniature.

—Albert Pike

I am not a human being; I am a human becoming.

—Author Unknown

Every human being is a repeated question asked to the spirit of the Universe.

—Mihai Eminescu

I sometimes think that God in creating man somewhat overestimated His ability.

—Oscar Wilde

We may be the intelligent species, but we are certainly not the smartest!

—Kyle Short

Man is the only creature that refuses to be what he is.

—Albert Camus

The universe may have a purpose, but nothing we know suggests that, if so, this purpose has any similarity to ours.

—Bertrand Russell

Adam ate the apple, and our teeth still ache.

—Hungarian Proverb

Not every great man is a grand human being.

—Marie Dubsky

In nature a repulsive caterpillar turns into a lovely butterfly. But with humans it is the other way around: a lovely butterfly turns into a repulsive caterpillar.

—Anton Chekhov

Only on paper has humanity yet achieved glory, beauty, truth, knowledge, virtue, and abiding love.

—George Bernard Shaw

Men are cruel, but Man is kind.

—Rabindranath Tagore

Monkeys are superior to men in this: When a monkey looks into a mirror, he sees a monkey.

—Malcolm de Chazal

Human beings cling to their delicious tyrannies and to their exquisite nonsense, till death stares them in the face.

—Sydney Smith

Human beings invent just as many ways to sabotage their lives as to improve them.

—Mark Goulston

I sometimes think of what future historians will say of us. A single sentence will suffice for modern man: He fornicated and read the papers.

—Albert Camus

That's it! When you come to know men, that's how they are: too sensitive in the wrong place.

—D.H. Lawrence

Man is the only animal that laughs and weeps; for he is the only animal that is struck with the difference between what things are and what they ought to be.

—William Hazlitt

Man talks about everything, and he talks about everything as though the understanding of everything were all inside him.

—Antonio Porchia

We are just an advanced breed of monkeys on a minor planet of a very average star.

—Stephen Hawking

Humility

Swallow your pride occasionally, it's non-fattening!

—Author Unknown

Humility is to make a right estimate of one's self.

—Charles Haddon Spurgeon

We are all worms, but I do believe I am a glowworm.

—Winston Churchill

None are so empty as those who are full of themselves.

—Benjamin Whichcote

The selfish man looks into the world as he looks into his mirror: only to see himself.

—James Lendall Basford (1845–1915), Sparks from the Philosopher's Stone, 1882

Don't look for more honor than your learning merits.

—Jewish Proverb

Humility is the mother of giants. One sees great things from the valley; only small things from the peak.

—G.K. Chesterton

We would rather speak ill of ourselves than not talk about ourselves at all.

—François VI de la Rochefoucault, Maxims

Modesty: The art of encouraging people to find out for themselves how wonderful you are.

—Author Unknown

Talking much about oneself can also be a means to conceal oneself.

—Friedrich Nietzsche

I believe that the first great test of a truly great man is his humility. I don't mean by humility, doubt of his power. But really great men have a curious feeling that the greatness is not of them, but through them. And they see something divine in every other man and are endlessly, foolishly, incredibly merciful.

—John Ruskin

The man who thinks he can live without others is mistaken; the one who thinks others can't live without him is even more deluded.

—Hasidic Saying

The trouble with most of us is that we would rather be ruined by praise than saved by criticism.

—Norman Vincent Peale

With people of only moderate ability modesty is mere honesty; but with those who possess great talent it is hypocrisy.

—Arthur Schopenhauer

Don't talk about yourself; it will be done when you leave.

—Wilson Mizner

Glory is largely a theatrical concept. There is no striving for glory without a vivid awareness of an audience.

—Eric Hoffer, The True Believer, 1951

One learns to ignore criticism by first learning to ignore applause.

—Robert Brault

Any party which takes credit for the rain must not be surprised if its opponents blame it for the drought.

—Dwight Morrow

I can't tell you if genius is hereditary, because heaven has granted me no offspring.

—James McNeill Whistler

Don't accept your dog's admiration as conclusive evidence that you are wonderful.

—Ann Landers

Humor

Humor is emotional chaos remembered in tranquility.

—James Thurber

I think the next best thing to solving a problem is finding some humor in it.

—Frank A. Clark

Humor is reason gone mad.

—Groucho Marx

Humor is perhaps a sense of intellectual perspective: an awareness that some things are really important, others not; and that the two kinds are most oddly jumbled in everyday affairs.

—Christopher Morley

Humor results when society says you can't scratch certain things in public, but they itch in public.

—Tom Walsh

Humor prevents one from becoming a tragic figure even though they are involved in tragic events.

—E.T. "Cy" Eberhart

Every survival kit should include a sense of humor.

—Author Unknown

There is more logic in humor than in anything else. Because, you see, humor is truth.

—Victor Borge

Humor is just another defense against the universe.

—Mel Brooks

Serious things cannot be understood without laughable things, nor opposites at all without opposites.

—Plato

Humor is not a mood, but a way of looking at the world.

—Ludwig Wittgenstein

In the whole New Testament there is not a single joke. That fact alone would invalidate any book.

—Friedrich Nietzsche

Humor is... despair refusing to take itself seriously.

—Arland Ussher

If you want to make people weep, you must weep yourself. If you want to make people laugh, your face must remain serious.

—Giacomo Casanova

If I had no sense of humor, I would long ago have committed suicide.

—Mahatma Gandhi

Comedy is simply a funny way of being serious.

—Peter Ustinov

If money makes the world go round, it's humor that keeps it from spinning out of control.

—Craig Kimberley

Humor is, I think, the subtlest and chanciest of literary forms. It is surely not accidental that there are a thousand novelists, essayists, poets or journalists for each humorist. It is a long, long time between James Thurbers.

—Leo Rosten

Question: What is the quality you most like in a woman?
Walter Cronkite: I'm strongly urged by advisers not to say "moral laxity," so let's say "sense of humor."

Ideas

Ideas come from space.

—Thomas Edison

If the idea is not at first absurd, then there is no hope for it.

—Albert Einstein

Two ideas are always needed: one to kill the other.

—Georges Braque

Ideas are information taking shape.

—Jim Rohn

There is one thing stronger than all the armies in the world, and that is an idea whose time has come.

—Victor Hugo

Serious people have few ideas. People with ideas are never serious.

—Paul Vallely

If you have an apple and I have an apple and we exchange them then you and I will still have one apple. But if you have an idea and I have an idea and we exchange these ideas, then each of us will have two ideas.

—George Bernard Shaw

An idea isn't responsible for the people who believe it.

—Don Marquis

Ideas are like rabbits. You get a couple and learn how to handle them, and pretty soon you have a dozen of them.

—John Steinbeck

Ideas can no more flow backward than can a river.

—Victor Hugo

When I am completely myself, entirely alone and of good cheer – say travelling in a carriage or walking after a good meal or during the night when I cannot sleep. It is on such occasions that my ideas flow best and most abundantly. Whence and how they come I know not, nor can I force them…

—Wolfgang Amadeus Mozart

Drawing is putting a line round an idea.

—Henri Matisse

We have separated ideas from action because ideas are always of the past and action is always the present – that is, living is always the present. We are afraid of living and therefore the past, as ideas, has become so important to us.

—J. Krishnamurti

An idea that is not dangerous is unworthy of being called an idea at all.

—Oscar Wilde

Money never starts an idea. It is always the idea that starts the money.

—Owen Laughlin

When you write down your ideas you automatically focus your full attention on them. Few if any of us can write one thought and think another at the same time. Thus a pencil and paper make excellent concentration tools.

—Michael Leboeuf

Marx, Darwin and Freud are the three most crashing bores of the Western world. Simplistic popularization of their ideas has thrust our world into a mental straightjacket from which we can only escape by the most anarchic violence.

—William Golding

What matters is not the idea a man holds, but the depth at which he holds it.

—Ezra Pound

Convictions are more dangerous enemies to truth than lies.

—Friedrich Nietzsche

A great many people think they are thinking, when they are merely rearranging their prejudices.

—William James

If you wish to find, you must search. Rarely does a good idea interrupt you.

—Jim Rohn

I can't understand why people are frightened of new ideas. I am frightened of the old ones.

—John Cage

The ideas I stand for are not mine. I borrowed them from Socrates. I swiped them from Chesterfield. I stole them from Jesus. And I put them in a book. If you don't like their rules, whose would you use?

—Dale Carnegie

Humor is a reminder that no matter how high the throne one sits on, one sits on one's bottom.

—Taki

Ignorance

The little I know, I owe to ignorance.

—Sacha Guitry

Some folks are wise and some are otherwise.

—Tobias Smollett

There is no darkness but ignorance.

—William Shakespeare

Not ignorance, but ignorance of ignorance, is the death of knowledge.

—Alfred North Whitehead

There is nothing new under the sun, but there are lots of old things we don't know.

—Ambrose Bierce

A person is never happy except at the price of some ignorance.

—Anatole France

The pleasures of ignorance are as great, in their way, as the pleasures of knowledge.

—Aldous Huxley

Before we work on artificial intelligence why don't we do something about natural stupidity?

—Steve Polyak

I know nothing, except the fact of my ignorance.

—Socrates

The greatest obstacle to discovery is not ignorance – it is the illusion of knowledge.

—Daniel J. Boorstin

It's innocence when it charms us, ignorance when it doesn't.

—Mignon McLaughlin

The trouble ain't that there is too many fools, but that the lightning ain't distributed right.

—Mark Twain

At the simplest level, only people who know they do not know everything will be curious enough to find things out.

—Virginia Postrel

If ignorance is bliss, there should be more happy people.

—Victor Cousins

Everybody is ignorant. Only on different subjects.

—Will Rogers

Whenever people attack not the idea—but its source—you know they've hit the brick wall of their intellectual limitations.

—Dr. Idel Dreimer

The trouble with the world is that the stupid are cocksure and the intelligent are full of doubt.

—Bertrand Russell

Light travels faster than sound. That's why most people seem bright until you hear them speak.

—Author Unknown

Jealousy

Jealousy is a mental cancer.

—B.C. Forbes

It is not love that is blind, but jealousy.

—Lawrence Durrell, Justine, 1957

Love looks through a telescope; envy, through a microscope.

—Josh Billings

Envy assails the noblest: the winds howl around the highest peaks.

—Ovid

It is in the character of very few men to honor without envy a friend who has prospered.

—Aeschylus

Envy is ignorance.

—Ralph Waldo Emerson

If envy were a fever, all the world would be ill.

—Danish Proverb

A show of envy is an insult to oneself.

—Yevgeny Alexandrovich Yevtushenko

Envy is the art of counting the other fellow's blessings instead of your own.

—Harold Coffin

Our envy always lasts longer than the happiness of those we envy.

—François de La Rochefoucauld

Envy is thin because it bites but never eats.

—Spanish Proverb

Calamities are of two kinds: misfortune to ourselves, and good fortune to others.

—Ambrose Bierce

Envy is the most stupid of vices, for there is no single advantage to be gained from it.

—Honore de Balzac

The truest mark of being born with great qualities is being born without envy.

—Francois Duc de la Rochefoucauld

Language

Language is the dress of thought.

—Samuel Johnson

To have another language is to possess a second soul.

—Charlemagne

A different language is a different vision of life.

—Federico Fellini

If a language is corruptible, then a constitution written in that language is corruptible.

—Robert Brault

Language forces us to perceive the world as man presents it to us.

—Julia Penelope

But if thought corrupts language, language can also corrupt thought.

—George Orwell

Language is by its very nature a communal thing; that is, it expresses never the exact thing but a compromise—that which is common to you, me, and everybody.

—Thomas Earnest Hulme, Speculations, 1923

Our major obligation is not to mistake slogans for solutions.

—Edward R. Murrow

Words signify man's refusal to accept the world as it is.

—Walter Kaufmann

A language is a dialect with an army and a navy.

—Max Weinrich

I personally believe we developed language because of our deep inner need to complain.

—Jane Wagner

Almost all words do have color and nothing is more pleasant than to utter a pink word and see someone's eyes light up and know it is a pink word for him or her too.

—Gladys Taber

Language was invented to ask questions. Answered may be given grunts and gestures, but questions must be spoken. Humanness came of age when man asked the first question.

—Eric Hoffer

I was reading the dictionary. I thought it was a poem about everything.

—Steven Wright

Words, too, have genuine substance—mass and weight and specific gravity.

—Tim O'Brien, Tomcat in Love

Broadly speaking, the short words are the best, and the old words best of all.

—Winston Churchill

No one means all he says, and yet very few say all they mean, for words are slippery and thought is viscous.
—Henry Brooks Adams, The Education of Henry Adams, 1907

My language is the common prostitute that I turn into a virgin.

—Karl Kraus

What words say does not last. The words last. Because words are always the same, and what they say is never the same.

—Antonio Porchia

Life and language are alike sacred. Homicide and verbicide—that is, violent treatment of a word with fatal results to its legitimate meaning, which is its life—are alike forbidden. Manslaughter, which is the meaning of the one, is the same as man's laughter, which is the end of the other.

—Oliver Wendell Holmes, Sr. (1809–1894)

If I could but entice you with sentences and tongue tie you with words.

—Jamie Lynn Morris

It is the task of the translator to release in his own language that pure language that is under the spell of another, to liberate the language imprisoned in a work in his re-creation of that work.

—Walter Benjamin

A word is not a crystal, transparent and unchanged, it is the skin of a living thought and may vary greatly in color and content according to the circumstances and the time in which it is used.

—Oliver Wendell Holmes

Some translators turn an author's words from gold to stone, others from stone to gold.

—Terri Guillemets

Language ought to be the joint creation of poets and manual workers.

—George Orwell

He who does not know foreign languages does not know anything about his own.

—Johann Wolfgang von Goethe, Kunst and Alterthum

He swore at us in German (which I should judge to be a singularly effective language for that purpose)...

—Jerome K. Jerome, Three Men in a Boat
(To Say Nothing of the Dog), 1889

Oaths are but words, and words but wind.

—Samuel Butler (1612–1680), Hudribas

"If you can't say something nice, say it in French," my mother advised...

—Vicki Linder, "In Praise of Gossip," Cosmopolitan, 1982

Whenever ideas fail, men invent words.

—Martin H. Fischer (1879–1962)

Learning preserves the errors of the past, as well as its wisdom. For this reason, dictionaries are public dangers, although they are necessities.

—Alfred North Whitehead

Anthropologically speaking, the human race can be said to have evolved from primitive ton civilized states, but there is no sign of language having gone through the same evolution. There are no 'bronze age' or 'stone age' languages.

—David Crystal

Love

Love is metaphysical gravity.

—R. Buckminster Fuller

A man is not where he lives, but where he loves.

—Latin Proverb

Love is what makes two people sit in the middle of a bench when there is plenty of room at both ends.

—Author Unknown

Less is more, unless it's love.

—Ben Mittleman

Love is an irresistible desire to be irresistibly desired.

—Robert Frost

Who, being loved, is poor?

—Oscar Wilde

True love is a delightful slavery.

—James Lendall Basford

An old man in love is like a flower in winter.

—Portuguese Proverb

I love you not because of who you are but because of who I am when I am with you.

—Roy Croft

Your task is not to seek for love, but merely to seek and find all the barriers within yourself that you have built against it.

—Rumi

Love is when you can be your true self with someone, and you only want to be your true self because of them.

—Terri Guillemets

True love is like ghosts, which everyone talks about and few have seen.

—François de la Rochefoucault

Love me and the world is mine.

—David Reed

I was half in love with her by the time we sat down. That's the thing about girls. Every time they do something pretty, even if they're not much to look at, or even if they're sort of stupid, you fall half in love with them, and then you never know where the hell you are.

—J.D. Salinger

Being deeply loved by someone gives you strength, while loving someone deeply gives you courage.

—Lao Tzu

Once a man has won a woman's love, the love is his forever. He can only lose the woman.

—Robert Brault

The Eskimos had fifty-two names for snow because it was important to them: there ought to be as many for love.

—Margaret Atwood

Love is a game that two can play and both win.

—Eva Gabor

You know it's true love when reality sets in and it doesn't change a thing.

—Robert Brault

True love is a discipline in which each divines the secret self of the other and refuses to believe in the mere daily self.

—William Butler Yeats

Great love affairs start with Champagne and end with tisane.

—Honoré de Balzac

You know you're in love when you don't want to fall asleep because reality is finally better than your dreams.

—Dr. Seuss

Forget love—I'd rather fall in chocolate!

—Sandra J. Dykes

We choose those we like; with those we love, we have no say in the matter.

—Mignon McLaughlin

He felt now that he was not simply close to her, but that he did not know where he ended and she began.

—Leo Tolstoy

We are not the same persons this year as last; nor are those we love. It is a happy chance if we, changing, continue to love a changed person.

—W. Somerset Maugham

You can give without loving, but you can never love without giving.

—Author Unknown

Love is a canvas furnished by Nature and embroidered by imagination.

—Voltaire

Lust fades, so you'd better be with someone who can stand you.

—Alan Zweibel

Love in action is a harsh and dreadful thing compared with love in dreams.

—Fyodor Dostoyevsky

Love is the word used to label the sexual excitement of the young, the habituation of the middle-aged, and the mutual dependence of the old.

—John Ciardi

Only in love are unity and duality not in conflict.

—Rabindranath Tagore

It would be impossible to "love" anyone or anything one knew completely. Love is directed towards what lies hidden in its object.

—Paul Valéry

Platonic love is love from the neck up.

—Thyra Smater Winsolow

If I love you, what business is it of yours?

—Johann Wolfgang von Goethe

You don't have to go looking for love when it's where you come from.

—Werner Erhard

Love is the magician that pulls man out of his own hat.

—Ben Hech

Sometimes it's a form of love just to talk to somebody that you have nothing in common with and still be fascinated by their presence.

—David Byrne

Love makes time pass; time makes love pass.

—French Proverb

If grass can grow through cement, love can find you at every time in your life.

—Cher

Love is only a dirty trick played on us to achieve continuation of the species.

—W. Somerset Maugham

I love you as you are, but do not tell me how that is.

—Antonio Porchia

Love cures people—both the ones who give it and the ones who receive it.

—Karl Menninger

Absence diminishes small loves and increases great ones.

—François de la Rochefoucault

Let your love be like the misty rains, coming softly, but flooding the river.

—Malagasy Proverb

The hunger for love is much more difficult to remove than the hunger for bread.

—Mother Teresa

We're all a little weird. And life is a little weird. And when we find someone whose weirdness is compatible with ours, we join up with them and fall into mutually satisfying weirdness—and call it love— true love.

—Robert Fulghum

Take love as a sober man takes wine; do not become a drunkard. If your mistress is sincere and faithful, love her for that; but if she is not, if she is merely young and beautiful, love her for that; if she is agreeable and spirituelle, love her for that; if she is none of these things but merely loves you, love her for that. Love does not come to us every day.

—Alfred de Musset

Love doesn't sit there like a stone, it has to be made, like bread; remade all of the time, made new.

—Ursula K. Le Guin

Love is the condition in which the happiness of another person is essential to your own.

—Robert Heinlein

Love does not make the world go round. It makes the ride worthwhile.
—Author Unknown

Life has taught us that love does not consist in gazing at each other but in looking outward together in the same direction.

—Antoine de Saint-Exupéry

Love can only end in indifference. If it ends in hate, it hasn't ended.
—Robert Brault

Love is friendship that has caught fire. It settles for less than perfection and makes allowances for human weaknesses.

—Ann Landers

When love is not madness, it is not love.

—Pedro Calderon de la Barca

Love is not blind—it sees more, not less. But because it sees more, it is willing to see less.

—Julins Gordon

He gave her a look you could have poured on a waffle.

—Ring Lardner

The lover is a monotheist who knows that other people worship different gods but cannot himself imagine that there could be other gods.

—Theodor Reik

Love is a gross exaggeration of the difference between one person and everybody else.

—George Bernard Shaw

I wish people love everybody else the way they love me. It would be a better world.

—Muhammad Ali

It is not that love is blind. It is that love sees with a painter's eye, finding the essence that renders all else background.

—Robert Brault

Memory

Memory is second sight.
    —James Lendall Basford (1845–1915), *Seven Seventy Seven Sensations*, 1897

God gave us memories so that we might enjoy roses in December.

—J.M. Barrie

Memory is time folding back on itself.

—Garth Stein, The Art of Racing in the Rain, 2008

Hmmm, how to "can a day?" You know, those days that seem just perfect you want access to them whenever the need arises.

—Jeb Dickerson

The difference between false memories and true ones is the same as for jewels: it is always the false ones that look the most real, the most brilliant.

—Salvador Dali

What are memories but dreams of a better past?

—Robert Brault

A memory is what is left when something happens and does not completely unhappen.

—Edward de Bono

Some people do not become thinkers simply because their memories are too good.

—Friedrich Nietzsche

Memory is a child walking along a seashore. You never can tell what small pebble it will pick up and store away among its treasured things.

—Pierce Harris, Atlanta Journal

Memory itself is an internal rumour.

—George Santayana, The Life of Reason

Things that were hard to bear are sweet to remember.

—Seneca

The best way to remember your wife's birthday is to forget it once.

—Joseph Cossman

Memory... is the diary that we all carry about with us.

—Oscar Wilde, "The Importance of Being Earnest"

It was one of those perfect English autumnal days which occur more frequently in memory than in life.

—P.D. James

You can be sad recalling sad times, but if you really want to be sad, recall happy times.

—Robert Brault

Those who receive with most pains and difficulty remember best; every one thing they learn being, as it were, burned and branded on their minds.

—Plutarch

Every man's memory is his private literature.

—Aldous Huxley

The next best thing to the enjoyment of a good time, is the recollection of it.

—James Lendall Basford (1845–1915)

To expect a man to remember everything he has read is like expecting him to carry about in his body everything that he has ever eaten.

—Arthur Schopenhauer

The work of memory collapses time.

—Walter Benjamin

There are lots of people who mistake their imagination for their memory.

—Josh Billings

I have memories—but only a fool stores his past in the future.

—David Gerrold

Recalling days of sadness, memories haunt me. Recalling days of happiness, I haunt my memories.

—Robert Brault

The past is never dead, it is not even past.

—William Faulkner

Your memory is a monster; you forget—it doesn't. It simply files things away. It keeps things for you, or hides things from you—and summons them to your recall with a will of its own. You think you have a memory; but it has you!

—John Irving, A Prayer for Owen Meany, 1989

Living in memories is an empty gesture.

—Bhagwan Shree Rajneesh

The happiest memories are of moments that ended when they should have.

—Robert Brault

All our lives we are engaged in preserving our experiences and keeping them fresh by artificially sprinkling the water of memory over them. They have ceased to retain their original smell and fragrance. Do you call it life—this effort at the preservation of a phantom freshness in something that is withered and gone?

—Vimala Thakar

The advantage of a bad memory is that one enjoys several times the same good things for the first time.

—Friedrich Nietzsche

Memory is a complicated thing, a relative to truth, but not its twin.

—Barbara Kingsolver, Animal Dreams

Nothing fixes a thing so intensely in the memory as the wish to forget it.

—Michel de Montaigne

Men

It's a man's world, and you men can have it.

—Katherine Anne Porter

Many a man owes his success to his first wife, and his second wife to his success.

—Jim Backus

A man can be short and dumpy and getting bald but if he has fire, women will like him.

—Mae West

What is the difference between men and women? A woman wants one man to satisfy her every need, and a man wants every woman to satisfy his one need.

—Author Unknown

A man who marries his mistress leaves a vacancy in that position.

—Oscar Wilde

God gave us all a penis and a brain, but only enough blood to run one at a time.

—Robin Williams

A gentleman is simply a patient wolf.

—Lana Turner

I wonder why men get serious at all. They have this delicate, long thing hanging outside their bodies which goes up and down by its own will. If I were a man I would always be laughing at myself.

—Yoko Ono

The more I see of men, the more I like dogs.

—Germaine de Staël

Part of the reason that men seem so much less loving than women is that men's behavior is measured with a feminine ruler.

—Francesca M. Cancian

Marrying a man is like buying something you've been admiring for a long time in a shop window. You may love it when you get it home, but it doesn't always go with everything else in the house.

—Jean Kerr

Women may be able to fake orgasms, but men can fake whole relationships.

—James Shubert

The old theory was "Marry an older man, because they're more mature." But the new theory is: "Men don't mature. Marry a younger one."

—Rita Rudner

All women become like their mothers. That is their tragedy. No man does. That's his.

—Oscar Wilde

The average man is more interested in a woman who is interested in him than he is in a woman with beautiful legs.

—Marlene Dietrich

Stop? I'm the guy. I don't stop! That's the woman's job. We're the gas, they're the brakes.

—Lowell Ganz and Babaloo Mandel

Men are only as loyal as their options.

—Bill Maher

Plain women know more about men than beautiful ones do.

—Katharine Hepburn

Why do men chase women they have no intention of marrying? The same urge that makes dogs chase cars they have no intention of driving.

—Author Unknown

The hardest task in a girl's life is to prove to a man that his intentions are serious.

—Helen Rowland

It takes a woman twenty years to make a man of her son, and another woman twenty minutes to make a fool of him.

—Helen Rowland

Never trust a husband too far, nor a bachelor too near.

—Helen Rowland

Men want the same thing from their underwear that they want from women: a little bit of support, and a little bit of freedom.

—Jerry Seinfeld

Men were made for war. Without it they wandered greyly about, getting under the feet of the women, who were trying to organize the really important things of life.

—Alice Thomas Ellis

Macho doesn't prove mucho.

—Zsa Zsa Gabor

You men are not our protectors.... If you were, who would there be to protect us from?

—Mary Edwards Walker

A man would create another man if one did not already exist, but a woman might live an eternity without even thinking of reproducing her own sex.

—Goethe

It's not the men in my life, it's the life in my men.

—Mae West

A retired husband is often a wife's full-time job.

—Ella Harris

They say women talk too much. If you have worked in Congress you know that the filibuster was invented by men.

—Clare Boothe Luce

Women are never disarmed by compliments; men always are.

—Oscar Wilde

When you see a woman who can go nowhere without a staff of admirers, it is not so much because they think she is beautiful, it is because she has told them they are handsome.

—Jean Giraudoux

He is every other inch a gentleman.

—Rebecca West

How beautiful maleness is, if it finds its right expression.

—D.H. Lawrence

Men are like a fine wine. They start out like grapes, and it's our job to stomp on them and keep them in the dark until they mature into something you'd like to have dinner with.

—Author Unknown

My theory is that men are no more liberated than women.

—Indira Gandhi

All men are not slimy warthogs. Some men are silly giraffes, some woebegone puppies, some insecure frogs. But if one is not careful, those slimy warthogs can ruin it for all the others.

—Cynthia Heimel

Men live by forgetting – women live on memories.

—T.S. Eliot

When a woman is very, very bad, she is awful, but when a man is correspondingly good he is weird.

—Minna Antrim

A single Man.... is an incomplete Animal. He resembles the odd Half of a Pair of Scissors.

—Benjamin Franklin

When a man of forty falls in love with a girl of twenty, it isn't her youth he is seeking but his own.

—Lenore Coffee

The first time you buy a house you see how pretty the paint is and buy it. The second time you look to see if the basement has termites. It's the same with men.

—Lupe Velez

I want a man who's kind and understanding. Is that too much to ask of a millionaire?

—Zsa Zsa Gabor

Men wake up aroused in the morning. We can't help it. We just wake up and we want you. And the women are thinking, "How can he want me the way I look in the morning?" It's because we can't see you. We have no blood anywhere near our optic nerve.

—Sean Morey

Women are the right age for just a few years; men, for most of their lives.

—Mignon McLaughlin

Passion

Passion is universal humanity. Without it religion, history, romance and art would be useless.

—Honoré de Balzac

Renew your passions daily.

—Terri Guillemets

Our passions are the true phoenixes; when the old one is burnt out, a new one rises from its ashes.

—Johann Wolfgang von Goethe

The passions are like fire, useful in a thousand ways and dangerous only in one: through their excess.

—Christian Nestell Bovee

Man is so made that when anything fires his soul, impossibilities vanish.

—Jean de la Fontaine

We got married in a fever hotter than a pepper sprout.

—June Carter Cash

Every civilization is, among other things, an arrangement for domesticating the passions and setting them to do useful work.

—Aldous Huxley

Passion, though a bad regulator, is a powerful spring.

—Ralph Waldo Emerson

If passion drives you, let reason hold the reins.

—Benjamin Franklin

No one really knows why they are alive until they know what they'd die for.

—Martin Luther King Jr.

The most beautiful make-up of a woman is passion. But cosmetics are easier to buy.

—Yves Saint Laurent

Don't ask yourself what the world needs; ask yourself what makes you come alive. And then go and do that. Because what the world needs is people who have come alive.

—Attributed to Howard Thurman

Passion makes the world go round. Love just makes it a safer place.
—Ice-T, The Ice Opinion

You can have anything you want if you want it desperately enough. You must want it with an exuberance that erupts through the skin and joins the energy that created the world.

—Sheila Graham

Love is often gentle, desire always a rage.
—Mignon McLaughlin, The Second Neurotic's Notebook, 1966

You taught me to be nice, so nice that now I am so full of niceness, I have no sense of right and wrong, no outrage, no passion.

—Garrison Keillor

Without passion man is a mere latent force and possibility, like the flint which awaits the shock of the iron before it can give forth its spark.
—Henri-Frédéric Amiel, Journal, December 17, 1856

Chase down your passion like it's the last bus of the night.

—Terri Guillemets

The only people for me are the mad ones, the ones who are mad to live, mad to talk, mad to be saved, desirous of everything at the same time, the ones who never yawn or say a commonplace thing, but burn, burn, burn, like fabulous yellow roman candles exploding like spiders across the stars.

—Jack Kerouac

Perfection

Gold cannot be pure, and people cannot be perfect.

—Chinese Proverb

Striving for excellence motivates you; striving for perfection is demoralizing.

—Harriet Braiker

Perfection is not attainable. But if we chase perfection, we can catch excellence.

—Vince Lombardi

It's better to be perfectly useful than uselessly perfect.

—Dr. Idel Dreimer

Certain flaws are necessary for the whole. It would seem strange if old friends lacked certain quirks.

—Goethe

I cling to my imperfection, as the very essence of my being.
—Anatole France, The Garden of Epicurus, 1894

Unless I accept my faults I will most certainly doubt my virtues.

—Hugh Prather

They say that nobody is perfect. Then they tell you practice makes perfect. I wish they'd make up their minds.

—Wilt Chamberlain

Nothing that is complete breathes.
—Antonio Porchia, Voces, 1943, translated from Spanish by
W.S. Merwin

Mistakes are the very base of human thought feeding the structure like root nodules. If we were not provided with the knack of being wrong, we could never get anything useful done.

—Lewis Thomas

You see, when weaving a blanket, an Indian woman leaves a flaw in the weaving of that blanket to let the soul out.

—Martha Graham

When you aim for perfection, you discover it's a moving target.

—George Fisher

Have no fear of perfection—you'll never reach it.

—Salvador Dali

To escape criticism—do nothing, say nothing, be nothing.

—Elbert Hubbard

Even the best needles are not sharp at both ends.

—Chinese Proverb

Only in grammar can you be more than perfect.

—William Safire

Always live up to your standards—by lowering them, if necessary.
—Mignon McLaughlin, The Second Neurotic's Notebook, 1966

Perfection is achieved, not when there is nothing more to add, but when there is nothing left to take away.

—Antoine de Saint-Exupéry

A man would do nothing if he waited until he could do it so well that no one could find fault.

—John Henry Newman

Better a diamond with a flaw than a pebble without.

—Confucius, Analects

It's not that perfection cannot be achieved. It's that it's so hard to stop there.

—Robert Brault

Once you accept the fact that you're not perfect, then you develop some confidence.

—Rosalynn Carter

Ideals are absolutes—they are like round holes of perfection into which the square, rough-hewn pegs of reality can never be successfully fitted.

—Dr. Idel Dreimer

There is a crack in everything. That's how the light gets in.

—Leonard Cohen

There are no perfect men in this world, only perfect intentions.

—Pen Densham, Robin Hood: Prince of Thieves

Sometimes... when you hold out for everything, you walk away with nothing.

—Author Unknown

The closest to perfection a person ever comes is when he fills out a job application form.

—Stanley J. Randall

Questions

Millions saw the apple fall, but Newton asked why.

—Bernard Baruch

Be curious always! For knowledge will not acquire you; you must acquire it.

—Sudie Back

'Why?' and 'How?' are words so important that they cannot be too often used.

—Napoleon Bonaparte

You can tell if a man is clever by his answers. You can tell if a man is wise by his questions.

—Naguib Mahfouz

It is better to know some of the questions than all of the answers.

—James Thurber

It is not the answer than enlightens but the question.

—Eugene Ionesco

I keep six honest serving-men. They taught me all I knew. Their names are What and Why and When and How and Where and Who.

—Rudyard Kipling

I have no special talents. I am only passionately curious.

—Albert Einstein

The great question that has never been answered, and which I have not yet been able to answer despite my thirty years of research into the feminine soul is: What does a woman want?

—Sigmund Freud

All that non-fiction can do is answer questions. It's fiction's business to ask them.

—Richard Hughes

The "silly" question is the intimation of some totally new development.

—A.N. Whitehead

There are innumerable questions to which the inquisitive mind can in this state receive no answer: Why do you and I exist? Why was this world created? Since it was to be created, why was it not created sooner?

—Samuel Johnson

Curiosity is a willing, a proud, an eager confession of ignorance.
—S. Leonard Rubinstein, Writing: A Habit of Mind

A sense of curiosity is nature's original school of education.
—Smiley Blanton

Every sentence that I utter must be understood not as an affirmation but as a question.
—Niels Bohr

The cure for boredom is curiosity. There is no cure for curiosity.
—Ellen Parr, quoted in Reader's Digest "Quotable Quotes," December 1980

To be curious about that which is not one's concern while still in ignorance of oneself is absurd.
—Plato

Be patient with all that is unresolved in your heart. And try to love the questions themselves. Do not seek for the answers that cannot be given. For you wouldn't be able to live with them. And the point is to live everything, live the questions now and perhaps without knowing it, you will live along someday into the answers.
—Rainer Maria Rilke

The outcome of any serious research can only be to make two questions grow where only one grew before.
—Thorstein Veblen

To realize that the question does not matter is the first step towards answering it correctly.
—G.K. Chesterton

The larger the island of knowledge, the longer the shoreline of wonder.
—Ralph W. Sockman

There are no foolish questions, and no man becomes a fool until he has stopped asking questions.

—Charles Proteus Steinmetz

In the search for truth, there are certain questions that are not important. Of what material is the universe constructed? Is the universe eternal? Are there limits or not to the universe? What is the ideal form of organization for human society? If a man were to postpone his search for Enlightenment until such questions were solved, he would die before he found the path.

—Buddha

Quotes

A proverb is an exploding atom of wisdom.

—Gaston Kaboré

Short sentences drawn from long experience.

—Miguel de Cervantes

A proverb is to speech what salt is to food.

—Arabic Proverb

Quotationality defines us. We are what we quote.

—Gary Saul Morson

Maybe our favorite quotations say more about us than about the stories and people we're quoting.

—John Green

There are gems of thought that are ageless and eternal.

—Cicero

I love quotations because it is a joy to find thoughts one might have, beautifully expressed with much authority by someone recognized wiser than oneself.

—Marlene Dietrich

A quotation at the right moment is like bread in a famine.

—Yiddish Proverb

Write a wise saying and your name will live forever.

—Author unknown

You might not be able to answer a question with a question but you can always answer a question with a quote!

—Hunter Brinkmeier

Some lines are born quotations, some are made quotations, and some have "quotation" thrust upon them.

—Gary Saul Morson

Proverbs are the literature of reason.

—French Proverb

The maxims of men disclose their hearts.

—French Proverb

When two seemingly conflicting thoughts have made it to proverb or aphorism status, usually, in the ambivalence of life, both are true.

—Robert Irvine Fitzhenry

Apothegms form a short cut to much knowledge.

—Thomas Hood

I always love to quote Albert Einstein because nobody dares contradict him.

—Studs Terkel

Nothing ever becomes real till it is experienced—even a Proverb is no proverb to you till your Life has illustrated it.

—John Keats, letter to George and Georgiana Keats, February 24, 1819

Stronger than an army is a quotation whose time has come.

—W. Gates

In quoting others we cite ourselves.

—Julio Cortázar (1914–1984), Around the Day in
Eighty Worlds

A picture, it is said, is worth a thousand words, but cannot a few well-spoken words convey as many pictures?

—Author Unknown

The proper proportions of a maxim: a minimum of sound to a maximum of sense.

—Mark Twain

I often quote myself. It adds spice to my conversation.

—George Bernard Shaw

There are but few proverbial sayings that are not true, for they are all drawn from experience itself, which is the mother of all sciences.

—Miguel de Cervantes

Centuries have not worm-eaten the solidity of this ancient furniture of the mind.

—Isaac D'Israeli

Proverbs are in the world of thought what gold coin is in the world of business—great value in small compass, and equally current among all people. Sometimes the proverb may be false, the coin counterfeit, but in both cases the false proves the value of the true.

—Attributed to D. March in A Dictionary of Thoughts:
A Cyclopedia of Laconic Quotations from the Best Authors of
the World, Both Ancient and Modern by Tryon Edwards, 1908

Colors fade, temples crumble, empires fall, but wise words endure.

—Agnes Sybil Thorndike (1882–1976)

Gnomic wisdom, however, is notoriously polychrome, and proverbs depend for their truth entirely on the occasion they are applied to. Almost every wise saying has an opposite one, no less wise, to balance it...

—George Santayana,

Proverbs are potted wisdom.

—Charles Buxton

Every book is a quotation; and every house is a quotation out of all forests and mines and stone quarries; and every man is a quotation from all his ancestors.

—Ralph Waldo Emerson, "Plato; or, The Philosopher"

A good conversationalist is not one who remembers what was said, but says what someone wants to remember.

—John Mason Brown

Quotes are nothing but inspiration for the uninspired.

—Attributed to Richard Kemph

An aphorism is never exactly true.
It is either a half-truth or a truth and a half.

—Karl Kraus

I quote others in order to better express myself.

—Michel de Montaigne

Different people have different quotational gravity.

—Willis Goth Regier

The lips of the wise are as the doors of a cabinet; no sooner are they opened, but treasures are poured out before thee. Like unto trees of gold arranged in beds of silver, are wise sentences uttered in due season.

—The Economy of Human Life,
from an Indian manuscript

Quotation is the highest compliment you can pay to an author.

—André-Marie Ampère

He picked something out of everything he read.

—Pliny

Quotations calcify into clichés.

—Willis Goth Regier

You may get a large amount of truth into a brief space.

—Attributed to Beecher in Edge-Tools of Speech
by Maturin M. Ballou, 1899

People will accept your idea more readily if you tell them Benjamin Franklin said it first.

—David H. Comins

I am fully conscious of the fact, that aphorisms are like wandering Gypsies. They must always be published without guarantee of the authenticity.

—Erkki Melartin

Most of those who make collections of verse or epigram are like men eating cherries or oysters: they choose out the best at first, and end by eating all.

—Sébastien-Roch Nicolas

The devil can cite scripture for his purpose.

—William Shakespeare, Merchant of Venice

Most collectors collect tangibles. As a quotation collector, I collect wisdom, life, invisible beauty, souls alive in ink.

—Terri Guillemets

The proverbs of a nation furnish the index to its spirit and the results of its civilization.

—Timothy Titcomb

Books are the beehives of thought; laconics, the honey taken from them.
—James Ellis, quoted in Edge-Tools of Speech
by Maturin M. Ballou, 1899

A quote is just a tattoo on the tongue.
—Attributed to William F. DeVault

It is a pleasure to be able to quote lines to fit any occasion...
—Abraham Lincoln

When a thing has been said, and said well, have no scruple. Take it and copy it.
—Anatole France

Reframing an extract as a quotation constitutes a kind of coauthorship. With no change in wording, the cited passage becomes different. I imagine that the thrill of making an anthology includes the opportunity to become such a coauthor.
—Gary Saul Morson

Anatole France frankly advised, "When a thing has been said and said well, have no scruple. Take it and copy it." Yes, indeed, but do more. Copy many well-said things. Pierce them together. Assimilate them. Make the process of reading them a way to form the mind and shape the soul. As anthologies can never be complete, we will never exhaust the ways quotations can enrich our lives.
—Gary Saul Morson

Life itself is a quotation.
—Jorge Luis Borges

Quotation brings to many people one of the intensest joys of living.... This innocent vanity often helps us over the hard places in life; it gives us a warm little glow against the coldness of the world and keeps us snug and happy.
—Bernard Darwin

He wrapped himself in quotations—as a beggar would enfold himself in the purple of Emperors.

—Rudyard Kipling

Have you ever observed that we pay much more attention to a wise passage when it is quoted, than when we read it in the original author?
—Philip Gilbert Hamerton, The Intellectual Life, 1873

Anyone can tell the truth, but only very few of us can make epigrams.
—W. Sommerset Maugham

A writer can get into a vast deal of trouble through misquotation. If you ever want to receive lots of mail, I recommend you get a Shakespeare quote wrong in a magazine or newspaper.

—Joseph Epstein

A book of quotations... can never be complete.
—Robert M. Hamilton

Many useful and valuable books lie buried in shops and libraries, unknown and unexamined, unless some lucky compiler opens them by chance, and finds an easy spoil of wit and learning.
—Samuel Johnson, 1760

I am not merely a habitual quoter but an incorrigible one. I am, I may as well face it, more quotatious than an old stock-market ticker-tape machine, except that you can't unplug me.

—Joseph Epstein

Language would be tolerable without spicy, epigrammatic sayings, and life could no doubt be carried on by means of plain language wholly bereft of ornament. But if we wish to relish language, if we wish to give it point and piquancy, and if we want to drive home a truth, to whip up the flagging attention of our listener, to point a moral or adorn a tale, we must flavour our speech with proverbs.
—John Christian, "Introduction," Behar Proverbs, 1891

Somewhere in this world there is an epigram for every dilemma.
—Hendrik Willem van Loon, The Liberation of Mankind, 1926

It is my belief that nearly any invented quotation, played with confidence, stands a good chance to deceive.
—Mark Twain

To be apt in quotation is a splendid and dangerous gift. Splendid because it ornaments a man's speech with other men's jewels; dangerous, for the same reason.
—Robertson Davies

The great writers of aphorisms read as if they had all known each other well.
—Elias Canetti

Many of the historical proverbs have a doubtful paternity.
—Ralph Waldo Emerson, "Quotation and Originality," Letters and Social Aims, 1876

Like your body your mind also gets tired so refresh it by wise sayings.
—Hazrat Ali

Fine phrases I value more than bank-notes. I have ear for no other harmony than the harmony of words. To be occasionally quoted is the only fame I care for.
—Alexander Smith

I suppose every old scholar has had the experience of reading something in a book which was significant to him, but which he could never find again. Sure he is that he read it there; but no one else ever read it, nor can he find it again, though he buy the book, & ransack every page.
—Ralph Waldo Emerson, c.1867

In places this book is a little over-written, because Mr Blunden is no more able to resist a quotation than some people are to refuse a drink.
—George Orwell, review of Cricket Country
by Edmund Blunden

The chief ingredients which go to make a true proverb are: sense, shortness, and salt.
—James Howell, Paroimiografia, 1659

The taste of the finely-worded truth rolled upon the tongue as its thought is revolved in the mind.
—William Francis Henry King, "Introduction," Classical and
Foreign Quotations, 1889

I have heard that nothing gives an Author so great Pleasure, as to find his Works respectfully quoted by other learned Authors.
—Benjamin Franklin, "Preface," Poor Richard Improved

The only way to read a book of aphorisms without being bored is to open it at random and, having found something that interests you, close the book and meditate.
—Prince Charles-Joseph de Ligne, 1796

My readers, who may at first be apt to consider Quotation as downright pedantry, will be surprised when I assure them, that next to the simple imitation of sounds and gestures, Quotation is the most natural and most frequent habitude of human nature. For, Quotation must not be confined to passages adduced out of authors. He who cites the opinion, or remark, or saying of another, whether it has been written or spoken, is certainly one who quotes; and this we shall find to be universally practiced.
—James Boswell, "The Hypochondriack," 1779

I enjoy collecting quotations. When I find a choice one I pounce on it like a lepidopterist. My day is made. When I lose one because I did not copy it out at once I feel bereft.

—R.I. Fitzhenry, preface to The David & Charles Book of
Quotations, September 1981

We love quotations; they strengthen us in our own belief; they show that some other spirit, perhaps a master-spirit, has gone thus far with us.

—S.J.W., "On Female Education," 1835

It is bad enough to see one's own good things fathered on other people, but it is worse to have other people's rubbish fathered upon oneself.

—Samuel Butler

When I hear or read a good line I can hardly wait to tell it to somebody else...

—Robert Byrne

Many moons ago dictionaries of quotations may have been less needed than they are today. In those good/bad old days, people walked around with entire poems and all the Shakespearean soliloquies in their heads....

—Joseph Epstein

A true quotation cannot be divorced from the character who uttered or scribbled it; it should say as much about the person quoted as about the particular subject referred to, and for this reason an anthology of quotations should be a kind of portrait gallery.

—Robert Andrews

Reality

Nothing exists except atoms and empty space; everything else is opinion.

—Democritus

It may be a good thing to copy reality; but to invent reality is much, much better.

—Giuseppe Verdi

Reality is merely an illusion, albeit a very persistent one.

—Albert Einstein

We are all captives of the picture in our head – our belief that the world we have experienced is the world that really exists.

—Walter Lippmann

Objectivity has about as much substance as the emperor's new clothes.

—Connie Miller

Reality leaves a lot to the imagination.

—John Lennon

Nothing exists but thoughts! The universe is composed of impressions, ideas, pleasures and pains!

—Sir Humphrey Davy

Few people have the imagination for reality.

—Johann Wolfgang von Goethe

If a dream is realistic, it's not really a dream. It's a to-do.

—Kim and Jason Kotecki

There is no way you can use the word "reality" without quotation marks around it.

—Joseph Campbell (1904–1987)

To treat your facts with imagination is one thing, but to imagine your facts is another.

—John Burroughs

Reality bites... and doesn't let go.

—Author Unknown

Seems like nothing ever brings you back to reality that makes you want to stay there.

—Robert Brault

One day it will have to be officially admitted that what we have christened reality is an even greater illusion than the world of dreams.

—Salvador Dali

Humankind cannot bear very much reality.

—T.S. Eliot

Illusion is the first of all pleasures.

—Voltaire

Being realistic is the most commonly traveled way to mediocrity.

—Will Smith

There are no facts, only interpretations.

—Friedrich Nietzsche

Did you ever wonder if the person in the puddle is real, and you're just a reflection of him?

—Calvin and Hobbes

What we call reality is an agreement that people have arrived at to make life more livable.

—Louise Nevelson

Reality is the leading cause of stress amongst those in touch with it.

—Jane Wagner

How reluctantly the mind consents to reality!

—Norman Douglas

It must be hard to be a model, because you'd want to be like the photograph of you, and you can't ever look that way.

—Andy Warhol

Listening to both sides of a story will convince you that there is more to a story than both sides.

—Frank Tyger

Disbelief in magic can force a poor soul into believing in government and business.

—Tom Robbins

All the mind's activity is easy if it is not subjected to reality.

—Marcel Proust, Remembrance of Things Past:
Cities of the Plain

Relationships

If you want to go fast, go alone. If you want to go far, go together.

—African Proverb

To know when to go away and when to come closer is the key to any lasting relationship.

—Doménico Cieri Estrada

Shared joy is a double joy; shared sorrow is half a sorrow.

—Swedish Proverb

Having someone wonder where you are when you don't come home at night is a very old human need.

—Margaret Mead

Remember that in giving any reason at all for refusing, you lay some foundation for a future request.

—Arthur Helps

Helping others out of trouble generally helps the helper into trouble.
    —James Lendall Basford (1845–1915), Seven Seventy Seven
Sensations, 1897

No road is long with good company.

—Turkish Proverb

Good company upon the road is the shortest cut.

—Author Unknown

Once you find someone to share your ups and downs, downs are almost as good as ups.

—Robert Brault

Only your real friends will tell you when your face is dirty.

—Sicilian Proverb

A partner is someone who makes you more than you are, simply by being by your side.

—Albert Kim

To truly know someone is to know the silence that stands for the thing they never speak of.

—Robert Brault

Are we not like two volumes of one book?
                —Marceline Desbordes-Valmore

The antidote for fifty enemies is one friend.

—Aristotle

A loyal friend laughs at your jokes when they're not so good, and sympathizes with your problems when they're not so bad.

—Arnold H. Glasgow

Assumptions are the termites of relationships.

—Henry Winkler

People change and forget to tell each other.

—Lillian Hellman

True friendship comes when silence between two people is comfortable.

—Dave Tyson Gentry

Sometimes it is the person closest to us who must travel the furthest distance to be our friend.

—Robert Brault

Lots of people want to ride with you in the limo, but what you want is someone who will take the bus with you when the limo breaks down.

—Oprah Winfrey

When something is missing in your life, it usually turns out to be someone.

—Robert Brault

The most beautiful discovery true friends make is that they can grow separately without growing apart.

—Elisabeth Foley

Self

If I didn't define myself for myself, I would be crunched into other people's fantasies for me and eaten alive.

—Audre Lorde

We are all primary numbers divisible only by ourselves.

—Jean Guitton

The world is not outside you.

—Ramana Maharshi

Every man is his own ancestor, and every man his own heir. He devises his own future, and he inherits his own past.

—H.F. Hedge

Man cannot remake himself without suffering, for he is both the marble and the sculptor.

—Dr. Alexis Carrel

I am sure that nothing has such a decisive influence upon a man's course as his personal appearance, and not so much his appearance as his belief in its attractiveness or unattractiveness.

—Leo Tolstoy

Before you diagnose yourself with depression or low self-esteem, first make sure that you are not, in fact, just surrounding yourself with assholes.

—William Gibson

There is nothing noble about being superior to some other person. The true nobility is in being superior to your previous self.

—Hindustani Proverb

You cannot be lonely if you like the person you're alone with.

—Wayne W. Dyer

The mirror will only lie, when you look at it through a mask.

—Anthony Liccione

I am a raging sea trapped in a raindrop.

—Author unknown

Why should we honor those that die upon the field of battle? A man may show as reckless a courage in entering into the abyss of himself.

—William Butler Yeats

If in the last few years you haven't discarded a major opinion or acquired a new one, check your pulse. You may be dead.

—Gelett Burgess

Be careful of selfish motives. You can mistake them for principles and end up dying for them.

—Robert Braul

We are the products of editing, rather than authorship.

—George Wald

There is a public me and a private me, who, if they were separate people, probably wouldn't exchange Christmas cards.

—Robert Brault

Do I contradict myself?
Very well, then, I contradict myself,
I am large—I contain multitudes.

—Walt Whitman, Leaves of Grass

Your burden is of false self-identifications—abandon them all.

—Nisargadatta Maharaj

A criminal becomes a popular figure because he unburdens in no small degree the consciences of his fellow man, for now they know once more where evil is to be found.

—Carl G. Jung

We must be our own before we can be another's.

—Ralph Waldo Emerson

The promises of this world are, for the most part, vain phantoms; and to confide in one's self, and become something of worth and value is the best and safest course.

—Michelangelo

The body is a house of many windows: there we all sit, showing ourselves and crying on the passers-by to come and love us.

—Robert Louis Stevenson

People aren't ignoring you. They are busy with their lives. And the way to stop feeling ignored is to get busy with yours.

—Robert Brault

Selfishness is not living as one wishes to live. It is asking others to live as one wishes to live.

—Oscar Wilde

Grace is within you. If it were external, it would be useless.

—Ramana Maharshi

We are sure to be losers when we quarrel with ourselves; it is civil war.

—Charles Caleb Colton

We all have to escape from this thing called life sometimes. Maybe we use substances to do it. Maybe we use religion. Maybe we use exercise. Maybe we use anger. But we all have to do it. How we do it is what defines us.

—Dan Pearce

Dig within. There lies the well-spring of good: ever dig, and it will ever flow.

—Marcus Aurelius

Every human has four endowments – self-awareness, conscience, independent will and creative imagination. These give us the ultimate human freedom… The power to choose, to respond, to change.

—Stephen Covey

I wish I could show you when you are lonely or in the darkness, the astonishing light of your own being.

—Hāfez

What we do flows from who we are.

—Paul Vitale

There is luxury in self-reproach.... When we blame ourselves we feel no one else has a right to blame us.

—Oscar Wilde

The importance and unimportance of the self cannot be exaggerated.
—Reginald H. Blyth

How easy it is to be "deep": all you have to do is let yourself sink into your own flaws.

—E.M. Cioran

Renew thyself completely each day; do it again, and again, and forever again.

—Chinese Proverb

Take your work seriously, but never yourself.
—Margot Fonteyn

It is often hard to bear the tears that we ourselves have caused.
—Marcel Proust

One must have chaos within one to give birth to a dancing star.
—Friedrich Nietzsche (1844–1900)

A wise man never loses anything if he have himself.
—Michel de Montaigne

I know not what phantom we take for self....
—Alexandre Vinet (1797–1847)

A man who finds no satisfaction in himself, seeks for it in vain elsewhere.
—François de la Rochefoucault

Having perfected our disguise, we spend our lives searching for someone we don't fool.

—Robert Brault

All men are sculptors, constantly chipping away the unwanted parts of their lives, trying to create their idea of a masterpiece.

—Eddie Murphy, 1979

To be happy is to be able to become aware of oneself without fright.

—Walter Benjamin

The words "I am" are potent words; be careful what you hitch them to. The thing you're claiming has a way of reaching back and claiming you.

—A.L. Kitselman

Almost always it is the fear of being ourselves that brings us to the mirror.

—Antonio Porchia, Voces, 1943

It's like, at the end, there's this surprise quiz: am I proud of me? I gave my life to become the person I am right now! Was it worth what I paid?

—Richard Bach

From birth to death every man is weaving destiny around himself, as a spider does his web.

—Helena P. Blavatsky (1831–1891)

At this very moment, you may be saying to yourself that you have any number of admirable qualities. You are a loyal friend, a caring person, someone who is smart, dependable, fun to be around. That's wonderful, and I'm happy for you, but let me ask you this: are you being any of those things to yourself?

—Phillip C. McGraw

What an odd, ruminating, noisy, self-interrupting conversation we conduct with ourselves from birth to death.

—Diane Ackerman, An Alchemy of Mind: The Marvel and Mystery of the Brain

It is not easy to find happiness in ourselves, and it is not possible to find it elsewhere.

—Agnes Repplier

There is great security in the prisons we create for ourselves.
—Stephen G. Scalese, The Whisper in Your Heart

A philosopher lives in your mind, a lover in your heart, an alchemist in your soul.
—Terri Guillemets

I said I could have done the thing, had the obstacles been removed, but after all else had been cleared away, there would still have been myself.
—Muriel Strode (1875–1964), My Little Book of Life, 1912

Man is never alone. Acknowledged or unacknowledged, that which dreams through him is always there to support him from within.
—Laurence van der Post

Everyone is a moon, and has a dark side which he never shows to anybody.
—Mark Twain

If you only live for yourself you are always in immediate danger of being bored to death with the repetition of your own views and interests.
—W. Beran Wolfe

Think positively about yourself.... ask God who made you to keep on remaking you.
—Norman Vincent Peale

I have had more trouble with myself than with any other man.
—Dwigh L. Moody

Each of us is something of a schizophrenic personality, tragically divided against ourselves.

—Martin Luther King, Jr.

Trying to define yourself is like trying to bite your own teeth.

—Alan Watts

I was right not to be afraid of any thief but myself, who will end by leaving me nothing.

—Katherine Anne Porter

There is as much difference between us and ourselves as between us and others.

—Michel De Montaigne

There are at least two kinds of cowards. One kind always lives with himself, afraid to face the world. The other kind lives with the world, afraid to face himself.

—Roscoe Snowden

The most excellent Jihad is that for the conquest of self.

—Cyril Connolly

And remember, no matter where you go, there you are.

—Confucius

The perfect man has no self.

—Zhuangzi

Self-destruction is the effect of cowardice in the highest extreme.

—Daniel Defoe

My life has been one great big joke,
A dance that's walked,
A song that's spoke,

I laugh so hard I almost choke,
When I think about myself.

—Maya Angelou

In a speech, the columnist Charles Krauthammer.... offered a new version of Socrates' famous saying, "The unexamined life is not worth living." In our age of bottomless self-love and obsession with our own feelings, Krauthammer suggested, "The too-examined life is not worth living either."

—John Leo

Sex

Sex is God's joke on human beings.

—Bette Davis

The natural man has only two primal passions, to get and beget.

—William Osler

Sex and sleep make me conscious that I am mortal.

—Alexander the Great

Why should we take advice on sex from the pope? If he knows anything about it, he shouldn't!

—George Bernard Shaw

The finest people marry the two sexes in their own person.

—Ralph Waldo Emerson

Love is a matter of chemistry, but sex is a matter of physics.

—Author Unknown

My wife is a sex object. Every time I ask for sex, she objects.

—Les Dawson

You know, of course, that the Tasmanians, who never committed adultery, are now extinct.

—W. Somerset Maugham, The Bread-Winner

The difference between sex and love is that sex relieves tension and love causes it.

—Woody Allen

The common thread that binds nearly all animal species seems to be that males are willing to abandon all sense and decorum, even to risk their lives, in the frantic quest for sex.

—Randy Thornhill and Craig T. Palmer

If you use the electric vibrator near water, you will come and go at the same time.

—Louise Sammons

Sex between a man and a woman can be a beautiful thing, provided you're between the right man and the right woman.

—Woody Allen

The tragedy is when you've got sex in the head instead of down where it belongs.

—D.H. Lawrence

It is not economical to go to bed early to save candles if the result is twins.

—Chinese Proverb

It was also Jacque who told me that children didn't come out of their mother's tummies. As she put it, "Where the ingredients go in is where the finished product comes out!"

—Anne M. Frank, letter, 1944

I thank God I was raised Catholic, so sex will always be dirty.

—John Waters

Sex hasn't been the same since women started enjoying it.
—Lewis Grizzard

My message to businessmen of this country when they go abroad on business is that there is one thing above all they can take with them to stop them catching AIDS, and that is the wife.
—Edwina Currie

Obscenity is whatever gives the Judge an erection.
—Author Unknown

Nymphomaniac: a woman as obsessed with sex as an average man.
—Mignon McLaughlin, The Neurotic's Notebook, 1960

Sex Education – A controversial course that parents argue about while their kids are out doing the lab work.
—Richard E. Turner

The hypothalamus is one of the most important parts of the brain, involved in many kinds of motivation, among other functions. The hypothalamus controls the "Four F's": fighting, fleeing, feeding, and mating.
—Marvin Dunnette

For women the best aphrodisiacs are words. The G-spot is in the ears. He who looks for it below there is wasting his time.
—Isabel Allende

The difference between pornography and erotica is lighting.
—Gloria Leonard

Having sex is like playing bridge. If you don't have a good partner, you'd better have a good hand.
—Woody Allen

Sex. In America an obsession. In other parts of the world a fact.
—Marlene Dietrich

I am always looking for meaningful one night stands.

—Dudley Moore

It isn't premarital sex if you have no intention of getting married.

—Drew Carey

While farmers generally allow one rooster for ten hens, ten men are scarcely sufficient to service one woman.

—Boccaccio

Do infants enjoy infancy as much as adults enjoy adultery?

—Murray Banks

I think I could fall madly in bed with you.

—Author Unknown

The sexual organs show more character than the actors' faces.... There are phalluses in porno whose distended veins speak of the integrity of the hardworking heart, but there is so little specific content in the faces! Hard core lulls after it excites, and finally it puts the brain to sleep.

—Norman Mailer

Playboy exploits sex the way Sports Illustrated exploits sports.

—Hugh Hefner

Desire is in men a hunger, in women only an appetite.

—Mignon McLaughlin, The Neurotic's Notebook, 1960

When authorities warn you of the sinfulness of sex, there is an important lesson to be learned. Do not have sex with the authorities.

—Matt Groening

Literature is mostly about having sex and not much about having children; life is the other way around.

—David Lodge, The British Museum Is Falling Down, 1965

Older women are best because they always think they may be doing it for the last time.

—Ian Fleming

Erotica is using the feather, pornography is using the whole chicken.

—Isabel Allende

An intellectual is someone who has discovered something more interesting than sex.

—Aldous Huxley

To know the difference between erotica and pornography you must first know the difference between naked and nude.

—Bernard Poulin

When a man talks dirty to a woman, it's sexual harassment. When a woman talks dirty to a man, it's $3.95 a minute.

—Author Unknown

Sex is one of the nine reasons for reincarnation. The other eight are unimportant.

—Henry Miller

Sex is something children never discuss in the presence of their elders.

—Arthur Roche

For the first time in history, sex is more dangerous than the cigarette afterward.

—Jay Leno

Simplicity

Simplicity is the ultimate sophistication.

—Leonardo Da Vinci

Men of few words are the best men.

—William Shakespeare

It is far more difficult to be simple than to be complicated.

—John Ruskin

All the great things are simple.

—Winston Churchill

The greatest step towards a life of simplicity is to learn to let go.

—Steve Maraboli

Besides the noble art of getting things done, there is the noble art of leaving things undone. The wisdom of life consists in the elimination of non-essentials.

—Lin Yutang

The ability to simplify means to eliminate the unnecessary so that the necessary may speak.

—Hans Hofmann, Introduction to the Bootstrap, 1993

I've adjectived up my life so much I forgot how to be simple and plain and quiet. Be. Just be.

—Terri Guillemets

Everything we possess that is not necessary for life or happiness becomes a burden, and scarcely a day passes that we do not add to it.

—Robert Brault

How many things are there which I do not want.

—Socrates

Any intelligent fool can make things bigger, more complex, and more violent. It takes a touch of genius—and a lot of courage—to move in the opposite direction.

—E.F. Schumacher

Simplicity and harmony are the ultimate conditions to be attained in all things.

—Horace Fletcher

The sculptor produces the beautiful statue by chipping away such parts of the marble block as are not needed—it is a process of elimination.

—Elbert Hubbard

Frugality is one of the most beautiful and joyful words in the English language, and yet one that we are culturally cut off from understanding and enjoying. The consumption society has made us feel that happiness lies in having things, and has failed to teach us the happiness of not having things.

—Elise Boulding

Very simple ideas lie within the reach only of complex minds.

—Rémy de Gourmont

Simplicity does not precede complexity, but follows it.

—Alan J. Perlis

You have succeeded in life when all you really want is only what you really need.

—Vernon Howard

The goal of life: simple but not empty.

—Terri Guillemets

Everything that is exact is short.

—Joseph Joubert

Our affluent society contains those of talent and insight who are driven to prefer poverty, to choose it, rather than submit to the desolation of an empty abundance.

—Michael Harrington

Maybe a person's time would be as well spent raising food as raising money to buy food.

—Frank A. Clark

If you haven't had at least a slight poetic crack in the heart, you have been cheated by nature.

—Phyllis Battelle

Reduce the complexity of life by eliminating the needless wants of life, and the labors of life reduce themselves.

—Edwin Way Teale

Truth is ever to be found in the simplicity, not in the multiplicity and confusion of things.

—Isaac Newton

When the solution is simple, God is answering.

—Albert Einstein

The greatest truths are the simplest: so likewise are the greatest men.

—Augustus William Hare

Simplicity of life is not a misery but the foundation of refinement.

—William Morris

Everything should be made as simple as possible, but not simpler.

—Albert Einstein

Live simply that others might simply live.

—Elizabeth Ann Seton

Material blessings, when they pay beyond the category of need, are weirdly fruitful of headache.

—Philip Wylie

Solitude

The happiest of all lives is a busy solitude.

—Voltaire

Conversation enriches the understanding, but solitude is the school of genius.

—Edward Gibbon

The man who goes alone can start today but he who travels with another must wait till the other is ready.

—Henry David Thoreau

Our language has wisely sensed the two sides of being alone. It has created the word loneliness to express the pain of being alone. And it has created the word solitude to express the glory of being alone.

—Paul Tillich

Solitude is a form of meditation.

—Terri Guillemets

One can acquire everything in solitude except character.

—Stendhal

We live in a very tense society. We are pulled apart... and we all need to learn how to pull ourselves together.... I think that at least part of the answer lies in solitude.

—Helen Hayes

Man loves company even if it is only that of a small burning candle.
—Georg Christoph Lichtenberg (1742–1799)

The thing that makes you exceptional, if you are at all, is inevitably that which must also make you lonely.

—Lorraine Hansberry

In a soulmate we find not company but a completed solitude.

—Robert Brault

With some people solitariness is an escape not from others but from themselves. For they see in the eyes of others only a reflection of themselves.

—Eric Hoffer

Reading well is one of the great pleasures that solitude can afford you.

—Harold Bloom

There are days when solitude is a heady wine that intoxicates you with freedom, others when it is a bitter tonic, and still others when it is a poison that makes you beat your head against the wall.

—Colette

Inside myself is a place where I live all alone, and that's where I renew my springs that never dry up.

—Pearl Buck

I went to the woods because I wished to live deliberately, to front only the essential facts of life, and see if I could not learn what it had to teach, and not, when I came to die, discover that I had not lived.

—Henry David Thoreau, 1854

I'm not anti-social. I'm pro-solitude.

—Author unknown

Loneliness can be conquered only by those who can bear solitude.

—Paul Tillich

It is only when we silence the blaring sounds of our daily existence that we can finally hear the whispers of truth that life reveals to us, as it stands knocking on the doorsteps of our hearts.

—K.T. Jong

You will not find a soulmate in the quiet of your room. You must go to a noisy place and look in the quiet corners.

—Robert Brault

Society shows us what we are. Solitude shows us what should be.

—Robert Cecil

What a commentary on civilization, when being alone is being suspect; when one has to apologize for it, make excuses, hide the fact that one practices it—like a secret vice.

—Anne Morrow Lindbergh

There is something in the nature of silence which affects me deeply. Why it is I know not; but I do know that I love to be alone at such an hour as this. I love to forget the outward world and hold communion with the beings of the mind.

—Charles Lanman, "Musings," 1840

I have a great deal of company in the house, especially in the morning when nobody calls.

—Henry David Thoreau

I owe my solitude to other people.

—Alan Watts

You will not find a soulmate in the quiet of your room. You must go to a noisy place and look in the quiet corners.

—Robert Brault

Stress

Tension is who you think you should be. Relaxation is who you are.

—Chinese Proverb

STRESS: Someone Trying to Repair Every Situation Solo.

—Dave Willis

Stress is nothing more than a socially acceptable form of mental illness.
—Richard Carlson

How beautiful it is to do nothing, and then to rest afterward.
—Spanish Proverb

To sit with a dog on a hillside on a glorious afternoon is to be back in Eden, where doing nothing was not boring—it was peace.
—Milan Kundera

The greatest weapon against stress is our ability to choose one thought over another.
—William James

Don't let your mind bully your body into believing it must carry the burden of its worries.
—Terri Guillemets

Take rest. A field that has rested gives a bountiful crop.
—Ovid

It's not the load that breaks you down. It's the way you carry it.
—Lou Holtz

The most anxious man in the prison is the governor.
—George Bernard Shaw

There is more to life than increasing its speed.
—Mahatma Gandhi

If your teeth are clenched and your fists are clenched, your lifespan is probably clenched.
—Terri Guillemets

To live in scarcity is to worry about the cost of food; to live in abundance is to worry about who else you can invite for dinner.
—Mike Dolan

A crust eaten in peace is better than a banquet partaken in anxiety.

—Aesop, Fables

How can a society that exists on instant mashed potatoes, packaged cake mixes, frozen dinners, and instant cameras teach patience to its young?

—Paul Sweeney

We live longer than our forefathers; but we suffer more from a thousand artificial anxieties and cares. They fatigued only the muscles, we exhaust the finer strength of the nerves.

—Edward George Bulwer-Lytton

Half our life is spent trying to find something to do with the time we have rushed through life trying to save.

—Will Rogers

Anxiety is fear of oneself.

—Wilhelm Stekel

Sometimes the most important thing in a whole day is the rest we take between two deep breaths.

—Etty Hillesum

I try to take one day at a time, but sometimes several days attack me at once.

—Jennifer Yane

The major cause of stress is the inability of people to discover their real nature.

—Author Unknown

The field of consciousness is tiny. It accepts only one problem at a time.

—Antoine de Saint-Exupéry

Slow down and everything you are chasing will come around and catch you.

—John De Paola

God didn't do it all in one day. What makes me think I can?

—Author Unknown

Stress is an ignorant state. It believes that everything is an emergency.

—Natalie Goldberg

The mark of a successful man is one that has spent an entire day on the bank of a river without feeling guilty about it.

—Author Unknown

Men for the sake of getting a living forget to live.

—Margaret Fuller

For fast-acting relief, try slowing down.

—Lily Tomlin

Thinking

What luck for rulers that men do not think.

—Adolph Hitler

A great many people think they are thinking when they are merely rearranging their prejudices.

—William James

It has been said that we have approximately 187,000 thoughts a day, 98 percent of which we had the day before, and the day before that.

—Ariel and Shya Kane

The trouble with most people is that they think with their hopes or fear or wishes rather than with their minds.

—Will Durant

A man is not idle because he is absorbed in thought. There is a visible labor and there is an invisible labor.

—Victor Hugo

Thinking is like loving and dying. Each of us must do it for himself.

—Josiah Royce

People seem not to see that their opinion of the world is also a confession of character.

—Ralph Waldo Emerson

Challenge your assumptions so that you can find your truths.

—Author Unknown

No matter where you go or what you do, you live your entire life within the confines of your head.

—Terry Josephson

Our most important thoughts are those which contradict our emotions.

—Paul Valéry

Some people get lost in thought because it's such unfamiliar territory.

—G. Behn

People do not like to think. If one thinks, one must reach conclusions. Conclusions are not always present.

—Helen Keller

Thinking up the Theory of Relativity was easy. Proving it was next to impossible.

—Albert Einstein

If you realized how powerful your thoughts are, you would never think a negative thought.

—Peace Pilgrim

At a certain age some people's minds close up; they live on their intellectual fat.

—William Lyon Phelps

Original thought is like original sin: both happened before you were born, to people you could not possibly have met.

—Fran Lebowitz

Isn't it strange that we talk least about the things we think about most?

—Charles A. Lindbergh

He who will not reason is a bigot; he who cannot is a fool; and he who dares not is a slave.

—William Drummond

The vitality of thought is in adventure. Ideas won't keep. SSSooomething must be done about them.

—A.N. Whitehead

Ours is the age which is proud of machines that think and suspicious of men who try to.

—Howard Mumford Jones

It is well for people who think, to change their minds occasionally in order to keep them clean.

—Luther Burbank

When one thinks clearly about thinking, one is present at the first instant of time.

—Edgar Allan Poe

You and I are not what we eat; we are what we think.

—Walter Anderson

There are thoughts which appear not to have come from the senses, but rather to have been forced through the skull.

—James Lendall Basford

As long as you are going to be thinking anyway, think big.

—Donald Trump

Great thinkers move slowly.

—James Lendall Basford

Don't think. Thinking is the enemy of creativity. It's self-conscious and anything self-conscious is lousy: You can't try to do things. You simply must do things.

—Ray Bradbury

Our minds are lazier than our bodies.

—François de la Rochefoucault

The average man never really thinks from end to end of his life. The mental activity of such people is only a mouthing of clichés.

—H.L. Mencken

Thoughts are like an open ocean, they can either move you forward within its waves, or sink you under deep into its abyss.

—Anthony Liccione

We are dying from overthinking. We are slowly killing ourselves by thinking about everything. Think. Think. Think. You can never trust the human mind anyway. It's a death trap.

—Anthony Hopkins

We are no more responsible for the evil thoughts which pass through our minds than a scarecrow for the birds which fly over the seed-plot he has to guard. The sole responsibility in each case is to prevent them from settling.

—John Churton Collins

Sometimes I think and other times I am.

—Paul Valéry

Practical gentlemen hate uncertainty, balancing of probabilities, skepticism or approximation. They have a number of bitterly satirical comments on persons whose minds are so open that their brains fall out. They are bent on getting to a conclusion.

—Max Radin

Opinion is that exercise of the human will which helps us to make a decision without information.

—John Erskine

Doubt is not a pleasant state of mind, but certainty is absurd.

—Voltaire

Men can live without air a few minutes, without water for about two weeks, without food for about two months—and without a new thought for years on end.

—Kent Ruth

Children are happy because they don't have a file in their minds called "All the things that could go wrong."

—Author Unknown

Truth

Truth, as any dictionary will tell you, is a property of certain of our ideas. It means their "agreement," as falsity means their disagreement, with "reality."

—William James

The high-minded man must care more for the truth than for what people think.

—Aristotle

Truth is the daughter of time, not of authority.

—Francis Beacon

All truth passes through three stages. First, it is ridiculed. Second, it is violently opposed. Third, it is accepted as being self-evident.

—Arthur Schopenhauer

Truth is a woman. One must not use force with her.

—Friedrich Nietzsche

There is nothing so powerful as truth – and often nothing so strange.

—Daniel Webster

To arrive at the simplest truth, as Newton knew and practiced, requires years of contemplation. Not activity. Not reasoning. Not calculating. Not busy behavior of any kind. Not reading. Not talking. Not making an effort. Not thinking. Simply bearing in mind what it is one needs to know.

—George Spencer Brown

An error does not become truth by reason of multiplied propagation, nor does truth become error because nobody sees it.

—Mahatma Gandhi

The truth shall make you free.

—John 8:32

In war, Truth is the first casualty.

—Aeschylus

If falsehood, like truth, had but one face, we would be more on equal terms. For we would consider the contrary of what the liar said to be certain. But the opposite of truth has a hundred thousand faces and an infinite field.

—Michel De Montaigne

The terrible thing about the quest for truth is that you find it.

—Rémy De Gourmont

Women

Being powerful is like being a lady. If you have to tell people you are, you aren't.

—Margaret Thatcher

Arguing with a woman is like reading the software license agreement. In the end, you ignore everything and click "I agree".

—Author Unknown

A man chases a woman until she catches him.

—American Proverb

Women speak two languages—one of which is verbal.

—William Shakespeare

Fighting is essentially a masculine idea; a woman's weapon is her tongue.

—Hermione Gingold

I like being a woman even in a man's world. After all, men can't wear dresses but we can wear the pants.

—Whitney Houston

Women always worry about the things that men forget; men always worry about the things women remember.

—Author Unknown

If men knew all that women think they would be twenty times more audacious.

—Alphonse Karr

A woman is like a tea bag. It's only when she's in hot water that you realize how strong she is.

—Nancy Reagan

No matter how happily a woman may be married, it always pleases her to discover that there is a nice man who wishes that she were not.

—H.L. Mencken

A woman should soften but not weaken a man.

—Sigmund Freud

Sometimes it takes balls to be a woman.

—Anonymous

Women cannot complain about men anymore until they start getting better taste in them.

—Bill Maher

She wasn't looking for a knight. She was looking for a sword.

—Atticus

A man is as good as he has to be and a woman is as bad as she dares.

—Elbert Hubbard

The man's desire is for the woman; but the woman's desire is rarely other than for the desire of the man.

—Samuel Taylor Coleridge

A woman should be an illusion.

—Ian Fleming

Women do not find it difficult nowadays to behave like men, but they often find it extremely difficult to behave like gentlemen.

—Compton Mackenzie

I would rather trust a woman's instinct than a man's reason.

—Stanley Baldwin

One is not born a woman, one becomes one.

—Simone de Beauvoir

Who loves not women, wine, and song, remains a fool his whole life long.

—German Proverb

A woman who cannot be ugly is not beautiful.

—Karl Kraus

Woman begins by resisting a man's advances and ends by blocking his retreat.

—Oscar Wilde

A woman need know but one man well, in order to understand all men, whereas a man may know all women and understand not one of them.

—Helen Rowland

Beauty is the first present Nature gives to women, and the first it takes away.

—Méré

Men look at themselves in mirrors. Women look for themselves.

—Elissa Melamed

Women dress alike all over the world: they dress to be annoying to other women.

—Elsa Schiaparelli

A pessimist is a man who thinks all women are bad. An optimist is a man who hopes they are.

—Chauncey Mitchell Depew

No woman wants to see herself too clearly.

—Mignon McLaughlin

The essence of life is the smile of round female bottoms, under the shadow of cosmic boredom.

—Guy de Maupassant

A woman wears her tears like jewelry.

—Author Unknown

To get to a woman's heart, a man must first use his own.

—Mike Dobbertin

There are women who do not like to cause suffering to many men at a time, and who prefer to concentrate on one man: These are the faithful women.

—Alfred Capus

A man never knows how to say goodbye; a woman never knows when to say it.

—Helen Rowland

Women are never stronger than when they arm themselves with their weakness.

—Marie de Vichy-Chamrond

In politics, if you want something said ask a man. If you want something done ask a woman.

—Margaret Thatcher

If women didn't exist, all the money in the world would have no meaning.

—Aristotle Onassis

Ah, women. They make the highs higher and the lows more frequent.
—Friedrich Nietzsche

Men really prefer reasonably attractive women; they go after the sensational ones to impress other men.

—Mignon McLaughlin

Whatever women do they must do twice as well as men to be thought half as good. Luckily, this is not difficult.

—Charlotte Whitton

You educate a man; you educate a man. You educate a woman; you educate a generation.

—Brigham Young

They may talk of a comet, or a burning mountain, or some such bagatelle; but to me a modest woman, dressed out in all her finery, is the most tremendous object of the whole creation.

—Oliver Goldsmith

Every woman is wrong until she cries, and then she is right—instantly.

—Sam Slick

Every girl should use what Mother Nature gave her before Father Time takes it away.

—Laurence J. Peter

Let us leave the beautiful women to men with no imagination.

—Marcel Proust

I hate women because they know where things are.

—James Thurber

Women like silent men. They think they're listening.

—Marcel Achard

The rarest thing in the world is a woman who is pleased with photographs of herself.

—Elizabeth Metcalf

Be to her virtues very kind,
Be to her faults a little blind.

—Matthew Prior

Even when they meet in the street, women look at each other like Guelphs and Guibellines.

—Arthur Schopenhauer

The average woman would rather have beauty than brains, because the average man can see better than he can think.

—Author Unknown

That's the trouble with us. We number everything. Take women, for example. I think they deserve to have more than twelve years between the ages of twenty-eight and forty.

—James Thurber

Whether they give or refuse, it delights women just the same to have been asked.

—Ovid

Biologically speaking, if something bites, it's more likely to be female.
—Desmond Morris

There is a special place in hell for women who do not help other women.

—Madeleine K. Albright

I should like to know what is the proper function of women, if it is not to make reasons for husbands to stay at home, and still stronger reasons for bachelors to go out.

—George Eliot

Women are like elephants to me. I like to look at them, but I wouldn't want to own one.

—W.C. Fields

Women rule the world. No man has ever done anything that a woman hasn't either allowed him to do, or encouraged him to do.

—Bob Dylan

Can you imagine a world without men? No crime and lots of happy fat women.

—Nicole Hollander

Women get the last word in every argument. Anything a man says after that is the beginning of a new argument.

—Author Unknown

A man's face is his autobiography. A woman's face is her work of fiction.

—Oscar Wilde

She wore a short skirt and a tight sweater and her figure described a set of parabolas that could cause cardiac arrest in a yak.

—Woody Allen

We are foolish, and without excuse foolish, in speaking of the superiority of one sex to the other, as if they could be compared in similar things! Each has what the other has not; each completes the other; they are in nothing alike; and the happiness and perfection of both depend on each asking and receiving from the other what the other only can give.

—John Ruskin

Words

Words are free. It's how you use them that may cost you.

— Author Unknown

Words are magic things. They hide secret life meanings. The very essence of the world…

—Danai Krokou

Words are loaded pistols.

—Jean-Paul Sartre

If I don't write to empty my mind, I go mad.

—Lord Byron

The road to hell is paved with adverbs.

—Stephen King

Words, like eyeglasses, blur everything that they do not make clearer.

—Joseph Joubert

The trouble with words is that you never know whose mouths they have been in.

—Dennis Potter

When writers die they become books, which is, after all, not too bad an incarnation.

—Jorge Luis Borges

It seems to me that those songs that have been any good, I have nothing much to do with the writing of them. The words have just crawled down my sleeve and come out on the page.

—Joan Baez

Words—so innocent and powerless as they are, as standing in a dictionary, how potent for good and evil they become in the hands of one who knows how to combine them.

—Nathaniel Hawthorne

It is not my sentence that I polish, but my thought. I pause until the drop of light that I need is formed and falls from my pen.

—Joseph Joubert

When we see a natural style we are quite amazed and delighted, because we expected to see an author and find a man.

—Blaise Pascal

Writers are not just people who sit down and write. They hazard themselves. Every time you compose a book your composition of yourself is at stake.

—E.L. Doctorow

Writers spend three years rearranging 26 letters of the alphabet. It's enough to make you lose your mind day by day.

—Richard Price

When something can be read without effort, great effort has gone into its writing.

—Enrique Jardiel Poncela

I love writing. I love the swirl and swing of words as they tangle with human emotions.

—James Michener

Words have no power to impress the mind without the exquisite horror of their reality. !

—Edgar Allan Poe

Don't tell me the moon is shining; show me the glint of light on broken glass.

—Anton Chekhov

The role of a writer is not to say what we all can say, but what we are unable to say.

—Anaïs Nin

Writing is my time machine, takes me to the precise time and place I belong.

—Jeb Dickerson

A critic can only review the book he has read, not the one which the writer wrote.

—Mignon McLaughlin

Writing became such a process of discovery that I couldn't wait to get to work in the morning: I wanted to know what I was going to say.

—Sharon O'Brien

In the course of life, I have often had to eat my words, and I must confess that I have always found it a wholesome diet.

—Winston Churchill

The process of writing has something infinite about it. Even though it is interrupted each night, it is one single notation.

—Elias Canetti

The best time for planning a book is while you're doing the dishes.

—Agatha Christie

Metaphors have a way of holding the most truth in the least space.

—Orson Scott Card

Every word born of an inner necessity—writing must never be anything else.

—Etty Hillesum

Always and never are two words you should always remember never to use.

—Wendell Johnson

The time to begin writing an article is when you have finished it to your satisfaction. By that time you begin to clearly and logically perceive what it is that you really want to say.

—Mark Twain

Many books require no thought from those who read them, and for a very simple reason. They made no such demand upon those who wrote them.

—Charles Caleb Colton

Write your first draft with your heart. Re-write with your head.

—From the movie Finding Forrester

A writer's mind seems to be situated partly in the solar plexus and partly in the head.

—Ethel Wilson

What no wife of a writer can ever understand is that a writer is working when he's staring out of the window.

—Burton Rascoe

Write down the thoughts of the moment. Those that come unsought for are commonly the most valuable.

—Francis Bacon

Writing is not apart from living. Writing is a kind of double living. The writer experiences everything twice. Once in reality and once in that mirror which waits always before or behind.

—Catherine Drinker Bowen

The right word may be effective, but no word was ever as effective as a rightly timed pause.

—Mark Twain

A word is not the same with one writer as with another. One tears it from his guts. The other pulls it out of his overcoat pocket.

—Charles Peguy

If there's a book you really want to read, but it hasn't been written yet, then you must write it.

—Toni Morrison

To me, the greatest pleasure of writing is not what it's about, but the inner music the words make.

—Truman Capote

The expression "to write something down" suggests a descent of thought to the fingers whose movements immediately falsify it.

—William Gass

What I like in a good author is not what he says, but what he whispers.

—Logan Pearsall Smith

Storytelling reveals meaning without committing the error of defining it.

—Hannah Arendt

A good style should show no signs of effort. What is written should seem a happy accident.

—W. Somerset Maugham

We write to remember our nows later.

—Terri Guillemets

Leadership

I am not afraid of an army of lions led by a sheep.
I am afraid of an army of sheep led by a lion.

—Alexander the Great

Leadership is often mistakenly perceived as a subcategory of Business. There is certain truth in this approach as leadership is a vital aspect of business. However, it is by perceiving leadership as an independent skill to be applied on all levels of one's life that people can reap its maximum benefits. Leadership is automatically at work whenever and wherever a group of people come together to work toward a common goal. Leadership is a mixture of art and science; depending on the situation the amounts of each ingredient vary. Sometimes a greater amount of art is required, while in other situations more science is needed. When applied in corporate contexts, leadership loses a large part of its core significance to meet goals and needs that are related to the management of people. Scholars group leadership styles into different categories. One of the most recurrent terms one comes across in business literature is *Transformational leadership*. Doesn't this term sound like a tautology? What else leadership can be if not transformational? There is, of course, a whole range of terms to describe various leadership styles. Autocratic, laissez-faire, participative, transactional, and so on. *Transformational leadership* though is pure redundancy. The very objective of leadership is to *transform* people and bring out the best in them. To stress the transformational power of leadership, I would go as far as to argue that leadership is alchemy at its highest degree. Alchemy is the medieval forerunner of modern chemistry. It was first developed in medieval Europe. It aimed to purify, mature, and perfect certain metals and its practice was based on the transformation of common, *base metals* such as copper, silver, iron or tin into *noble metals*, especially gold. I consider this a very accurate metaphor for the kind of magic that can take place when great leadership is at work as it is only under great leadership that ordinary people can be transformed into extraordinary individuals. It is under great leadership that teams of common people can be turned into productive, powerful groups, thus forming a whole much greater than the sum of its parts. If leadership is not magic in motion, if it does not transform and enrich people's lives, work, and relationships, then it should not be called leadership. It is mere management. I am absolutely not arguing that leadership is nobler than management. Managing people is a great challenge in itself. All I am suggesting is that Leadership and Management are two different domains whose methods and goals happen to converge at times.

Leadership more than a mere organizational technique is the ability to cut through the crowd, get in front of the crowd, and give them a good reason why you should keep standing there, in front of them. I've noticed there is a common denominator in all people I am seduced by, be it professionally, intellectually, or physically. Whether they are historic figures, politicians, influential CEOs, thought leaders or romantic partners, these people have a very powerful presence. I believe that being seduced by any figure, person or idea involves an essential ingredient. Fascination. I would not be able to notice, let alone give my attention to someone who does not stand out of the crowd. Leadership too is about igniting fascination. Leadership is about seduction. It is an affair. A polygamous one. An affair you develop gradually with different people, at the same time. These can be a small or large group of people you might not have direct contact with, yet you want to have continuous impact on them. Such people can be your colleagues, business partners, clients, members of your community, people you mentor, supporters or social media followers. There is no way you can ever be influential unless you are able to make these people to *sustainably* perceive things the way you do, then encourage them to act accordingly. By sustainably I mean continuously and systematically. As a leader you have projects in your head waiting to take shape. Projects need long-term commitment to materialize, so it is long-term supporters that you need to help you transform them into reality.

Even if you are not currently a leader—even if you harbor no special interest or desire to ever be one—you may still be tired of being invisible or underappreciated. Tired of having your ideas, suggestions and opinions dismissed by your boss, clients, colleagues, or friends. It hurts to be ignored. Especially while other people—which might hold less compelling ideas—receive more positive reactions or win a better hearing in meetings and negotiations. Whether you currently occupy a leadership role or aspire to one, speaking like a leader is paramount. Unless you have already achieved a special status within your industry and people know you through your work and accomplishments, you should regard speaking and communicating plans, ideas, goals and visions as the most essential part of your job description as a leader. Leaders are not like other people. At least not when it comes to communicating ideas. Leaders are performers. It is a show leaders have to deliver in front of an audience to captivate their *attention*, then ignite fascination, before fueling them with enough motivation and desire for action toward a specific goal. Leaders are individuals capable of taking precedence over other mortals, perceiving trends far ahead of others. Their vision and goals are so clear that they often feel compelled to act even at the risk of being perceived as reckless or stupid. They can be very confident in what others perceive as a crazy vision but they are extremely careful when it comes to communicating that vision to their audience.

The gateway to people's mind are their eyes and ears. Therefore, if you aspire to become a leader or a better leader, it is crucial that you look and sound like one. Why do leaders need to be magnetic though? Simply because audiences and followers do not want their leaders to speak and act like everyone else. Would you accept as a leader someone who speaks and acts like the person next door? People hold their leaders to a higher standard, so they naturally demand more of them. At the same time leaders expect more of themselves too. They want their speeches to strengthen their personal status and further their organization's success. It is in times of major change and crisis that people turn to leaders for direction and insight. In such situations a lot is at stake, so expectations are higher. For instance, it is after a national tragedy that a whole country waits for their president to speak. By the same token, when a brand releases a new product, who better to herald it than the head of the company? Following a merger or an acquisition, panicked employees don't know where they stand until they hear the organization's plans from the CEO's mouth. The progress of any organization—whether it is a team operation, a department, an NGO, a start-up, or a large corporation—depends on its leader's ability to fascinate and persuade.

Overcoming Bucephalus' Complex: A Leader's Greatest Challenge

I have a tremendous admiration for great historical figures. Since early childhood my parents and grand-parents instilled in me a love for greatness and epic accomplishments through storytelling and Greek mythology. One of my favorite—real—stories about Alexander the Great, king of the ancient Greek kingdom of Macedonia is his taming of Bucephalus. Bucephalus is considered by many the most famous horse in history. Alexander fought all his battles on this horse. Their initial encounter was very eventful though and took place when the Greek prince was only 12 years old. This incident revealed the true character of a young boy who, a few years later, would become one of the greatest conquerors in history. It also demonstrated that a leader's greatest challenge is to be the masterful regulator of people's emotions.

Bucephalus was a giant, magnificent black stallion. His name literally means "ox head" in Ancient Greek. Bucephalus was initially brought to Macedonia in 346 BC. The horse was presented to Alexander's father, King Philip II with a price tag three times the norm of the time. There was a major issue though and it was not his price tag. Bucephalus was too wild and was rearing up anyone who came near him. No one had been able to ride, tame or even approach him. Alexander loved this horse at first sight.

None of King Philip's attendants managed to mount Bucephalus. As they were leading him away as totally useless, Alexander, who stood by, famously exclaimed "What an excellent horse do they lose for want of address and boldness to manage him!" Philip at first took no notice of what his son said, but when he saw how vexed Alexander was to see the horse sent away, he turned to his son, saying "Do you reproach those who are older than yourself, as if you knew more, and were better able to manage him than they." "I could manage this horse, better than others do" Alexander replied. "And if you do not, what will you forfeit for your rashness?" Philip asked. "I will pay the whole price of the horse" answered Alexander.[1]

As soon as the wager was settled, Alexander ran to the horse. After observing his behavior he noticed that the horse was not afraid of humans

---

[1] Dialogue from *Source of the History of Western Civilization*, p. 151.

like others thought. It was afraid of its own shadow. Alexander came up with a totally original approach in taming it. He took hold of the bridle and turned the horse's face directly toward the sun, having observed that the horse was afraid of the motion of its own shadow. He then let him go a little forward, still holding the reins in his hands, and stroking the horse gently when he found him begin to grow eager. He let fall his upper garment softly and with one nimble leap he mounted him. When he felt Bucephalus *free from all rebelliousness and impatient for the course, he let him go at full speed, inciting him with a commanding voice and urging him also with his heel.* Philip and his attendants looked on at first in silence and anxiety for the result, till seeing him turn at the end of his career and come back rejoicing and triumphing for what he had performed, they all burst out into acclamations of applause.

Historians claim that the taming of the wild Bucephalus was a turning point in the young prince's life, demonstrating the fearlessness, sharp perception and determination he was to show later in his conquest of Asia and other continents. Bucephalus and Alexander were inseparable; only Alexander could ride that horse. This is precisely what I call the "Bucephalus' Complex." Aside from horses it can be applied to us, modern humans. This is what I regard as the noblest and most powerful skill a leader can ever possess: skillfully turning people's heads toward the sun to distract them away from their own shadows that is, away from self-doubt, self-sabotaging attitudes, unreasonable fears and risk-aversion to lead them toward challenges, goals and projects. Like Alexander managed to free the wild Bucephalus from his rebelliousness, leaders need to break through people's defense barriers before guiding them toward their desired goals.

Your team, the people you are in charge of, the people you mentor are your Bucephalus. Once you manage to help them get rid of their insecurities and fears, once you help them develop skills they will be ready to "go to battle" and execute your orders. Fighting against people's inner devils can sometimes feel like Don Quixote fighting against windmills though. But it does pay off. It is only after you've freed people of their fears and insecurities and after you've made them discover their full potential that they will pledge allegiance to you and your vision much more promptly than they would otherwise do.

Alexander the Great: A Quintessential Leader

Alexander the Great (356 BC–323 BC) was the son of King Philip II of Macedonia. He grew up not only in great privilege but also in great learning, with the renowned Greek philosopher Aristotle being his personal tutor. He admired Homer's mythic heroes and slept beside a copy of the Iliad, annotated by Aristotle himself. Wise well beyond his age, he acted fast to secure Macedonian hegemony. In the space of only 11 years he conquered the then-known world, from Macedon, through Greece, across Persia to India then down to North Africa. In geographic terms he achieved within a decade what other empires took centuries to achieve. He became king at the age of 20, when his father was assassinated, and he was 32 years old when he died. In an unparalleled 11-year journey of conquest he rode more than 10,000 miles and fought 70 battles without losing a single one. His remarkable speed of movement was revealed in the short time he took to seize the then-known world; a time when expeditions were carried out exclusively on foot.

A few centuries later, the year Julius Caesar celebrated his 32nd birthday, as he was reading the life of Alexander the Great, he suddenly burst into tears. Perhaps the most ambitious of us ought to cry with him! His friends were surprised. On being asked the reason, he famously told them "Do you not think, it is matter for sorrow that while Alexander, at my age, was already king of so many peoples, I have as yet not achieved no brilliant success?" Indeed, Alexander set the bar high. In a very short time he became the role model of all subsequent military leaders. He was the first person who had a vision of conquering the whole world. Within that vision he wanted to know everything. He wanted to have seen everything and to have done everything by the time his life was finished. On many levels he did accomplish that. Above all, he wanted to acquire knowledge and then disseminate it.

Aside from being a great military leader and statesman, he was one of the greatest intellects of his time. Surprisingly, the size of his army never went over 40,000 soldiers. In his military tactics, Alexander prioritized mobility and speed which both gave his army military advantage over opponents who outnumbered him. He surrounded himself with all sorts of people. During his expeditions he traveled with members of the court which included engineers, poets, scientists, philosophers, doctors, and slave traders, and most importantly a personal historian who wrote his exploits which were then sent far and wide, so that his name would be forever respected.

Far from becoming obsolete in modern times, Alexander's leadership skills have become increasingly relevant to anyone holding a leadership position or aspiring to one, including politicians and those operating in corporate and nonprofit organizations. The question is, what did Alexander do differently from the rest? How did he manage to achieve virtual worldwide success in the space of a decade without losing a single battle? How can modern leaders get inspired by his achievements to succeed in their respective arenas? How does his leadership strategy apply to modern life?

Speed in Decision and Action

From early childhood, Alexander mastered the lesson that problems should be faced, not avoided. He demonstrated flexibility and would eagerly abandon his comfort zone when needed, often modifying his strategy to accommodate new conditions. Alexander did not have the luxury of time in the battlefield. His course of action involved a series of critical decisions that would either lead to victory or defeat. He had long battles with Darius III of Persia. Despite being surprised by Darius' strategic moves, he displayed speed of mind by turning his army around and arriving at the battleground before the enemy had fully prepared their defense.

Innovative, Daring, and Excellent Strategist

The capacity to come up with innovative and unconventional ideas was Alexander's major hallmark. He always managed to find alternative solutions to problems that represented deadlocks for others. He was cunning in military strategy and excellent at reading the battlefield, the two qualities which led him to a phenomenal record of consecutive battle conquests. Alexander was a genius in the art of planning. Before every campaign he would spend time anticipating his opponent's possible moves and developing tactics to prevent their actions. This reduced the possibilities of unpleasant surprises and led to decisive and swift actions. He overcame armies far more powerful and numerous than his by being more determined, smarter, and more resourceful than his opponents. Amazingly, Alexander built his empire with an army that numbered no more than 40,000 soldiers. This means he had to make optimal use of his forces to overcome the overwhelming numbers that opposed him.

Astute Negotiator

Alexander was willing to negotiate and build strategic alliances whenever they were possible and convenient for his objectives. However, he always kept in mind what alternatives to negotiation he had. He preferred to receive a friendly surrender proposal from his opponents, rather than spend significant amounts of energy, time, and resources fighting against each city and country. Although he worked to befriend the people of the nations he conquered, he always made sure that Macedonians were in overall charge.

Led and Fought by Example

"A boss says 'Go!' A leader says 'Let's go!'" This well-known quote by E.M. Kelly applies here. Alexander led his people to conquer the world by providing an example. He never asked from his soldiers anything that he would not do himself, which explains why his men were fiercely loyal. Unlike most military leaders, he always led from front in battle where he was easily recognizable. Although this made him an easier target for the enemy, he was a stirring inspiration for his own troops. He was injured countless times, but being unceasingly courageous, he continually pushed himself to physical limits.

Cross-Cultural Intelligence

Alexander was extremely sensitive to the cultural differences of the diverse nations he conquered and early on realized that varied cultures required different leadership styles. He spoke several languages and always customized his leadership style to match the values and culture of each nation. At the same time, he was careful to win over religious figures and was never too proud to bow before the gods of other nations.

Bold and Clear Goals

Alexander's obsession with glory led him to set ambitious, bold, and clear goals for himself and his people. Holder of a cloudless vision, he was masterful in communicating that vision and convincing those around him to embrace his goals. Alexander is remembered for his unbendable will and persistence in besieging impregnable cities. Every city eventually fell under the perseverance of his various attacks. Alexander concentrated his resources on the task at hand. And only when the task was finished, would he focus his efforts on the next objective.

He Understood PR Very Well and Wrote His Own History

If we think in numbers, he lived no longer than 32 years. He built his empire within less than 12 years and his legend has been lasting more than 24 centuries. So, Alexander obviously did a phenomenal job managing his reputation. He founded 12 cities bearing his name in the various countries he conquered—he gave to all 12 the name of "Alexandria." He associated his name with excellence, power, unbendable will, and knowledge. Alexander was tremendously ambitious. He surrounded himself with symbols that built his image. His obsession for long-lasting glory helped him endure virtually everything for the sake of achieving his life goals. It was precisely this obsession that strengthened his determination, spreading confidence among his people and fear among his enemies. He represented the type of leader that every soldier would like to have: courageous, determined, and undefeated. However, unlike other major military leaders—like Genghis Khan or Ivan the Terrible—Alexander was never seen as a tyrant. Amazingly, his was the only conqueror in history people were proud to be conquered by. Throughout his Asiatic expedition Alexander carried with him an influential historian of the time, Callisthenes of Olynthus, the nephew of Aristotle. Callisthenes' main duty was to write the *Deeds of Alexander* which were then sent to every corner of his empire to secure posthumous fame.

He Surrounded Himself with the Right People

He selected his people very carefully, particularly the companions who fought around him and helped him make crucial decisions. He displayed exceptional emotional intelligence. Knowing his people thoroughly, Alexander developed a keen sense of their problems, fears, and needs. He empowered them so they could develop their full potential. Those he selected helped him achieve his outrageous dreams and guarded the destiny of his empire until his death. He paid attention to meritocracy, making sure that he generously rewarded loyalty and superb behavior. He gave his men incentives to conquer new lands by making them feel like owners of the conquered territories.

He Was Merciless with Those Who Opposed or Betrayed Him

Alexander's use of reward and coercive power increased with his success. To promote teamwork and cohesion, Alexander established compensation for units and for the whole army. He was, however, ruthless with those who opposed or betrayed his trust. The Siege of Tyre is a very representative example. Tyre was the largest Phoenician city built on an "impregnable" island. Alexander's siege of it took seven months in which 7,000 Tyrians died in its defense. After conquest, Alexander crucified 2,000 more and the remaining 30,000 were sold into slavery.

The Leadership Pyramid

We humans are pattern-based. We form habits and do not like disruptions to what we have been used to. People have expectations, especially when they function in a pattern-based fashion. Napoleon Bonaparte was an expert in *expectation management*. He always advocated the "say what you mean" principle. Be responsible for your words and actions. Responsibility is, in fact, a major leadership task. As the word itself suggests responsibility goes far beyond mere commitment to a project or ownership of one's actions. "Responsibility," as the Latin root of the word suggests, is the ability to *respond*. Responsibility is also about responding efficiently to adversity, challenges, risks and opportunities. The larger the number of people, projects and risks you are in charge of or involved in, the greater the power of *responsibility* is. Notice that I am not talking about the *need* for responsibility. I am talking about the *power* of responsibility. Napoleon's art of responsibility and the "say what you mean" communication strategy inspired confidence and trust in his soldiers and people and made them follow him wherever he led them.

Your leadership style and communication skills form integral part of your Corporate Fingerprint and your Unique Skill Pairings, a personal theory I live by and which I am proud to share with you in the next section. It is, therefore, important for your people to see your sincerity as a leader. By choosing your words carefully you can show that you mean serious business. Who you are is inseparable from the message you communicate as well as the way you choose to deliver that message to your audience. By this, I don't simply mean that your actions must speak louder than your words. This speaks by itself! I mean that your particular character, who you are, what you preach, your actions and values should shape the message that your audience hears. False hopes and empty promises are not what you would hear from good leaders, and here's a key paradox: leaders must be centered on themselves in order to construct a powerful message that reflects their unique personality, charisma and vision, yet when they speak to their audiences they speak not for themselves but for their people, teams and wider organizations. The trust that followers, supporters or team members place on you functions pretty much like an emotional money box. We all know how money boxes work. You save up money by making deposits and when you need to use part of that money you withdraw *some* of it. The same goes with a leader's trust account. It is an account based on how reliable people feel you are, how much and how far they feel they can trust you. There are countless ways—and even more excuses!—to make emotional withdrawals from your trust account: being inconsistent, speaking in a way while acting otherwise, changing your mind, strategy or direction too often. So, withdrawals from that trust account must be reasonable, and it is important that you never reach a zero balance as, unlike with real bank accounts, it is very hard to restore credibility.

Being consistent and demonstrating integrity is the moral floor upon which trusting and lasting relationships can be built in life and business. Leaders can only have an impact when they operate from a solid basis that allows people to feel comfortable listening and trusting their word. Getting people to *actively* listen to you is the very foundation and perhaps the hardest and most decisive stage of the Leadership Pyramid. Once you have captivated people's attention and convinced them that your message is *worth* listening to, you can move on to the next stage. It is only after people have bought into your vision that they can start aligning their beliefs and actions to your message. It's only after you've managed to gain people's active listening and built trust that you can move on to the third level of the Leadership Pyramid, which involves other people's action and much less your own. It is important that you give your best self in the first two stages where you have the most control, as in the following four stages leading to the top of the pyramid, most control passes to your followers, the people who carry and propagate your message. The clearer, sharper, and the more meticulously framed your message is at the initial stage and the more momentum and drive it carries, the more chances it has to make it to the top of the pyramid. There is an additional advantage to a clear, well-defined, sharp message. In this social media-dominated world we all live in, tons of messages are produced, liked, shared, and … forgotten daily. Every day millions of messages are produced, aimed at millions of people. Don't allow yours to be one among thousands of other messages. Social media marketers have established a growing trend: to maintain presence and visibility of their brands, they literally bombard their customers, followers and subscribers with infotainment posts several times a day. While this strategy can be effective for short-term sales, it is far from being a smart way for leaders to empower their personal brand and communicate their message. As a leader you want to make a long-term impact. It is therefore important that every single one of your messages is a firework. It must be eventful and long-awaited.

When crafting a message, it is important to identify the best channels to reach your target audience. The combination of channels you need to leverage varies based on the type of message you want to share and the kind of audience you are trying to reach. However, no matter what type of message you want to communicate or what type of audience you target, your message must ideally combine a strategic mix of key elements to increase in strength and momentum: a core idea, down-to-earth pragmatism, a revolutionary idea, and a call to action to overcome a challenge.

People KEEP following your vision when you are no longer there (after your death)

People PROPAGATE your vision through ACTIONS

People PROPAGATE your vision through WORDS

People ALIGN their ACTIONS to your vision

People TRUST you

People LISTEN to you

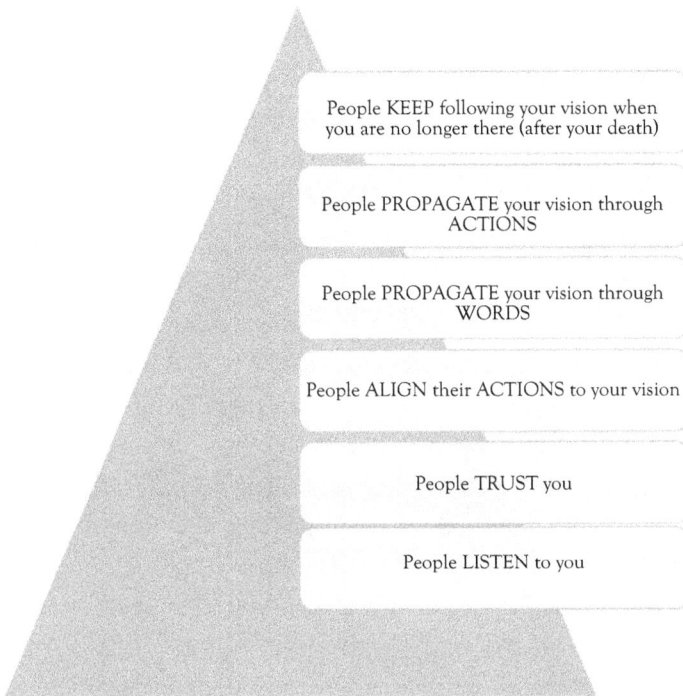

To be inspiring and gain a maximum reach, to propagate and endure through time, a message needs to be engaging, value-adding and must urge people to act. Words, be it written or spoken, are not enough to make your message endure. While a smart mix of these elements can make your message appealing, it's not enough to engage people so that they act on it. Action can take the form of a lifestyle change, the acquisition of a new set of skills, or a change of perception that pushes people to make adjustments to their lives. A message that endures is one that defies time and space. Such messages are more enduring than the leaders who have uttered them. They often remain in people's minds when the leader is not physically present and for a long time after their death. Examples include ideas one can find in famous speeches such as Martin Luther King's "I have a dream" speech, John F. Kennedy's famous "ask not what your country can do for you, ask what you can do for your country." or Deng Xiaoping's famous "to be rich is glorious!", a historic statement that inaugurated a series of market reforms that turned communist China into the global economic superpower it is now.

Crafting Your Corporate Fingerprint: The Power of Unique Skill Pairings (USP)

As human beings we serve no purpose on this planet if we have no value to add to our species. It is impossible to find two human beings with the same fingerprint or DNA blueprint and there is a good reason for this. If two people are exactly the same, one is not needed. The way to bring value to the human race is to be unique, one of a kind. The way every species on earth survives, evolves, and thrives is by adding value to its collective progression. The greater the value you bring to the species, the more valuable and irreplaceable you become as a part of a greater whole. As a result, the more reliant the species becomes on you for survival, evolution and progression. When this principle is applied in the wider economy, it means that the more you serve and produce for others through your unique talents, skills and creativity—the more and bigger the problems you solve for others—the greater is the value you add to your own life and career progression.

It is through acts of creativity that we add unique value to the species, the market and the wider economy. The economy is an interconnected web of values brought to the table by individuals that share the desire to add value using their unique skills and talents. The amount and quality of the ingredients you contribute to the "pie" adds or detracts from the economy, its evolution and ultimately its progress. Selling is serving others; it's about offering solutions to consumers' needs through fair exchange. Buying is serving others; it's all about offering a monetary round of applause to a business producing a value-adding product or service. Earning money is serving others; it's about being remunerated a share of the overall economy. Hiring people to work for you is serving others; it means that you support their subsistence, your local economy and that you contribute to taxes.

All value-adding acts lead to more exchange and to a greater economy, thus functioning as a platform for others to serve in return. Uneven contribution of unique value explains why wealth is not evenly distributed. As ideological and ethical socialism and communism might sound, they don't encourage people to stand out and create unique value, which explains why capitalism is nowadays more prevalent in most political systems across the world. By offering incentives for personal growth and achievement it balances self-interest with the interconnected benefit of serving and adding value to the greater whole. When it comes to leadership things are no different than species evolution or the economy. Your leadership style is a core part of your Corporate Fingerprint (CF). It is specific to you and makes you unique. A leader must be unique. They must stand out and it is an uncommon combination of skills and personality traits that is required for a leader to become unique.

Skill acquisition is an integral part of learning. It starts the moment we take our first breath and ends when we have ended. Everyone has the ability to learn new skills and acquire new competences but it is the use we make of them and how smartly we combine them that makes all the difference. A smart combination of skills will propel you to stardom within your organization or industry. I came up with the concept of *Unique Skill Pairings* (USP) to define an *uncommon combination of distant qualities and skills* that I have applied in my own life and career. That is, a combination of skills that is hard to find in *one same* person. Possessing a single competence, skill or a group of skills that are closely related (e.g., software engineering and graphic design) won't help you reap maximum benefits in terms of career advancement. You need to develop unique, hard to copy talents to distinguish yourself from other people and create your own, unique, impossible to copy Corporate Fingerprint (CF). If you look in any organization, business, or industry it is not hard to notice that the amount of people who represent the best in what they do is indeed very limited. These are the industry giants. People you hear or read about in the media and professional journals. What few people seem to know is that you don't need extraordinary talents to be extraordinary. What you actually need is a mix, a cocktail of skills. Most extraordinary people do not possess extraordinary skills. Rather, they have developed a mix of *distant skills*.

The more "you" you are, the more unique and authentic, the more extraordinary and happier you end up feeling in your career and life. Talent is a terrible thing to waste. Each one of us has the potential to add unique value to their organization, team and community by developing a smart set of Unique Skill Pairings (USP). Examples of USP abound. Some are more known than others but the formula remains the same. Steve Jobs mixed technology and aesthetics and Apple products came into being. His love for distinctive design—clean, fun, and friendly—fueled a design revolution in high technology. Ferran Adrià, a Michelin-starred chef from Barcelona, is one of the best and perhaps the most controversial and experimental chefs in the world. The type of guy who can turn asparagus into bread and almonds into cheese. His restaurant *El Bulli* was rated the best restaurant in the world 4 years in a row. It receives up to 1,000,000 reservation requests every year but only a few hundred are accepted. Ferran Adrià is a molecular cuisine chef and his dish inventions have revolutionized the face of modern gastronomy. If you deconstruct him the way he deconstructs food, you will discover that he is a cook, an artist, a scientist, a designer, a philosopher, an inventor, and an anarchist. All at the same time. He managed to mix distant skills, talents, interests, and personality traits to combine gastronomy and chemistry. The result is explosive.

How do you know the ingredients of your own mix? It is crucial that you know exactly what your mixable skills and talents are. Knowing the exact ingredients is crucial when it comes to developing your Unique Skill Pairings (USP) formula. Adding a touch of eccentricity to the mix is a great plus. It is important that you make your own Unique Skill Pairings (USP) list. Work on this list as diligently as you would for a professional project. I suggest that you take a paper and write down five things *you* think you are good at. Not great or excellent but good at. Once you write those down, ask *at least* three family members, three friends, and three coworkers to add elements to your list. Once they suggest you are good at a particular skill please don't argue with them! It is important that these people do not belong in the same group. Family and close relatives know hidden aspects of your personality and life story that few people do. Colleagues are familiar with your technical and teamwork skills while friends can bring insightful feedback on other facets of your personality such as your social ability and soft skills. These three categories of people combined will help you gain a 360-degree view of yourself. You should welcome both positive and negative feedback. This will help you see your personal attributes, your strengths, weaknesses and abilities. Apart from helping you discover what your potential Unique Skill Pairings (USP) are, seeing youself from different angles will give you the opportunity to understand how you are perceived by those around you. It will also help you understand your reputation and take action accordingly to reach your goals. Make sure to take note of everything they will add to your list, then take these skills into account before sitting down alone to construct your USP formula. Do keep in mind that you need to mix distant ingredients. Remember. The more distant the ingredients, the stronger your cocktail mix. Think about it! Mixing Coke and Pepsi is unlikely to give an impressive result. Originality is a key element when it comes to developing your Corporate Fingerprint.

When deciding to build a new set of skills or wondering which existing ones to further develop, it is crucial to take into account the Unique Skill Pairings (USP) principle. It will help you stand out of the competition and propel you to a much higher level of success and exposure to better quality business and life opportunities. Possessing Unique Skill Pairings (USP) won't only make you more employable and more competitive within your field. It will make you *irreplaceable*. Irreplaceability is the greatest, most valuable asset one can possibly possess, not only in the job market but also as a leader in any corporate or life setting. Your Unique Skill Pairings (USP) are an invaluable asset that will follow you everywhere you go. Financial assets are volatile, your unique intellectual assets are not. In the aftermath of a hard-to-overcome failure, a bankruptcy or any form of financial misfortune, your Unique Skill Pairings (USP) will still be there, at your service, ready to put in smart use existing resources or create new ones from scratch.

People who can only master one skill are replaceable. If you are a good salesman, there is not much to be proud of. Why? Because you are replaceable! If you are a great engineer or doctor, you are still replaceable. The same applies to personality traits. If you are just funny, you are replaceable. If you are just ambitious, you are replaceable. If all you are is a serious, knowledgeable talker, you are also replaceable. It is only when you start combining distant skill sets *and* personality traits that you can seriously increase your chances to achieve legendary status within your field. Having said that, acquiring similar skills will still make you a better version of yourself, more competitive in the job market but by no means will it make you irreplaceable. Irreplaceability is at the top of the pyramid and aside from a high salary, recognition and authority, it will offer two additional benefits: more bargaining power and better opportunities in Life and Business. It is pretty common to see professionals developing similar sets of skills. You might, for instance, see people that have studied computer engineering to further their industry skills by acquiring a competence in software development.

Good job. But to become unique within their field one should be acquiring distant skills; That is, skills that seem unrelated to each other. Very often the sort of skills that are regarded as irrelevant to their field.

There is a reason why I find job titles and labels very limiting. A title is a pretty static thing. We evolve every day and learning is a never-ending affair. Many people choose to overspecialize in an aspect of their job, field or industry. It is, however, by navigating across different fields and industries that you will discover unexpected things, push your limits and become more than you have ever thought. In short, by defining yourself you are limiting yourself. We are well aware of how necessary it is to possess a concrete job title in the corporate world, especially when attending networking events or introducing yourself to people who try to make sense of what your company stands for and what is your expertise. In reality, however, *limiting your intellectual capacity, skills, competences and actions to your job title can be extremely damaging, not to say destructive, to your career.* It can impede your growth, prevent you from venturing into new territories and getting seriously creative. Creativity is the common denominator that drives great leaders and all types of outstanding professionals from entrepreneurs to artists, scientists or life coaches. A key question here is: Can we reach a super high level of creativity without being geniuses? Yes. By developing distant, opposite-side-of-the-spectrum skills. Creative people are often paradoxical. In his seminal book *Creativity: the Work and Lives of 91 Prominent People*, professor of Psychology and Management Mihaly Csikszentmihalyi (Yes. Croatian names can be as tough as this to pronounce!) writes:

"I have devoted thirty years of research to how creative people live and work, to make more understandable the mysterious process by which they come up with new ideas and new things. If I had to express in one word what makes their personalities different from others, it's *complexity*. They show *tendencies of thought and action that in most people are segregated.* They contain *contradictory extremes*; instead of being an individual, *each of them is a multitude.*"

To engineer your Corporate Fingerprint, to become seriously creative and add real value to the market, your business or organization, you have to learn, do and be different things. One cannot be creative, say in physics by only acquiring a great education in physics. To be creative in physics it takes *another* education. Creativity requires that we use mental patterns and mechanisms we have learned elsewhere. We have to immerse ourselves into a different universe for extra inspiration. In a sense, we need to alienate ourselves in a positive, constructive way. It is astonishing to see how overspecialized employees have become over the past few decades. It is sad to see how successful the job industry are at shaping people's minds and limiting their potential, skills and career choices by mass-producing overspecialized, disposable staff that can be replaced anytime. We are sacrificing well-rounded members of society by transforming them into gullible worker bees ready to submit to the dictates of their boss, the job industry or large corporations. While this serves the interest of large corporations, it doesn't serve yours. Whatever you do, strive to become *a one-of-a-kind art of craftsmanship.* Unique Skill Pairings (USP) are combinations of professional skills and qualities that do not normally fall on the same side of the spectrum. You have surely met or worked with great professionals who are leading figures in their respective fields. Becoming a category of your own and achieving legendary status within a specific field requires a combination of Unique Skill Pairings (USP) *and* Unique Personality Pairings (UPP).

Corporate Fingerprint Formula

CORPORATE FINGERPRINT = USP(UNIQUE SKILL PAIRINGS) + UPP(UNIQUE PERSONALITY PAIRINGS)

	Examples of USP and UPP
Unique Skill Pairings (USP)	• Project Management + Graphic Arts + Fluency in Mandarin • Software Engineering + Marketing+ Fluency in German • Business Development + Public Speaking + Fluent in French and Hindi • Sales + Graphic design + Music Composer
Unique Personality Pairings (UPP)	• Playful + Disciplined • Down-to-earth + Creative • Rebellious + Conservative • Proud + Humble • Passionate + Objective • Cocky + Sensitive • Responsible + Laissez-faire
Corporate Fingerprint	• Down-to-earth + Creative + Business Development + Public Speaking + Fluent in French and Hindi • Passionate + Objective + Software Engineering + Marketing + Fluency in German • Cocky + Sensitive + Sales + Graphic Design + Music Composer

Would you rather hire a project manager or a Down-to-Earth and Creative Project Manager who is passionate about Painting and is Fluent in English and Mandarin? The possible USP and UPP combinations are countless. The ones on the table are but a few examples and for the sake of clarity are limited to three elements. Your Corporate Fingerprint (CF) is yours to design. Variety remains key here. Possessing three *distant* skills makes you more competitive than possessing six closely related skills. A combination of Unique Skill Pairings (USP) and Unique Personality Pairings (UPP) will result into something unprecedented. People will want to be associated to you, not merely for *what* you do, but for *who* you are. Possessing uncommon personality traits, being drawn to variety, welcoming change, having a mind filled with curiosity and a mass of contradictions helps. A lot. If this doesn't sound like you, it's still fine. You might lack that natural drive but not the ambition and common sense required to chart a strategic route to developing a smart skill mix essential to your success as a leader.

If a strong set of Unique Skill Pairings (USP) is the key ingredient to developing a strong Corporate Fingerprint (CF), Skill Layering (SL) is the core ingredient when it comes to solidifying your Unique Skill Pairings (USP) edifice through a smart combination of existing and new skills.

Absolute skill mastery is not necessary to develop a successful *skill layering strategy*. Skill layering requires, though, a few primary skills. I have decided to call this type of skills Access Skills (AS). That is, basic micro-skills that cannot be used independently, unless they are applied in a wider, macro-skills context. It is about building new sets of skills based on the ones that have been already acquired. Access Skills (AS) function pretty much like *cement,* holding your skills edifice together. These skills help you expand your competence sets. Using them will help you combine and cement different sets of skills and competences into a *whole*, thus forming your Unique Corporate Fingerprint. Access Skills (AS) are very valuable at the initial stage when learning a new skill, by considerably reducing confusion as well as the cognitive and communicative load that comes hand in hand with the development of a new competence. Access Skills (AS) include your memory and the ability to observe patterns based on existing skills. Remember this: It's easier to sidestep than climb. Access Skills (AS) can take many shapes and forms depending on the number of skills you have developed so far and on how well you master those. Such skills won't only make you more adaptable to new situations. Access Skills (AS) have a compounding effect; they save you time and energy and double your efficiency. Examples of Access Skills include:

1. Team-building
2. Problem-solving skills
3. Cross-cultural intelligence
4. Analytical/Quantitative skills
5. Strong work ethic
6. Flexibility/Adaptability
7. Initiative
8. Written communication skills
9. Verbal communication skills

I love to immerse myself into different cultures and learn foreign languages. I have always considered cross-cultural intelligence and communication a key aspect of my Corporate Fingerprint and personal expansion strategy. Both literally and metaphorically. Expansion in the sense of personal development through active exposure to different cultures, reasoning patterns and ways of perceiving the world. Expansion, also, in concrete geographic country and market terms, that is, expansion of career opportunities, and growth of financial assets. Economic growth has slowed down significantly in recent years, especially after the 2008 financial crisis. On top of this, markets in the Western world have become alarmingly saturated.

Going the extra mile and becoming fluent in another language will inevitably offer you a strong competitive advantage over those entering a new market with basic knowledge and minimal understanding of the local culture. There are still pristine market territories to be explored in emerging economies across the world. Don't limit yourself to what has now become a confined place. I was a Humanities student when I was at senior high school. Ancient Greek and Latin were two courses that most people would try to avoid, for two reasons. They looked "Chinese" to them, or they simply regarded them as dead languages, a mere waste of time. I had a different way of seeing things. Learning dead Latin actually helped me learn better, faster and effortlessly a bunch of modern, living languages, such as French, Spanish, Italian, and Portuguese and gain access to a full range of career opportunities that come hand in hand with having access to these cultures, countries and markets. If you can already see the pattern, I used Latin as an *access skill* (a skill that cannot be used independently in the modern world) to help me learn faster and more efficiently four other languages which I *actually* use daily to expand my professional and social network, my business, client base, professional projects and career opportunities. Most importantly, developing strong cross-cultural communication skills offered me extra freedom and flexibility. If a hurricane or financial crisis strikes tomorrow, I still have plenty of options in terms of geographic locations and business opportunities through access to familiar markets. Lesson of the story: never underestimate any skill, as outdated or old-fashioned as it may seem.

I was 17 years old when my parents expressed a real concern after realizing how irrevocable I was in my decision to move to Paris and study French Linguistics and Literature at university. Relatives wouldn't stop asking me what kind of career I was hoping to pursue with this major, considering that I was not dreaming of a school teacher career. Such nonsense questions allowed me to see for the first time how people limit their own life choices. My answer was the same to everyone: "Relax people. I am not planning to *only* study this major. I am planning to do *much more*. I am actually planning to *become* much more. This is only the beginning!" In theory everyone likes to have freedom of choice. In practice though, people don't like to face many choices. Making a choice requires action and the willingness to adapt to a new context. New choices lead to unfamiliar paths forcing people to step out of their comfort zone, which is something many are not willing to do. When I was studying Language and Literature in the department of Humanities at Sorbonne University in Paris, I was part of a world that holds its own values, rules, patterns of thought and of course its own stereotypes. Humanities scholars have a sort of aversion for the corporate world. They regard corporate professionals (business people, bankers, traders, etc.) as uncultured, profoundly unscrupulous, greedy egomaniacs in pursuit of high job titles and fat bonuses. The kind of people that deserve to be looked with a certain disdain and which they regard as the root cause of all the unfortunate things that happen in this world, from environmental pollution to the recent financial crisis and so on. On the other side you have corporate people and entrepreneurs who have a totally different set of values and who in their turn regard intellectuals and educators as failures. They see them as not smart enough to actually do something other than teaching, writing, or spend time criticizing society. Although there might be some truth there, these are stereotypes. But real stereotypes affecting real lives nonetheless. If you have experienced both worlds you know what I am talking about.

Developing Unique Skill Pairings (USP) requires an almost schizophrenic way of being, thinking and operating. So, don't be afraid to *be many people at the same time.* Don't be afraid of a bit of confusion. Don't be afraid to be a walking contradiction. Above all, don't feel you are being disloyal to yourself when dealing with different sorts of people or when operating in unfamiliar environments. Adaptability is the business of a leader. Be a chameleon of all colors and shades … and, of course, make sure you enjoy it! I am proud of the fact that I belong simultaneously to different worlds and groups of people. You might sometimes feel overwhelmed by the work that is involved in building these "chameleon skills." The key is to not feel intimidated by the task. For this reason it is essential that you choose very carefully the skills you will be investing time and energy in. It is sad to see how many people are struggling to improve at things they will never be good at. Don't make this same mistake. It's important to focus your energy, time and resources into becoming great in something you are already good at, instead of struggling to become average or decent in something that is not your cup of tea.

Make sure that you invest in those skills that are right for you, always taking into account your natural talents and inclinations. I was never fond of science classes at school. Instead of spending extra time to improve myself in those areas I had no interest nor talent in, I chose to invest most of my time getting great at those things I was already very good at–which also happen to be the ones I enjoyed studying the most. This is a rule I still live by. It is in perfect alignment with the 80/20 rule or Pareto's Principle[2] which I am discussing in detail in the Business section.

In the process of building your own Corporate Fingerprint the main goal is to be perceived as a bargain, the real deal. You should aim to become an addiction to those around you. As Steve Martin famously said "Be so good, they can't ignore you," I would like to take this a bit further and say "Be so good, they can't get over you." Developing a magnetic personality means that you become a person people are drawn toward, then get *addicted* to. Not simply attracted to or seduced by. I am talking about addiction here. If you think about it, it is in specific product categories and brands that people who manifest various forms of addiction get addicted to. Smokers tend to be addicted to a specific cigarette brand. Alcoholics to a particular type of liquor. Studies have shown that video gambling addicts are only addicted to this form of gambling and wouldn't be interested in say, roulette betting.

There is a key concept in the food industry. The *bliss point*. When manufacturing food, producers look for the optimal sweetness/acidity ratio, the bliss point. Striking the perfect flavor balance prevents consumers from feeling satiated and full. As a result, they consume a lot more food than they normally would. The ratio that keeps you wanting to eat more at a point where you overeat. It is interesting to use this as an analogy and apply the optimal ratio principle to the development of your Corporate Fingerprint (CF). The bliss point formula applies perfectly to the development of Unique Skill Pairings (USP).

It teaches us how building an "addictive" Corporate Fingerprint can make you irreplaceable and make people ask for more. More of your talents, time, skills, experience, guidance. More of you! You should always look at the bliss point ratio when crafting your personal brand. The optimal level of "sweetness" and "acidity." For instance, if you are overly disciplined and conservative in the way you lead your company, your career or life, that might be at the extreme of the salty side of the flavor spectrum. Have you thought what sort of ingredients you need to put

---

[2] The 80/20 principle is known as the path of least effort to maximum results. It was named after economist Vilfredo *Pareto*. It specifies an unequal relationship between inputs and outputs.

into your Unique Skill Pairings (USP) mix to draw people to you over and over again. An important element to consider when embarking in any skill learning adventure is the level of mastery we aim to achieve. It is a high level of competence that will allow you to make a real difference. The Writing Spectrum can be used as a reference for developing any new skill. It is important to break down your skill learning goals into milestones during the whole process. The darker the shade, the higher one's level of competence.

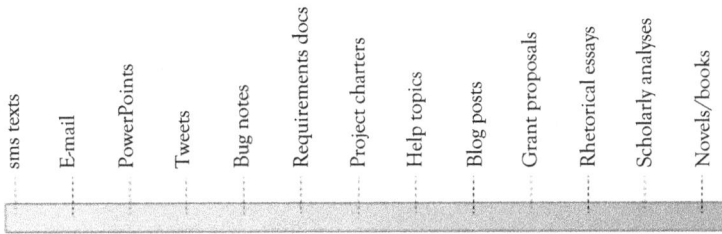

The writing spectrum

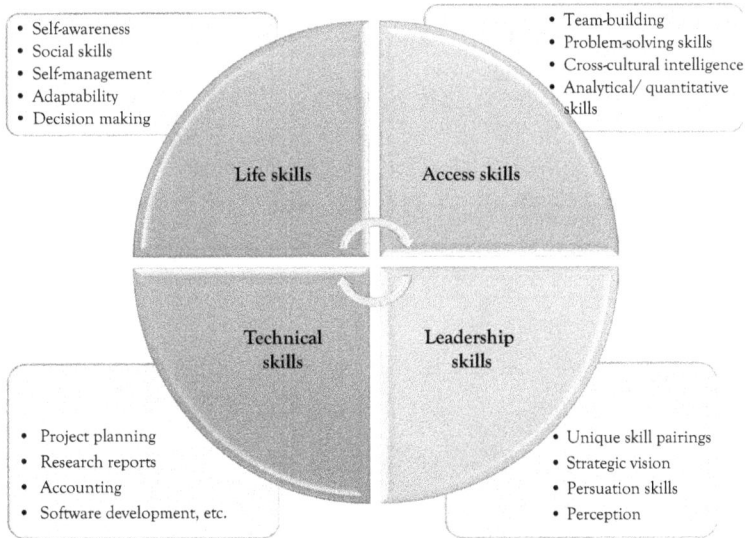

Skills Wheel: the list on each section is non-exhaustive.

Now open an Excel chart and create your own Unique Skill Pairings Wheel. The more elements it combines and the more colorful it is, the strongest your Corporate Fingerprint.

Leadership Quotes

Leadership is not a noun. It is a verb. It's action. It's movement.
—John Maxwell

Don't just get involved. Fight for your seat at the table. Better yet, fight for a seat at the head of the table.
—Barack Obama

It is not titles that honor men, but men that honor titles.
—Niccolò Machiavelli

You can't lead anyone else further than you have gone yourself.
—Gene Mauch

Very often a change of self is needed more than a change of scene.
—Arthur Christopher Benson

A good leader takes care of those in their charge. A bad leader takes charge of those in their care.
—Simon Sinek

A true hero isn't measured by the size of his strength but by the strength of his heart.
—Hercules

I learned that a great leader is a man who has the ability to get other people to do what they don't want to do and like it.
—Harry S. Truman

One measure of leadership is the caliber of people who choose to follow you.
—Dennis A. Peer

Leaders don't create followers, they create more leaders.

—Tom Peters

To lead the people, walk behind them.

—Lao-Tzu

A leader is a dealer in hope.

—Napoleon Bonaparte, attributed

You can like people without leading them but you cannot lead people well without liking them.

—John C. Maxwell

No man will even be a great leader who wants to do it all himself, or to get all the credit for doing it.

—Andrew Carnegie

Leaders are visionaries with a poorly developed sense of fear and no concept of the odds against them.

—Robert Jarvik

A good leader is a person who takes a little more than his share of the blame and a little less than his share of the credit.

—John C. Maxwell

I praise loudly, I blame softly.

—Catherine the Great

Great leaders are almost always great simplifiers, who can cut through argument, debate and doubt to offer a solution everybody can understand.

—Colin Powell

Effective leadership is putting first things first. Effective management is discipline, carrying it out.

—Stephen Covey

The way to get people to build a ship is not to teach them carpentry, assign them tasks and give them schedules to meet; but to inspire them to long for the infinite immensity of the sea.

—Antoine se Saint-Exupéry

Leadership is action, not position.

—Donald H. McGannon

Remember the difference between a boss and a leader; a boss says "Go!" - a leader says "Let's go!"

—E.M. Kelly

A chief is a man who assumes responsibility. He says "I was beaten," he does not say "My men were beaten."

—Antoine de Saint-Exupery

Management is the art of making problems so interesting that everyone wants to get to work and deal with them.

—Paul Hawken

Charlatanism of some degree is indispensable to effective leadership.

—Eric Hoffer

The promise given was a necessity of the past. The word broken is a necessity of the present.

—Niccolo Machiavelli

Attitude

With the right attitude self-imposed limitations vanish.

—Alexander the Great

It's so hard when I have to, and so easy when I want to.

—Annie Gottlier

A happy person is not a person in a certain set of circumstances, but rather a person with a certain set of attitudes.

—Hugh Downs

Become a possibilitarian. No matter how dark things seem to be or actually are, raise your sights and see possibilities—always see them, for they're always there.

—Norman Vincent Peale

Leaders who don't listen will eventually be surrounded by people who have nothing to say.

—Author Unknown

How can something bother you if you won't let it?

—Terri Guillemets

Life is not happening to you. Life is responding to you.

—Author Unknown

The impossible can always be broken down into possibilities.

—Author Unknown

The human spirit is stronger than anything that can happen to it.

—C.C. Scott

Never be ashamed of a scar. It simply means you are stronger than whatever tried to hurt you.

—Author unknown

It is easy to keep things at a distance; it is hard to be naturally beyond them.

—Bunan

Happiness is an attitude. We either make ourselves miserable, or happy and strong. The amount of work is the same.

—Francesca Reigler

Defeat is not bitter unless you swallow it.

—Joe Clark

Physical strength is measured by what we can carry; spiritual by what we can bear.

—Author Unknown

We always think we'd be happier in some faraway place, as if you could catch a plane to a state of mind.

—Robert Brault

The only disability in life is a bad attitude.

—Scott Hamilton

Your life is your garden,
Your thoughts are the seeds.
If your life isn't awesome,
You've been watering the weeds.

—Author Unknown

Pain and suffering are inevitable in our lives but misery is an option.

—Chip Beck

Things turn out best for the people who make the best out of the way things turn out.

—Author unknown

There are two types of people—those who come into a room and say, "Well, here I am!" and those who come in and say, "Ah, there you are."

—Frederick L. Collins

If you have nothing to be grateful for check your pulse.
Anywhere is paradise; it's up to you.

—Author Unknown

I am an optimist. It does not seem too much use being anything else.

—Winston Churchill

They may destroy your rose gardens, but no harm has been done, so that they have not destroyed your urge for roses.
—Muriel Strode Lieberman (1875–1964), "Much in a Basket: VIII," At the Roots of Grasses, 1923

If the skies fall, one may hope to catch larks.

—Francis Rabelais

The sun won't shine until you put the umbrella away. Be free.

—Author unknown

The man who has no inner life is a slave to his surroundings.

—Henri Frédéric Amiel

A good speaker is a good listener who hears what lesser speaker fails to.

—Sommers White

Turn your face to the sun and the shadows fall behind you.

—Maori Proverb

Unhappiness is best defined as the difference between our talents and our expectations.

—Edward de Bono, Observer, June 12, 1977

People seem not to see that their opinion of the world is also a confession of character.

—Ralph Waldo Emerson, "Worship,"
The Conduct of Life, 1860

Swallow a toad in the morning and you will encounter nothing more disgusting the rest of the day.

—Nicholas Chamfort

Consider how much more you often suffer from your anger and grief, than from those very things for which you are angry and grieved.

—Marcus Antonius

Keep a green tree in your heart and perhaps a singing bird will come.

—Chinese Proverb

Nothing is interesting if you're not interested.

—Helen MacInness

Excellence is not a skill. It is an attitude.

—Ralph Marston

Don't find fault. Find a remedy.

—Henry Ford

The problem is not that there are problems. The problem is expecting otherwise and thinking that having problems is a problem.

—Theodore Rubin

A bad attitude is like a flat tire. You can't go anywhere until you change it.

The greatest discovery of my generation is that a human being can alter his life by altering his attitudes of mind.

—William James

Attitude is more important than the past, than education, than money, than circumstances, than what other people think or say or do. It is more important than appearance, giftedness or skill. It will make or break a company, a church, a home. The remarkable thing is, we have a choice every day regarding the attitude we will embrace for that day. We cannot change the past. We cannot change the fact that people will act in a certain way. We cannot change the inevitable. The only thing we can do is play the one string we have, and that is our attitude.

—Chuck Swindoll

I am more and more convinced that our happiness or unhappiness depends far more on the way we meet the events of life, than on the nature of those events themselves.

—Alexander Von Humbold

Change

When the winds of change blow, some people build walls and others build windmills.

—Chinese Proverb

Change, before you have to.

—Jack Welch

If you want to make enemies, try to change something.

—Woodrow Wilson

Faced with the choice between changing one's mind and proving that there is no need to do so, almost everyone gets busy on the proof.

—John Kenneth Galbraith

Things alter for the worse spontaneously, if they be not altered for the better designedly.

—Francis Bacon

There is nothing more difficult to take in hand, more perilous to conduct or more uncertain in its success, than to take the lead in the introduction of a new order of things.

—Niccolo Machiavelli

Every beginning is a consequence—every beginning ends something.

—Paul Valery

We all have big changes in our lives that are more or less a second chance.

—Harrison Ford

If you want to truly understand something, try to change it.

—Kurt Lewin

Changing and actually improving are two quite different skills.

—Dr. SunWolf, 2015 tweet

The man who never alters his opinion is like standing water, and breeds reptiles of the mind.

—William Blake

What you have become is the price you paid to get what you used to want.

—Mignon McLaughlin, The Neurotic's Notebook, 1960

All change is not growth, as all movement is not forward.
—Ellen Glasgow

After you've done a thing the same way for two years, look it over carefully. After five years, look at it with suspicion. And after ten years, throw it away and start all over.
—Alfred Edward Perlman, New York Times, July 3, 1958

If you would attain to what you are not yet, you must always be displeased by what you are. For where you are pleased with yourself there you have remained. Keep adding, keep walking, keep advancing.
—Saint Augustine

The goal of any culture is to decay through overcivilization. The factors of decadence—luxury, scepticism, weariness and superstition are constant. The civilization of one epoch becomes the manure of the next.
—Cyril Connolly

The bamboo that bends is stronger than the oak that resists.
—Japanese Proverb

Our only security is our ability to change.
—John Lilly

It's the most unhappy people who most fear change.
—Mignon McLaughlin, The Second Neurotic's Notebook, 1966

It's humbling to start afresh. It takes a lot of courage.... You just have to put your ego on a shelf and tell it to be quiet.
—Jennifer Ritchie Payette

It is not the strongest of the species that survive, nor the most intelligent, but the one most responsive to change.
—Author unknown, commonly misattributed to
Charles Darwin

Every possession and every happiness is but lent by chance for an uncertain time, and may therefore be demanded back the next hour.

—Arthur Schopenhauer

The only man I know who behaves sensibly is my tailor; he takes my measurements anew each time he sees me. The rest go on with their old measurements and expect me to fit them.

—George Bernard Shaw

Perhaps there should be one day a week when you tackle your "Things I Gotta Undo" list.

—Robert Brault

When you create change you can be wrong, but always believe that you are doing it for the right reasons.

—Richard Gerver

The goal of every culture is to decay through overcivilization; the factors of decadence—luxury, skepticism, weariness, and superstition—are constant. The civilization of one epoch becomes the manure of the next.

—Cyril Connolly

Change will not come if we wait for some other person or some other time. We are the ones we've been waiting for. We are the change that we seek.

—Barack Obama

Every day of our lives we are on the verge of making those slight changes that would make all the difference.

—Mignon McLaughlin

He who rejects change is the architect of decay.

—Harold Wilson

Things do not change; we change.

—Henry David Thoreau

It is not necessary to change. Survival is not mandatory.
                                        —W. Edwards Deming

If you want to make enemies try to change something.
                                        —Woodrow Wilson

You can recognize a pioneer by the arrows in his back.
                                        —Beverly Rubick

To exist is to change, to change is to mature, to mature is to go on creating oneself endlessly.
                                        —Henri Bergson

Consider how hard it is to change yourself and you will understand what little chance you have in trying to change others.
All change is not growth, as all movement is not forward.
                                        —Ellen Glasgow

There is a certain relief in change, even though it be from bad to worse! As I have often found in travelling in a stagecoach, that it is often a comfort to shift one's position, and be bruised in a new place.
                                        —Washington Irving

Things alter for the worse spontaneously, if they be not altered for the better designedly.
                                        —Francis Bacon

The devil could change. He was once an angel and may be evolving still.
                                        —Laurence J. Peter

Growth is the only evidence of life.
                                        —John Henry Newman, Apologia pro vita sua, 1864

Just because everything is different doesn't mean anything has changed.
                                        —Irene Peter

The circumstances of the world are so variable that an irrevocable purpose or opinion is almost synonymous with a foolish one.

—William H. Seward

Continuity gives us roots; change gives us branches, letting us stretch and grow and reach new heights.

—Pauline R. Kezer

He that will not apply new remedies must expect new evils; for time is the greatest innovator.

—Francis Bacon, "On Innovation," Essays, 1597

Few can accept happiness if it means change. We want the life we have now, only happier.

—Robert Brault

Every beginning is a consequence—every beginning ends something.

—Paul Valery

You must welcome change as the rule but not as your ruler.

—Denis Waitley

Character

Character is destiny.

—Heraclitus

The same boiling water that softens the potato hardens the egg. It's about what you are made of, not the circumstances.

—Author Unknown

Persons with weight of character carry, like planets, their atmospheres along with them in their orbits.

—Thomas Hardy

Your smile is your logo, your personality is your business card, how you leave others feeling after an experience with you is your trademark.

—Author Unknown

Character is higher than intellect.

—Ralph Waldo Emerson

Leadership is a potent combination of strategy and character but if you must be without one, be without strategy.

—Norman Swartzkopf

Hire for character, train for skills.

—Peter Schutz

A man never discloses his character so clearly as when he describes another's.

—Jean Paul Richter

Every one of us has in him a continent of undiscovered character. Blessed is he who acts the Columbus to his own soul.

—Author Unknown

There is something in every person's character that cannot be broken— the bony structure of his character.

—Georg Christoph Lichtenberg (1742–1799)

A man may be born a jackass; but it is his business if he makes himself a double one.

—Martin H. Fischer (1879–1962)

No man can climb out beyond the limitations of his own character.

—John Morley

Circumstances are moulds in which characters are run.

—James Lendall Basford (1845–1915), Seven Seventy Seven Sensations, 1897

Fortune does not change men; it unmasks them.

—Suzanne Necker

In each human heart are a tiger, a pig, an ass and a nightingale. Diversity of character is due to their unequal activity.

—Ambrose Bierce

There is a great deal of self-will in the world, but very little genuine independence of character.

—Frederick W. Faber

We're seldom drawn to a character we admire; only to a personality we like.

—Mignon McLaughlin, The Second Neurotic's Notebook, 1966

She was not quite what you would call refined. She was not quite what you would call unrefined. She was the kind of person who keeps a parrot.

—Mark Twain

Charisma

People buy into the leader before they buy into the vision.

—John C. Maxwell

Charm is... a way of getting the answer yes without having asked any clear question.

—Albert Camus, The Fall, 1956

Charisma is not so much getting people to like you as getting people to like themselves when you're around.

—Robert Brault, rbrault.blogspot.com

It is absurd to divide people into good and bad. People are either charming or tedious.

—Oscar Wilde

Charisma is a fancy name given to the knack of giving people your full attention.

—Robert Brault

When you do common things in life in an uncommon way, you will command the attention of the world.

—George W. Carver

I want minimum information given with maximum politeness.

—Jackie Kennedy

Confidence

Don't major in minor things.

—Author unknown

It's not who you are that holds you back, it's who you think you're not.

—Attributed to Hanoch McCarty

If you are going to doubt something, doubt your limits.

—Don Ward

It is folly for a man to pray to the gods for that which he has the power to obtain by himself.

—Epicurus

Without a humble but reasonable confidence in your own powers you cannot be successful or happy.

—Norman Vincent Peale

Life marks us all down, so it's just as well that we start out by overpricing ourselves.

—Mignon McLaughlin, The Neurotic's Notebook, 1960

I quit being afraid when my first venture failed and the sky didn't fall down.

—Allen H. Neuharth

If you hear a voice within you say "you cannot paint," then by all means paint, and that voice will be silenced.

—Vincent Van Gogh

I will release all the confined forces of my soul and apply them directly to that which I may be. I will release all my thousand possibilities and send them broadside against life.

—Muriel Strode Lieberman (1875–1964), "A Soul's Faring: XXIV," A Soul's Faring, 1921

Success comes in cans, not cant's.

—Author Unknown

I am not a has-been. I am a will be.

—Lauren Bacall

If you really put a small value upon yourself, rest assured that the world will not raise your price.

—Author Unknown

Confidence comes not from always being right but from not fearing to be wrong.

—Peter T. McIntyre

You have to expect things of yourself before you can do them.

—Michael Jordan

Thousands of geniuses live and die undiscovered—either by themselves or by others.

—Mark Twain

Nothing splendid has ever been achieved except by those who dared believe that something inside of them was superior to circumstance.

—Bruce Barton

Confidence is preparation. Everything else is beyond your control.

—Richard Kline

Sex appeal is fifty percent what you've got and fifty percent what people think you've got.

—Sophia Loren

If you doubt yourself, then indeed you stand on shaky ground.

—Henrik Ibsen

Anyone who ever gave you confidence, you owe them a lot.

—Truman Capote, Breakfast at Tiffany's, 1958,
spoken by the character Holly Golightly

Pay no attention to what the critics say. A statue has never been erected in honor of a critic.

—Jean Sibelius

When there is no enemy within, the enemies outside cannot hurt you.

—African proverb

Men are not against you; they are merely for themselves.

—Gene Fowler, Skyline, 1961

Courage

Life shrinks or expands in proportion to one's courage.

—Anaïs Nin, Diary, 1969

Courage is knowing what not to fear.

—Plato

I will win not immediately but definitely.

—Author Unknown

A great deal of talent is lost to the world for want of a little courage. Every day sends to their graves obscure men whose timidity prevented them from making a first effort.

—Sydney Smith

If you get tired learn to rest, not quit.

—Author Unknown

Optimism is the foundation of courage.

—Nicholas Murray Butler

Sometimes even to live is an act of courage.

—Lucius Annaeus Seneca, Letters to Lucilius

Courage is the power to let go of the familiar.

—Raymond Lindquis

It is curious—curious that physical courage should be so common in the world, and moral courage so rare.

—Mark Twain

Courage is as often the outcome of despair as of hope; in the one case we have nothing to lose, in the other everything to gain.

—Diane de Poitiers

It's hard to fight an enemy who has outposts in your head.

—Sally Kempton, Esquire, 1970

Courage doesn't always roar. Sometimes courage is the little voice at the end of the day that says I'll try again tomorrow.

—Mary Anne Radmacher

Your value is the product of your thoughts. Do not miscalculate your self-worth by multiplying your insecurities.

—Dodinsky

Courage is a love affair with the unknown.

—Osho

Bravery is being the only one who knows you're afraid.

—Franklin P. Jones

Courage is resistance to fear, mastery of fear—not absence of fear.

—Mark Twain

Courage is what it takes to stand up and speak; courage is also what it takes to sit down and listen.

—Winston Churchill

My endurance may be born of courage, but I will not forget that it may also be born of that most pitiable of human things—weakness.

—Muriel Strode-Lieberman (1875–1964),
My Little Book of Life, 1912

Courage is reckoned the greatest of all virtues; because, unless a man has that virtue, he has no security for preserving any other.

—Samuel Johnson

Necessity does the work of courage.

—Nicholas Murray Butler

Courage is almost a contradiction in terms. It means a strong desire to live taking the form of readiness to die.

—G.K. Chesterton

Courage is the fear of being thought a coward.

—Horace Smith

A hero is no braver than an ordinary man, but he is braver five minutes longer.

—Ralph Waldo Emerson

A timid person is frightened before a danger, a coward during the time, and a courageous person afterward.

—Jean Paul Richter

It is easier to find a score of men wise enough to discover the truth than to find one intrepid enough, in the face of opposition, to stand up for it.

—A.A. Hodge

Decisions

May your choices reflect your hopes, not your fears.

—Nelson Mandela

Unsuccessful people make decisions based on their current situation. Successful people make decisions based on where they want to be.

—Author Unknown

It is only in our decisions that we are important.

—Jean-Paul Sartre

Life is the sum of all your choices.

—Albert Camus

A mistake repeated more than once is a decision.

—Paolo Coelho

You are the CEO of your own life. Start making executive decisions today.

—Stephen Luke

When you have to make a tough decision flip a coin. Why? Because when the coin is in the air, you suddenly know what you are hoping for.

—Author Unknown

Never base your life decisions on advice from people who don't have to deal with the results.
If decision-making is a science, judgement is an art.

—Author Unknown

A wise man makes his own decisions. An ignorant man follows public opinion.

—Chinese Proverb

Design is nothing, if not decision-making.

—Henry Petroski

You are always one decision away from a totally different life.

—Author Unknown

I try not to make decisions I am not excited about.

—Jake Nickell

It is better to be approximately right than precisely wrong.

—Warren Buffett

You are free to choose but you are not free from the consequence of your choice.

—Author Unknown

Learn to say "no" to the good, so you can say "yes" to the best.

—John C. Maxwell

With time, our indecisions become decisions that life takes for us.

—Roxana Jones

Excellence represents the wise choice of many alternatives. Choice, not chance determines your destiny.

—Aristotle

One of the hardest parts of life is deciding whether to walk away or try harder.

—Author Unknown

The doors we open and close each day decide the lives we live.

—Flora Whittemore

To be suspicious is not a fault. To be suspicious all the time without coming to a conclusion is the defect.

—Lu Xun

The hardest thing to learn in life is which bridge to cross and which to burn.

—David Russell

Making a decision takes a moment. Living a decision takes a lifetime.

—A. El-Mawardy

Some persons are very decisive when it comes to avoiding decisions.

—Brendan Francis

It's not hard to make decisions when you know what your values are.

—Roy Disney

Good decisions come from experience, and experience comes from bad decisions.

—Author Unknown

I must have a prodigious quantity of mind; it takes me as much as a week sometimes to make it up.

—Mark Twain

When one bases his life on principle, 99 percent of his decisions are already made.

—Author Unknown

Effort

Those at the top of the mountain didn't fall there.

—Author Unknown

Sweat is the cologne of accomplishment.

—Heywood Hale Broun

About the only thing that comes to us without effort is old age.

—Gloria Pitzer

I've got a theory that if you give 100 percent all of the time, somehow things will work out in the end.

—Larry Bird

Put in 5% more effort than "there's only so much I can do" and you'll be way ahead of the game.

—Terri Guillemets

There are no shortcuts to any place worth going.
Character is what emerges from all the little things you were too busy
to do yesterday, but did anyway.
—Mignon McLaughlin, The Second Neurotic's Notebook, 1966

One saves oneself much pain, by taking pains; much trouble, by
taking trouble.
—Augustus William Hare and Julius Charles Hare, Guesses at
Truth, by Two Brothers, 1827

Give your dreams all you've got and you'll be amazed at the energy
that comes out of you.
—William James

Effort is only effort when it begins to hurt.
—José Ortega y Gassett

To eat an egg, you must break the shell.
—Jamaican Proverb

Put your heart, mind, intellect and soul even to your smallest acts.
This is the secret of success.
—Swami Sivananda

Men are made stronger on realization that the helping hand they need
is at the end of their own arm.
—Sidney J. Phillips

Things may come to those who wait, but only the things left by those
who hustle.
—Abraham Lincoln

Look at a day when you are supremely satisfied at the end. It's not
a day when you lounge around doing nothing; it's when you've had
everything to do, and you've done it.
—Margaret Thatcher

The only thing that ever sat its way to success was a hen.

—Sarah Brown

The artist is nothing without the gift, but the gift is nothing without work.

—Emile Zola

You're either changing your life or you're not. No waiting for this or that or better weather or other hurdles. Hurdles are the change.

—Terri Guillemets

No matter what it is, if you aren't happy striving for it, you won't be happy achieving it.

—Robert Brault

People know you for what you've done, not for what you plan to do.

—Author Unknown

We gain no easier advantage than by relentlessly pursuing our goal while others pursue an advantage.

—Robert Brault

Focus

The main thing is to keep the main thing the man thing.

—Stephen Covey

Sometimes we must unfocus our way to clarity.

—Terri Guillemets

Tell me what you pay attention to and I will tell you who you are.

—José Ortega y Gasset

An arrow can only be shot by pulling it backward. When life is dragging you back with difficulties, it means it's going to launch you into something great. So just focus, and keep aiming.

—Author unknown

Your most important work is always ahead of you, never behind you.
—Stephen Covey

The capacity for delight is the gift of paying attention.
—Julia Margaret Cameron

Your priorities are your character.
—Author Unknown

Life is denied by lack of attention, whether it be to cleaning windows or trying to write a masterpiece.
—Nadia Boulanger

The moment one gives close attention to anything, even a blade of grass, it becomes a mysterious, awesome, indescribably magnificent world in itself.
—Henry Miller

The waste of life occasioned by trying to do too many things at once is appalling.
—Orison Marden

Genius

Genius is an African who dreams up snow.
—Robert Schumann

Men of genius are meteors destined to burn themselves out in lighting up their age.
—Napoleon Bonaparte, Discours de Lyon, 1771

Every great genius has an admixture of madness.
—Aristotle

Genius is childhood recovered at will.
—Charles Baudelaire

The function of genius is not to give new answers but to pose new questions – which time and mediocrity can solve.

—Hugh Trevor Roper

An idea can turn to dust or magic, depending on the talent that rubs against it.

—William Bernbach

So much of our time is preparation, so much is routine, and so much retrospect, that the path of each man's genius contracts itself to a very few hours.

—Ralph Waldo Emerson

The reluctance to put away childish things may be a requirement of genius.

—Rebecca Pepper Sinkler

Everybody is a genius. But, if you judge a fish by its ability to climb a tree, it will spend its whole life believing that it is stupid.

—Albert Einstein

Talent is that which is in a man's power; genius is that in whose power a man is.

—James Russell Lowell, Literary Essays

Thousands of geniuses live and die undiscovered—either by themselves or by others.

—Mark Twain

I put all my genius into my life. I put only my talent into my works.

—Oscar Wilde

Men of genius are often dull and inert in society; as the blazing meteor, when it descends to earth, is only a stone.

—Henry Wadsworth Longfellow, Kavanagh:
A Tale, 1849

Genius ain't anything more than elegant common sense.

—Josh Billings

Everyone is born a genius, but the process of living de-geniuses them.

—R. Buckminster Fuller

If children grew up according to early indications, we should have nothing but geniuses.

—Johann Wolfgang von Goethe

What moves men of genius, or rather what inspires their work, is not new ideas, but their obsession with the idea that what has already been said is still not enough.

—Eugene Delacroix

A genius is someone who has two great ideas.

—Jacob Bronowski

Everyone is a genius at least once a year. A real genius has his ideas closer together.

—G.H. Lichtenberg

Nothing has been more difficult than to be curious about an object or a person, without being obstructed by preconceived ideas. Occasionally the veil is lifted, and the one who lifts it is called a genius.

—Theodore Zeldin

The greatest thing by far is to be a master of metaphor. It is the one thing that cannot be learned from others and it is also a sign of genius, since a good metaphor implies an intuitive perception of the similarity in the dissimilar.

—Aristotle

Any intelligent fool can make things bigger, more complex, and more violent. It takes a touch of genius—and a lot of courage—to move in the opposite direction.

—E.F. Schumacher

Ideals

The ideal is the enemy of the possible.

—Dr. Idel Dreimer

Mankind aspires to a perfection not permitted by his genetic legacy— nor by the competitive necessities of his circumstance. He is condemned to endless aspiration—a persistent purgatory of failed ideals.

—Dr. Idel Dreimer

An idealist is one who, on noticing that roses smell better than a cabbage, concludes that it will also make better soup.

—Henry L. Mencken

It's a cruel world: idealistic dreams usually end up costing as much as regular stupidity.

—Dr. Idel Dreimer

Quality marks the search for an ideal after necessity has been satisfied and mere usefulness achieved.

—John Ruskin

It is a golden rule that one should never judge men by their opinions, but rather by what these opinions lead them to be.

—Georg Christoph Lichtenberg (1742–1799), translated by Norman Alliston, 1908

We have our ideals now, but when they are mentioned we feel self-conscious and uncomfortable, like a school-boy caught praying.

—Arnold Bennett (1867–1931)

Living up to ideals is like doing everyday work with your Sunday clothes on.

—Ed Howe

Idealism increases in direct proportion to one's distance from the problem.

—John Galsworthy

A man of personality can form ideals but only a person of character can achieve them.

—Herbert Read

Though I believe in liberalism, I find it difficult to believe in liberals.

—G.K. Chesterton

Every dogma has its day, but ideals are eternal.

—Israel Zangwill, speech, November 13, 1892

The soul mounts ever toward nobler things, but seldom is it strong enough to carry along with it the human clay.

—Bernard G. Richard, "Life and the Theories of Life," To Morrow, June 1905

Our ideals, like the gods of old, are constantly demanding human sacrifices.

—George Bernard Shaw

There is nothing the matter with Americans except their ideals. The real American is all right; it is the ideal American who is all wrong.

—G.K. Chesterton

Nobody grows old merely by living a number of years. We grow old by deserting our ideals. Years may wrinkle the skin but to give up enthusiasm wrinkles the soul.

—Samuel Ullman

Imagination

Everything you can imagine is real.

—Pablo Picasso

Imagination is intelligence with an erection.

—Victor Hugo

It's not what you look at that matters, it's what you see.

—Henry David Thoreau

To unpathed waters, undreamed shores.

—William Shakespeare

Anyone who can be replaced by a machine deserves to be.

—Dennis Gunton

When patterns are broken, new worlds emerge.

—Tuli Kupferberg

Creative minds have always been known to survive any kind of bad training.

—Anna Freud

I like nonsense. It wakes up the brain cells. Fantasy is a necessary ingredient in living, it's a way of looking at life through the wrong end of a telescope. Which is what I do, and that enables you to laugh at life's realities.

—Theodore Geisel

Fiction reveals truths that reality obscures.

—Jessamyn West

The strongest nation on earth is your imagi-nation.

—Matt Furey

Sometimes I've believed as many as six impossible things before breakfast.

—Lewis Carroll

I admit to having an imagination feverish enough to melt good judgment.

—Dean R. Koontz, Seize the Night

Some stories are true that never happened.

—Elie Weisel

Fantasy abandoned by reason produces impossible monsters; united with it, she is the mother of the arts and the origin of marvels.

—Francisco Goya

Creativity represents a miraculous coming together of the uninhibited energy of the child with its apparent opposite and enemy, the sense of order imposed on the disciplined adult intelligence.

—Norman Podhoretz

The man who can't visualize a horse galloping on a tomato is an idiot.

—André Breton

They who dream by day are cognizant of many things which escape those who dream only by night.

—Edgar Allan Poe, "Eleonora"

Don't expect anything original from an echo.

—Author Unknown

There are no rules of architecture for a castle in the clouds.

—G.K. Chesterton

Never tell people how to do things. Tell them what to do and they will surprise you with their ingenuity.

—George Smith Patton, War as I Knew It, 1947

Imagination acts upon man as really as does gravitation, and may kill him as certainly as a dose of prussic acid.

—Sir James Frazer

The creative person is both more primitive and more cultivated, more destructive, a lot madder and a lot saner, than the average person.

—Frank Barron, Think, November-December 1962

I paint objects as I think them, not as I see them.

—Pablo Picasso

Perhaps imagination is only intelligence having fun.

—George Scialabba

I am now and have always been a stranger to the realm of practical matters.

—Anton Chekhov

Integrity

Never rob your character to enrich your pocket.
—James Lendall Basford (1845–1915), Seven Seventy Seven Sensations, 1897

Live in such a way that you would not be ashamed to sell your parrot to the town gossip.

—Will Rogers

Integrity has no need of rules.

—Albert Camus

The man who has won millions at the cost of his conscience is a failure.
—B.C. Forbes

You do not wake up one morning a bad person. It happens by a thousand tiny surrenders of self-respect to self-interest.

—Robert Brault

Take care that no one hates you justly.

—Publilius Syrus

To know what is right and not do it is the worst cowardice.

—Confucius

There is no pillow so soft as a clear conscience.

—French Proverb

Goodness is the only investment that never fails.

—Henry David Thoreau

There is only one way to achieve happiness on this terrestrial ball,
And that is to have either a clear conscience or none at all.

—Ogden Nash

Somebody once said that in looking for people to hire, you look for three qualities: integrity, intelligence and energy. But if you don't have the first, the other two could kill you.

—Warren Buffett

The right to do something does not mean that doing it is right.

—William Safire

Character is doing the right thing when nobody's looking. There are too many people who think that the only thing that's right is to get by, and the only thing that's wrong is to get caught.

—J.C. Watts

It takes less time to do a thing right, than it does to explain why you did it wrong.

—Henry Wadsworth Longfellow

The measure of a man's real character is what he would do if he knew he never would be found out.

—Thomas Babington Macaulay

Better keep yourself clean and bright; you are the window through which you must see the world.

—George Bernard Shaw

Dignity consists not in possessing honors, but in the consciousness that we deserve them.

—Aristotle

One does evil enough when one does nothing good.

—German Proverb

The time is always right to do what is right.

—Martin Luther King, Jr.

Character is much easier kept than recovered.

—Thomas Paine

The only exercise some people get is jumping to conclusions, running down their friends, side-stepping responsibility, and pushing their luck!

—Author Unknown

Laws control the lesser man. Right conduct controls the greater one.

—Chinese Proverb

Conscience warns us before it reproaches us.

—Comtesse Diane (Marie Josephine de Suin de Beausacq), Maximes de la vie, 1908

To speak ill of others is a dishonest way of praising ourselves.

—Will Durant

If we are ever in doubt what to do, it is a good rule to ask ourselves what we shall wish on the morrow that we had done.

—John Lubbock, "The Happiness of Duty," 1887

Let me be thankful first, because I never was robbed before; second, because although they took my purse, they did not take my life; third, although they took my all, it was not much; and fourthly, because it was I who was robbed, and not I who robbed.

—Matthew Henry (1662–1714)

Never let your sense of morals prevent you from doing what is right!
—Isaac Asimov

I am prepared to die, but there is no cause for which I am prepared to kill.
—Mahatma Gandhi

Every time I've done something that doesn't feel right, it's ended up not being right.
—Mario Cuomo

The only correct actions are those that demand no explanation and no apology.
—Red Auerbach

If we cannot live so as to be happy, let us at least live so as to deserve it.
—Immanuel Hermass von Fichte

In matters of principle, stand like a rock; in matters of taste, swim with the current.
—Thomas Jefferson

I will follow the right side even to the fire, but excluding the fire if I can.
—Michel de Montaigne, translated

There is an ongoing battle between conscience and self-interest in which, at some point, we have to take sides.
—Robert Brault

It's impossible to be loyal to your family, your friends, your country, and your principles, all at the same time.
—Mignon McLaughlin, The Neurotic's Notebook, 1960

If a man is not rising upwards to be an angel, depend upon it, he is sinking downwards to be a devil.
—Samuel Taylor Coleridge

Man is the only animal that blushes. Or needs to.

—Mark Twain

When you choose the lesser of two evils, always remember that it is still an evil.

—Max Lerner, Actions and Passions, 1949

Aspire to a lower level of harm.

—Terri Guillemets

Intelligence

Common sense is not so common.

—Voltaire

It's not that I'm so smart, it's just that I stay with problems longer.

—Albert Einstein

If the human brain were so simple that we could understand it, we would be so simple that we couldn't.

—Emerson M. Pugh

The measure of intelligence is the ability to change.

—Albert Einstein

No matter the situation, never let your emotions overpower your intelligence.

—Jean Houston

Knowing others is intelligence; knowing yourself is true wisdom. Mastering others is strength; mastering yourself is true power.

—Lao Tzu (604–531 BC)

We should not only use the brains we have, but all that we can borrow.

—Woodrow Wilson

We should take care not to make the intellect our god; it has, of course, powerful muscles, but no personality.

—Albert Einstein

If the Aborigine drafted an I.Q. test, all of Western civilization would presumably flunk it.

—Stanley Garn

The first method for estimating the intelligence of a ruler is to look at the men he has around him.

—Niccolo Machiavelli

All men have a reason, but not all men can give a reason.

—John Henry Cardinal Newman

What a distressing contrast there is between the radiant intelligence of the child and the feeble mentality of the average adult.

—Sigmund Freud

Primitive does not mean stupid.

—S.A. Sach

Intelligence is the ability to avoid doing work, yet getting the work done.

—Linus Torvalds

It is hard to challenge an idiot idea, because people think you're challenging their right to idiocy.

—Robert Brault

Intelligence is like underwear. It is important that you have it, but not necessary that you show it off.

—Author Unknown

Intelligence is quickness in seeing things as they are.

—George Santayana

Intuition

Instinct is the nose of the mind.

—Delphine de Girardin

Intuition is what you know for sure without knowing for certain.

—Weston Agor

Intuition is the new physics. It's an Einsteinian seven-sense, practical way to make tough decisions. The crazier the times are, the more important it is for leaders to develop and trust their intuition.

—Tom Peters

We all have spiritual DNA; wisdom and truth are part of our genetic structure even if we don't always access it.

—Lama Surya Das

Instead of penetrating the mystery we let ourselves be penetrated by the mystery.

—Wendy Palmer

Instinct is untaught ability.

—Alexander Bainon. Tom Peters

Logic, which alone can give certainty, is the instrument of demonstration; intuition is the instrument of invention.

—Henri Poincare

A leader or a man of action in a crisis almost always acts subconsciously and then thinks of the reasons for his action.

—Jawaharlal Nehru

Sell your cleverness and buy bewilderment. Cleverness is mere opinion, bewilderment is intuition.

—Rumi

Life is a school where you learn how to remember what your soul already knows.

—Author Unknown

Intuition is instinct humanized.

—F.B. Dowd

I would rather trust a woman's instinct than a man's reason.

—Stanley Baldwin

Knowledge

Knowledge is the true organ of sight, not the eyes.

—Panchatantra

Seek knowledge, even if it be in China.

—Muhammad, the Koran

Real knowledge is to know the extent of one's ignorance.

—Confucius

If we would have new knowledge, we must get a whole world of new questions.

—Susanne K. Langer

Knowledge is haunted by the ghost of past opinion.

—Author Unknown

I am not young enough to know everything.

—J.M. Barrie

Abundance of knowledge does not teach men to be wise.

—Heraclitus

A love affair with knowledge will never end in heartbreak.

—Michael Garrett Marin

Knowledge comes, but wisdom lingers.

—Lord Alfred Tennyson

Since we cannot know all that is to be known of everything, we ought to know a little about everything.

—Blaise Pascal

It's silly when any man assumes that he knows it all. It's tragic when he does!

—Martin H. Fischer (1879–1962)

Some drink deeply from the river of knowledge. Others only gargle.

—Woody Allen

The greatest obstacle to discovering the shape of the earth, the continents and the ocean was not ignorance but the illusion of knowledge.

—Daniel J. Boorstin, The Discoverers

To be master of any branch of knowledge, you must master those which lie next to it; and thus to know anything you must know all.

—Oliver Wendell Holmes, Jr.

Of course there's a lot of knowledge in universities: the freshmen bring a little in; the seniors don't take much away, so knowledge sort of accumulates.

—Abbott Lawrence Lowell

The larger the island of knowledge, the longer the shoreline of wonder.

—Ralph W. Sockman

Knowledge has a beginning but no end.

—Geeta S. Iyengar

Know Thy Self

Search others for their virtue, and yourself for your vices.

—R. Buckminster Fuller

A single event can awaken within us a stranger totally unknown to us. To live is to be slowly born.

—Antoine de Saint-Exupéry

Man stands in his own shadow and wonders why it's dark.

—Zen Proverb

He who knows others is learned; He who knows himself is wise.

—Lao-tzu, Tao te Ching

Resolve to be thyself; and know that he who finds himself, loses his misery.

—Matthew Arnold

You can out-distance that which is running after you, but not what is running inside you.

—Rwandan Proverb

Men go abroad to wonder at the heights of mountains, at the huge waves of the sea, at the long courses of the rivers, at the vast compass of the ocean, at the circular motions of the stars, and they pass by themselves without wondering.

—St. Augustine

Know thyself, or at least keep renewing the acquaintance.

—Robert Brault

Always do right. That will gratify some of the people and astonish the rest.

—Mark Twain

He that does good for good's sake seeks neither paradise nor reward, but he is sure of both in the end.

—William Penn

Nothing is more unpleasant than a virtuous person with a mean mind.

—Walter Bagehot

I can teach anybody how to get what they want out of life. The problem is that I can't find anybody who can tell me what they want.

—Mark Twain

I have had more trouble with myself than with any other man I have ever met.

—Dwight Lyman Moody

When you blame and criticize others, you are avoiding some truth about yourself.

—Deepak Chopra

I know well what I am fleeing from but not what I am in search of.

—Michel de Montaigne

Not until we are lost do we begin to understand ourselves.

—Henry David Thoreau

Never mind searching for who you are. Search for the person you aspire to be.

—Robert Brault

Take the time to come home to yourself every day.

—Robin Casarjean

I am more afraid of my own heart than of the pope and all his cardinals. I have within me the great pope, Self.

—Martin Luther

Before I can live with other folks I've got to live with myself. The one thing that doesn't abide by majority rule is a person's conscience.

—Harper Lee, To Kill a Mockingbird

You grow up the day you have your first real laugh, at yourself.
— Ethel Barrymore

Everyone complains of his memory, but no one complains of his judgment.
— Francois de La Rochefoucauld, Maxims, 1665

Know well what leads you forward and what holds you back, and choose the path that leads to wisdom.
— Buddha

I may not have gone where I intended to go, but I think I have ended up where I intended to be.
— Douglas Adams

Biographies are but the clothes and buttons of the man—the biography of the man himself cannot be written.
— Mark Twain, Autobiography, 1924

We did not change as we grew older; we just became more clearly ourselves.
— Lynn Hall

One day I will count my possessions, and they will include me.
— Muriel Strode

Don't bother just to be better than your contemporaries or predecessors. Try to be better than yourself.
— William Faulkner

Just let awareness have its way with you completely.
— Scott Morrison

There is part of us that stands in quiet witness to what we do, taking notes, waiting for a solitary moment to bring up the subject.
— Robert Brault

Not being able to govern events, I govern myself.

—Michel de Montaigne

We confess to little faults only to persuade ourselves that we have no great ones.

—François VI de la Rochefoucault, Maxims

There comes a morning in life when you wake up a new person; that is to say, you wake up the same person but you realize it's your own fault.

—Robert Brault

We judge ourselves by what we feel capable of doing, while others judge us by what we have already done.

—Henry Wadsworth Longfellow, Kavanagh, 1849

I am convinced all of humanity is born with more gifts than we know. Most are born geniuses and just get de-geniused rapidly.

—Buckminster Fuller

Our remedies oft in ourselves do lie
Which we ascribe to heaven.

—William Shakespeare, All's Well That Ends Well

The study of crime begins with the knowledge of oneself.

—Henry Miller

People are like stained-glass windows. They sparkle and shine when the sun is out, but when the darkness sets in their true beauty is revealed only if there is light from within.

—Elisabeth Kübler-Ross

The things we hate about ourselves aren't more real than things we like about ourselves.

—Ellen Goodman

If you are tuned out of your own emotions, you will be poor at reading them in other people.

—Daniel Goleman

Once your awareness becomes a flame, it burns up the whole slavery
that the mind has created.

—Osho

Other people's opinion of you does not have to become your reality.

—Les Brown

Self-love seems so often unrequited.

—Anthony Powell

You have brains in your head.
You have feet in your shoes.
You can steer yourself in any direction you choose.
You're on your own.
And you know what you know.
You are the guy who'll decide where to go.

—Dr. Seuss

Don't be distracted by criticism. Remember—the only taste of success
some people have is when they take a bite out of you.

—Zig Ziglar

I am,
indeed,
a king,
because I know how
to rule myself.

—Pietro Aretino, 1537

Of all our infirmities, the most savage is to despise our being.

—Michel de Montaigne

Men are not punished for their sins, but by them.
—Elbert Hubbard, A Thousand and One Epigrams, 1911

One of the "lost arts" is that of minding one's own business.
—James Lendall Basford (1845–1915), Sparks from the
Philosopher's Stone, 1882

God may forgive your sins, but your nervous system won't.

—Alfred Korzyybski

If it was necessary to tolerate in other people everything that one permits oneself, life would be unbearable.

—Georges Courteline, La philosophie de
Georges Courteline, 1917

Some luck lies in not getting what you thought you wanted but getting what you have, which once you have got it you may be smart enough to see is what you would have wanted had you known.

—Garrison Keillor

Put your ear down next to your soul and listen hard.

—Anne Sexton

Mind

A man must be big enough to admit his mistakes, smart enough to profit from them and strong enough to correct them.

—John C. Maxwell

How long has it been since someone touched part of you other than your body?

—Terri Guillemets

The mind is like a parachute. It doesn't work if it's not open.

—Frank Zappa

Be very, very careful what you put into that head because you will never, ever get it out.

—Cardinal Wolsey

Your mind is a dangerous neighborhood and you shouldn't go in there alone at night.

—Christiane Northrup

Every time you think the problem is 'out there,' that very thought is the problem.

—Stephen Covey

To he who is right in mind, he can do all the wrong things and it will still turn out right. To he who is wrong in mind, he can do all the right things and it will still turn out wrong.

—Derek Rydall

Be careful of your thoughts, they may become words at any moment.

—Iara Gassen

It is the mark of an educated mind to be able to entertain a thought without accepting it.

—Aristotle

The best cure for the body is a quiet mind.

—Napoleon Bonaparte

The man who acquires the ability to take full possession of his own mind may take possession of anything else to which he is justly entitled.

—Andrew Carnegie

Mother Nature is the most powerful force on the planet—but in the human realm, it's the Mind.

—Terri Guillemets

Here in your mind you have complete privacy. Here there's no difference between what is and what could be.

—Chuck Palahniuk, Choke

To a mind that is still, the whole universe surrenders.

—Zhuangzi

I will not let anyone walk through my mind with their dirty feet.
—Mahatma Gandhi

Wouldn't it be wonderful if our mind growled like our stomach does when it is hungry?
—Zig Ziglar

The vacation we often need is freedom from our own mind.
—Jack Adam Weber

You can stand tall without standing on someone. You can be a victor without having victims.
—Harriet Woods

You're picky about the car you drive. You're picky about what you wear. You're picky about what you put in your mouth. We want you to be pickier about what you think.
—Abraham-Hicks

The energy of the mind is the essence of life.
—Aristotle

Men harm others by their deeds, themselves by their thoughts.
—Augustus William Hare and Julius Charles Hare,
Guesses at Truth, by Two Brothers, 1827

A person can grow only as much as his horizon allows.
—John Powell

What is right is often forgotten by what is convenient.
—Bodie Thoene, Warsaw Requiem

It is a man's own mind, not his enemy or foe, that lures him to evil ways.
—Buddha

Pain of mind is worse than pain of body.

—Latin Proverb

Misery is almost always the result of thinking.

—Joseph Joubert

Body and mind, like man and wife, do not always agree to die together.
—Charles Caleb Colton

What if there are not only two nostrils, two eyes, two lobes, and so forth, but two psyches as well, and they are separately equipped? They go through life like Siamese twins inside one person.
—Norman Mailer, Harlot's Ghost, 1991

Don't let it be all in your head, nor all in your body.

—Terri Guillemets

Man's mind, once stretched by a new idea, never regains its original dimensions.

—Oliver Wendell Holmes

Minds, like bodies, will often fall into a pimpled, ill-conditioned state from mere excess of comfort.

—Charles Dickens, Barnaby Rudge

Chaos is a name for any order that produces confusion in our minds.
—George Santayana

Great Minds Discuss Ideas; Average Minds Discuss Events; Small Minds Discuss People.

—Socrates

Our life is shaped by our mind. We become what we think. Suffering follows an evil thought as the wheels of a cart follow the oxen that draws it.

—Buddha

The mind sleeps in the mineral kingdom, breathes in the vegetable kingdom, dreams in the animal kingdom and awakes in man.

—Teilhard de Chardin

Perseverance

Great souls have wills, feeble ones have only wishes.

—Chinese Proverb

It's not that I'm so smart, it's just that I stay with problems longer.

—Albert Einstein

The difference between perseverance and obstinacy is that one comes from a strong will, and the other from a strong won't.

—Henry Ward Beecher

People often say that motivation doesn't last. Well, neither does bathing—that's why we recommend it daily.

—Zig Ziglar

He conquers who endures.

—Persius

Where the willingness is great, the difficulties cannot be great.

—Niccolo Machiavelli

The only thing that stands between a man and what he wants from life is often the will to try it and the faith to believe that it is possible.

—Richard M. Devos

Stubbornly persist, and you will find that the limits of your stubbornness go well beyond the stubbornness of your limits.

—Robert Brault

Saints were sinners who kept on going.

—Robert Louis Stevenson

In the absence of willpower the most complete collection of virtues and talents is wholly worthless.

—Aleister Crowley

Perseverance is not a long race; it is many short races one after another.

—Walter Elliott

The road to success is dotted with many tempting parking places.

—Author Unknown

Perseverance is the hard work you do after you get tired of doing the hard work you already did.

—Newt Gingrich

If you have the will to win, you have achieved half your success; if you don't, you have achieved half your failure.

—David Ambrose

Sometimes you feel like giving up, but then you look at other people who have given up, and the results aren't that good.

—Robert Brault

It's not that some people have willpower and some don't. It's that some people are ready to change and others are not.

—James Gordon

While I might find pleasure in your approval, your disapproval will not deter me.

—Muriel Strode

I am convinced that about half of what separates the successful entrepreneurs from the non-successful ones is pure perseverance.

—Steve Jobs

Fall seven times, stand up eight.

—Japanese Proverb

There is no telling how many miles you will have to run while chasing a dream.

—Author Unknown

But the moment you turn a corner you see another straight stretch ahead and there comes some further challenge to your ambition.

—Oliver Wendell Holmes, Jr.

One may go a long way after one is tired.

—French proverb

You can't go through life quitting everything. If you're going to achieve anything, you've got to stick with something.

—Author Unknown

If we are facing in the right direction, all we have to do is keep on walking.

—Buddhist Saying

Perspective

If you do not raise your eyes you will think that you are the highest point.

—Antonio Porchia, Voces, 1943, translated from Spanish by W.S. Merwin

What we see depends mainly on what we look for.

—John Lubbock

There is nothing either good or bad but thinking makes it so.

—William Shakespeare, Hamlet, 1600

It isn't that they can't see the solution. It is that they can't see the problem.

—G.K. Chesterton

A hen is only an egg's way of making another egg.

—Samuel Butler

Every exit is an entrance somewhere else.

—Tom Stoppard

It isn't so much that hard times are coming; the change observed is mostly soft times going.

—Groucho Marx

The urge to save humanity is almost always only a false-face for the urge to rule it.

—H.L. Mencken, Minority Report, 1956

There is only one pretty child in the world, and every mother has it.

—Chinese Proverb

Every man regards his own life as the New Year's Eve of time.

—Jean Paul Richter

Advertising is selling Twinkies to adults.

—Donald R. Vance

At high tide the fish eat ants; at low tide the ants eat fish.

—Thai Proverb

The real voyage of discovery consists not in seeking new landscapes, but in having new eyes.

—Marcel Proust

Necessity is not an established fact, but an interpretation.

—Friedrich Nietzsche

If you think you are too small to have an impact, try going to bed with a mosquito.

—Anita Roddick

Exceptions do not always prove the rule; they may be even the first germs of a new rule.
—Marie Dubsky, Freifrau von Ebner-Eschenbach (1830–1916), translated by Mrs Annis Lee Wister, 1882

The reverse side also has a reverse side.
—Japanese Proverb

The grass may be greener on the other side of the fence, but you still have to mow it.
—Author Unknown

There's an alternative. There's always a third way, and it's not a combination of the other two ways. It's a different way.
—David Carradine

Eventually you realize that not all opposing viewpoints come from people who oppose you.
—Robert Brault

An exhibitionist is nothing without a voyeur.
—S.A. Sachs

An unattempted woman cannot boast of her chastity.
—Michel de Montaigne

Nothing's a gift, it's all on loan.
—Wisława Szymborska (1923–2012), "Nothing's a Gift," The End and the Beginning, 1993, translated from the Polish by Stanisław Barańczak and Clare Cavanagh

What is true by lamplight is not always true by sunlight.
—Joseph Joubert

Won't you come into the garden? I would like my roses to see you.
—Richard Brinsley Sheridan

If a man could have half his wishes accomplished, he would double his troubles.

—Benjamin Franklin

I'm right-handed, whereas the fellow in my mirror is left-handed. I start shaving from the left; he starts from the right. Differences only in perception, but religious wars have been fought over such.

—Robert Brault

Efficiency is intelligent laziness.

—David Dunham

The ancient law 'an eye for an eye' will make all people blind. It is immoral because it is trying to subdue the enemy, and not to achieve his understanding. It seeks to destroy, not to win over.

—Martin Luther King

In the ideal sense nothing is uninteresting; there are only uninterested people.

—Brooks Atkinson

The poor never estimate as a virtue the generosity of the rich.
—Marie Dubsky, Freifrau von Ebner-Eschenbach (1830–1916), translated by Mrs Annis Lee Wister, 1882

Advice to children crossing the street: damn the lights. Watch the cars. The lights ain't never killed nobody.

—Moms Mabley

No object is mysterious. The mystery is your eye.
—Elizabeth Bowen, The House in Paris, 1935

Don't think of organ donations as giving up part of yourself to keep a total stranger alive. It's really a total stranger giving up almost all of themselves to keep part of you alive.

—Author Unknown

People who look through keyholes are apt to get the idea that most things are keyhole shaped.

—Author Unknown

There is no burnt rice to a hungry person.

—Philippine Proverb

But such a tiny and trivial thing as an umbrella can deprive you of the sight of such a stupendous fact as the sun.

—Meher Baba

The rich would have to eat money if the poor did not provide food.

—Russian proverb

If the only tool you have is a hammer, you tend to see every problem as a nail.

—Abraham Maslow

Each act is virgin, even the repeated ones.

—René Char

Disappointment is as inevitable as hope is necessary.

—Dr. Idel Dreimer

The guy who invented the first wheel was an idiot. The guy who invented the other three, he was a genius.

—Sid Caesar

If I had been around when Rubens was painting, I would have been revered as a fabulous model. Kate Moss? Well, she would have been the paintbrush.

—Dawn French

Every man takes the limits of his own field of vision for the limits of the world.

—Arthur Schopenhauer, "Studies in Pessimism," Psychological Observations, 1851

Events and external objects are, so to speak, but a neutral substance, which receives its colour and its significance from our soul.
—Alexandre Vinet (1797–1847)

The shadows: some hide, others reveal.
—Antonio Porchia, Voces, 1943, translated from Spanish by W.S. Merwin

An abridgement may be a bridge: it may help us over the water: but it keeps us from drinking.
—Augustus William Hare and Julius Charles Hare, Guesses at Truth, by Two Brothers, 1827

The most amazing things that can happen to a human being will happen to you, if you just lower your expectations.
—"Phil's-osophy" by Phil Dunphy (Christopher Lloyd, Steven Levitan, and Dan O'Shannon, Modern Family, "Schooled," original airdate October 10, 2010)

Why assume so glibly that the God who presumably created the universe is still running it? It is certainly conceivable that He may have finished it and then turned it over to lesser gods to operate.
—H.L. Mencken

If you see a whole thing—it seems that it's always beautiful. Planets, lives... But up close a world's all dirt and rocks. And day to day, life's a hard job, you get tired, you lose the pattern.
—Ursula K. Le Guin

Everything is best until we know better.
—James Lendall Basford (1845–1915), Seven Seventy Seven Sensations, 1897

The same fence that shuts others out shuts you in.
—Bill Copeland

Power

The measure of a man is what he does with power.

—Plato

Mastering others is strength, mastering oneself is true power.

—Lao Tzu

Power doesn't corrupt people. People corrupt power.

—William Gaddis

We know that anyone ever seizes power with the intention of relinquishing it.

—George Orwell

Power is domination, control and therefore a very selective form or truth, which is a lie.

—Wole Soyinka

Such a waste of talent. He chose money over power. In this town a mistake nearly everyone makes. Money is the McMansion in Sarasota that starts falling apart after 10 years. Power is the old stone building that stands for centuries. I cannot respect someone who doesn't see the difference.

—House of Cards, Political Drama TV series

Power is domination, control and therefore a very selective form or truth, which is a lie.

—Wole Soyinka

We have the best government that money can buy.

—Mark Twain

Make the best of what is in your power and take the rest as it happens.

—Epictetus

The intangible represents the real power of the universe. It is the seed of the tangible.

—Bruce Lee

Skepticism, like wisdom, springs out in full panoply only from the brain of a god, and it is little profit to see an idea in its growth, unless we track its seed to the power which sowed it.

—James Anthony Froude

When you choose to forgive those who have hurt you, you take away their power.

—Author Unknown

Democracy is the best school to learn soft power.

—Joseph Nye

No one is you and that is your power.

—Author Unknown

Purpose

The man who is happy is fulfilling the purpose of existence.

—Fyodor Dostoyevsky

The purpose of life is a life of purpose.

—Robert Byrne

A useless life is an early death.

—Johann Wolfgang von Goethe

We should all be obliged to appear before a board every five years, and justify our existence... on pain of liquidation.

—George Bernard Shaw

Everything happens for a reason. If you can't find a reason for something, there's a reason for that.

—Chris Levi

I don't think life is absurd. I think we are all here for a huge purpose. I think we shrink from the immensity of the purpose we are here for.

—Norman Mailer

If Heaven made him—earth can find some use for him.

—Chinese Proverb

When you walk in purpose, you collide with destiny.

—Ralph Buchanan

Purpose is understanding why you do what you do. Purpose will wake you up early and keep you up late.

—Author Unknown

Every morning is destiny's way of telling you that your purpose in life is yet to be fulfilled.

—Author Unknown

There is one thing we all must do. If we do everything else but that one thing, we will be lost. And if we do nothing else but that one thing, we will have lived a glorious life.

—Rumi

An "unemployed" existence is a worse negation of life than death itself.

—José Ortega y Gasset

Do not promote products. Promote their purpose.

—Michael Kouly

Every man is visited by the suspicion that the planet on which he is riding is not really going anywhere; that the Force which controls its measured eccentricities hasn't got anything special in mind. If he broods on this somber theme long enough he gets the doleful idea that the laughing children on a merry-go-round or the thin, fine hands of a lady's watch are revolving more purposely than he is.

—James Thurber

If today were the last day of your life, would you want to do what you are about to do today?

—Steve Jobs

I don't know why we are here but I am pretty sure that it is not in order to enjoy ourselves.

—Ludwig Wittgenstein

You can accept reality, or you can persist in your purpose until reality accepts you.

—Robert Brault

To have no set purpose in one's life is the harlotry of the will.

—Stephen MacKenna

Man's ideal state is realized when he has fulfilled the purpose for which he is born. And what is it that reason demands of him? Something very easy – that he lives in accordance to his own nature.

—Seneca

In the dim background of our mind we know what we ought to be doing but somehow we cannot start.

—William James

If you ask me why I came to this earth, I'll tell you: I came to live out loud.

—Emile Zola

To have a grievance is to have a purpose in life.
—Alan Coren, The Sanity Inspector, 1974

The purpose of life is to be defeated by greater and greater things.
—Rainer Maria Rilke

Reputation

The reputation of a thousand years may be determined by the conduct of one hour.

—Japanese Proverb

Live in such a way that, if someone spoke badly of you, no one would believe it.

—Author Unknown

You can't build a reputation on what you're going to do.

—Henry Ford

Reputation is an idle and most false imposition, often got without merit and lost without deserving. You have lost no reputation at all unless you repute yourself such a loser.

—William Shakespeare

Many a man's reputation would not know his character if they met on the street.

—Elbert Hubbard

Glass, china and reputation are easily cracked and never well-mended.
—Benjamin Franklin

Worry about your character rather than your reputation, because your character is who you are and your reputation only what people think of you.

—Author Unknown

You can't buy a good reputation. You must earn it.

—Harvey Mackay

My reputation was a bit exaggerated. Things were written in newspapers, then copied, the doubled. One of the reasons I never disclaimed that, was because I found it amusing. But I also constructed such an image for myself in order to gain more of a private life.

—Thomas Kretschmann

Our names are labels, plainly printed on the bottled essence of our past behavior.

—Logan Pearsall Smith

Character is like a tree and reputation like a shadow. The shadow is what we think of it; the tree is the real thing.

—Abraham Lincoln

Reputation is character minus what you've been caught doing.

—Michael Iapoce, A Funny Thing Happened on the Way to the Boardroom

Your brand is what other people say when you are not in the room.

—Jeff Bezos

Laugh at a bad reputation. Fear a good one that you could not sustain.

—Robert Bresson

Strategy

You cannot change your destination overnight but you can change your direction.

—Jim Rohn

Every battle is won before it is fought.

—Sun Tzu

I base my calculations on the expectation that luck will be against me.

—Napoleon Bonaparte

A vision without a strategy remains an illusion.

—Lee Bolman

Strategy without tactics is the slowest route to victory. Tactics without strategy is the noise before defeat.

—Sun Tzu

If you don't have a competitive advantage, don't compete.

—Jack Welch

There is no avoiding war. It can only be postponed to the advantage of the others.

—Niccolo Machiavelli

You must take your opponent into a dark forest where 2+2=5, and the path leading out is only wide enough for one.

—Mikhail Tal, World chess champion

Strategy is not the consequence of planning but its starting point.

—Henry Mitzberg

The key is not to prioritize what's on your schedule, but to schedule your priorities.

—Stephen Covey

Life is a game board. Time is your opponent. If you procrastinate, you will lose the game. You must take the move to be victorious.

—Napoleon Hill

Pick out industries that don't have celebrities—then become the first one. Big ponds are overrated.

—Scott Ginsberg

Sometimes you must cross a bridge and other times you need to burn it.

—Dodinsky

The offenses one does to a man should be such that one does not fear revenge for it.

—Nicolo Machiavelli

Advice to big business: Don't buy the patent; hire the guy who got it.

—Martin H. Fischer

Give a man a fish and he will eat for a day. Teach a man to fish and he will eat for a lifetime. Teach a man to create an artificial shortage of fish and he will eat steak.

—Jay Leno

Without knowledge, skill cannot be focused. Without skill strength cannot be brought to bar and without strength, knowledge my not be applied.

—Alexander the Great

Tactics is knowing what to do when there is something to do. Strategy is knowing what to do when there is nothing to do.

—Savielly Tartakower

Without strategy execution is aimless, without execution strategy is useless.

—Morris Chang

Hope is not a strategy.

—Author Unknown

Effort and courage are not enough without purpose and direction.

—J.F. Kennedy

The essence of strategy is choosing what not to do.

—Michael Porter

Strategy is the art of making use of time and space. I am less concerned about the latter than the former. Space we can recover, lost time never.

—Napoleon Bonaparte

Strategy is thinking about a choice and choosing to stick with your thinking.

—Jeroen De Flander

A fine line separates a fighter from a warrior. One is motivated by reason, the other, by purpose. One fights to live, the other lives to fight.

—Author Unknown

The difference between what you are and what you want to be is what you do.

—Author Unknown

Each step in the right direction allows you to see further in that direction.

—Tom Ziglar

When a man does not know what harbor he is making for, no wind is the right wind.

—Seneca

Lack of direction not lack of time is the problem. We all have twenty-four hour days.

—Author Unknown

Sometimes I feel like I'm going nowhere, in opposite directions.

—Terri Guillemets

When everything is coming your way, you are in the wrong lane.

—Author Unknown

Management is efficiency in climbing the ladder of success; leadership determines whether the ladder is leaning against the right wall.

—Stephen Covey

Amateurs talk tactics, dilettantes talk strategy, professionals talk logistics.

—Author Unknown

If you don't have the time to do it right what makes you think you'll have the time to do it over?

—Seth Godin

Never interrupt your enemy when he is making a mistake.

—Napoleon Bonaparte

The supreme art of war is to subdue the enemy without fighting.

—Sun Tzu

Strategy is buying a bottle of fine wine when you take a lady out for dinner. Tactics is getting her to drink it.

—Frank Muir

If you surrender to the wind, you can ride it.

—Toni Morrison

The indispensable first step to getting the things you want out of life is this: decide what you want.

—Ben Stein

Victorious warriors win first and then go to war, while defeated warriors go to war first and then seek to win.

—Sun Tzu

You must do fight too often with one enemy, or you will teach him all your art of war.

—Napoleon Bonaparte

Strategy requires thought, tactics requires observation.

—Max Euve

Vision

The only thing worse than being blind is having sight but no vision.

—Helen Keller

We are gambling on our vision, and we would rather do that than make "me too" products. Let some other companies do that. For us, it's always the next dream.

—Steve Jobs

Vision is but a picture of the future that produces passion.

—Bill Hybels

Vision stands on the shoulders of what is actual to get a better view of what is possible.

—Mary Ann Radmacker

Vision is the art of seeing what is invisible to others.

—Jonathan Swift

A vision is often something that nags inside you and becomes so insistent that you must act upon it.

—Richard Gerver

I dream. I test my dreams against my beliefs. I dare to take risks and I execute my vision to make those dreams come true.

—Walt Disney

Leadership is having a vision, sharing that vision and inspiring others to support your vision while creating their own.

—Mindy Gibbins-Klein

If you don't have a vision you're going to be stuck in what you know. And the only thing you know is what you've already seen.

—Iyanla Vanzant

Vision is a destination, a fixed point to which we focus all effort. Strategy is a root – an adaptable path to get us where we want to go.

—Simon Sinek

A man without vision for his future, always returns to his past.

—Author Unknown

Stop expecting your job to fund your vision. Your vision is probably bigger than your paycheck.

—Bishop TD Jakes

Create the highest, grandest vision possible for your life, because you become what you believe.

—Oprah Winfrey

If you can't find any joy I life, perhaps you have a vision problem.

—Tim Fargo

Wisdom

Wisdom comes from experience. Experience is often a result of lack of wisdom.

—Terry Pratchett

Where fear is present, wisdom cannot be.

—Lactantius

Wisdom is knowing what to do next; virtue is doing it.

—David Star Jordan, The Philosophy of Despair

The wise are always at peace.

—Arabic Proverb

The wise man can pick up a grain of sand and envision a whole universe.

—Jack Handey

Wisdom doesn't necessarily come with age. Sometimes age just shows up all by itself.

—Tom Wilson

We don't receive wisdom; we must discover it for ourselves after a journey that no one can take for us or spare us.

—Marcel Proust

Knowledge is proud that he has learned so much, wisdom is humble that he knows no more.

—William Cowper

Keep me away from the wisdom which does not cry, the philosophy which does not laugh and the greatness which does not bow before children.

—Kahlil Gibran

Ninety percent of all human wisdom is the ability to mind your own business.

—Robert A. Heinlein

It's so simple to be wise. Just think of something stupid to say, and then don't say it.

—Sam Levenson

He swallowed a lot of wisdom, but it seemed as if all of it had gone down the wrong way.

—G.C. Lichtenberg

We can be knowledgeable with other men's knowledge but we cannot be wise with other men's wisdom.

—Michel de Montaigne

Wise men speak because they have something to say; Fools because they have to say something.

—Plato

Wisdom comes to us when it can no longer do any good.

—Gabriel Garcia

A wise man ... proportions his belief to the evidence.

—David Hume (1711–1776)

Sometimes one likes foolish people for their folly, better than wise people for their wisdom.

—Elizabeth Gaskell (1810–1865)

The saddest aspect of life right now is that science gathers knowledge faster than society gathers wisdom.

—Isaac Asimov (1920–1972)

I don't think much of a man who is not wiser today than he was yesterday.

—Abraham Lincoln

*It requires wisdom to understand wisdom: The music is nothing if
the audience is deaf.*

—Walter Lippmann (1889–1974)

*Wisdom is meaningless until your own experience has given it mean-
ing... and there is wisdom in the selection of wisdom.*

—Bergen

Business

Business Is Life

Business is a bit like Russian nesting dolls: many worlds packed into one. Business is much more than just business. It's an infinite universe made up of multiple galaxies. It requires a combination of technical skills, leadership, talent, inspiration, persuasion skills, drive, curiosity, competition, diplomacy, thick skin, adrenaline rushes, creative obsession with an idea or a product, resistance to pressure, tolerance for failure, love for risk, appetite for success, ambition, empathy, self-discipline, inflated egos put in good use, the art of transforming people's desires into needs, and the list goes on. Business demands that you function in beast mode. You have to be a mental athlete and it goes beyond beating the competition. Above all, it's about beating your own last record performance. In fact, it's about an endless marathon, an operation that requires alertness of all five senses. Sometimes even a sixth sense is needed, as intuition is the human version of animal instinct and does play a big role in business.

There's something else I love about business. Business is an act of optimism. You cannot embrace business and fully invest yourself into it without an optimistic outlook or at least without the willingness to overcome fears and self-doubt. Competing in the business arena has a cathartic effect. To enter this arena one must first purge oneself from a lot of their emotional bucket. There is no such thing as a pessimistic entrepreneur. It would be a contradiction in terms. Can you imagine a pessimist trying to start a business? It's an oxymoron! He would see the potential for failure every step of the way. Business, by its very nature, is a risky place. True innovation requires doing something that has never been done before and for this a good amount of optimism is needed. To believe you can convince enough people to part with a good amount of their hard-earned cash to support your idea and create a business than can survive among five billion others is proof enough. There are millions of people who, out of convenience, choose to work nine-to-five jobs they feel completely unpassionate about. On the other hand, there is not a single entrepreneur out there who does believe in what they are doing.

It is precisely this enthusiasm that encourages entrepreneurs to take the risks others don't. Where figures, statistics, and advisers suggest they will fail, entrepreneurs believe they can actually succeed. That's what pushes them to look for opportunities where others dare not look. They seek sales in places where others don't even bother pitching. They form partnerships and ventures with people others dismiss and get the deals and discounts others don't bother asking for. The very act of doing business breeds confidence, whether through the natural hope of increasing one's income, achieving a better standard of living or through one's forced determination to prove wrong the people who doubt their business idea. When realism overrides optimism a business is left with an unhealthy culture of fear. Smart business owners understand the value and necessity of maintaining healthy amounts of both optimism and caution when it comes to decision-making. They're neither hopelessly naïve in the pursuit of their goals nor reluctant to experiment with new concepts and products. Instead, they fight to keep creativity and innovation at the heart of the game.

Business is the most elemental form of exchange. It is about give and take. Some times more "giving" is involved, while at other times more "taking" takes place. In many ways, business is about maintaining a certain balance. A balance that is hard–almost impossible–to maintain at all times and on all levels. In both Life and Business everyone is competing for the same thing. Attention. Everyone is trying to rise above the crowd and get noticed, preferred over, chosen, hired, or purchased from… out of an infinite pool of similar-seeming options.

Business is Life!

In fact, I can't conceive Life without Business. I have often come across people arguing that either you have a natural inclination, a talent for business, or you don't. Whichever career path you choose to take in life, you will soon realize that business is an essential part of whatever it is you do daily, even if your job title suggests otherwise. It can be a product, a service, a particular skill, an idea or a point of view that you trade. A number of people set out in business quite early in life, through family tradition, genuine interest or personal inclination. Others through academic qualifications in economics, finance, and management, while a larger number set out through other routes, circumstances, financial needs or the pursuit of a hobby that ends up being a profession. Obviously, some are more successful than others. However, all of them have to follow similar paths when it comes to monetizing the product of their labor. In your social and professional life you have met people with hobbies and passions. Some make a living out of them, while others don't seem to be very successful at reaping any financial benefits. Perhaps, the most challenging part when people are passionate about something is that it's often difficult to make it a profession. Many people argue that it is best for you to follow your passion and everything else will follow... But, is it that simple?

Following one's passion sounds good but it is far more complicated than this. It would be great if life was as easy as to deciding what it is we like to do, then simply start doing it and make a living out of it. What people miss when they encourage you to follow your passion is that–*aside* from your passion–there is a whole set of skills that is required to *enable* you to make a living–or a business!–out of that passion. Unless you master that set of skills, doing what you love for a living will remain mere wishful thinking. Each one of us lives in a real world with real obligations to be met and real expenses to be covered. Ignoring all these responsibilities and simply do what we love is unfortunately not realistic. People often say that money does not matter, but in our world it *actually does*. Money does not *mean everything*, but it *does matter*. Numerous studies have shown that past a certain point of financial security and living standards, money does not affect happiness. Before *that* level of financial security is achieved though, money *does* in fact have a massive impact on our mental health and happiness.

Lack of financial security makes people feel out of control. As a result, rather than looking forward to the future, they fear it. Even worse, anxiety coming from financial insecurity won't let you enjoy life. It will, in fact, make you miserable. I have always been a supporter of the idea that a physically and mentally healthy life requires *congruent living*. By congruent living I mean that your skills, talents, belief system, physical, intellectual and spiritual needs and what you spend most of your waking time on must be aligned. For instance, being a personal trainer or musician and having to live in the shoes of an executive on a nine-to-five schedule is pure misery. The opposite also holds true. In the first chapter of this book we discussed how important meaning and a sense of purpose are in Life. If you decided that it is a meaningful life you want to live, then making a living out of something you are passionate about is the only way to go about in life. If, on the other hand, you are not able to make money out of your passion, it won't be long till you stop enjoying it. Learning business skills in order to better enjoy your passion and make a living out of something you love is far more motivating than learning business skills just for the sake of it. The key question is: can you make your passion work for you? It is essential that you are passionate about the product or service you sell. The problem is that many people who are passionate about a product and great at making it are not equally passionate about selling it. Simply because they don't see themselves as sales people.

The moment you start a business you are automatically required to be a sales person. This idea is hard for many people to reconcile with. Sales people are often looked down upon. Most professionals regard their job role as separate from sales. They tend to *only* see themselves as personal trainers, engineers, educators, lawyers and so on. There is not a single time in life when people are not selling though. I love the process of selling. I love the idea of selling. The reason you have to like sales is simple: you can't afford to not like sales in Life. If you take a close look at your everyday life, you will notice that selling is what you do most of your time, even in moments where you are not at all aware of the fact. People sell their products, their ideas, and their labor on a daily basis, not necessarily to customers but to every single person they interact with in their personal, professional and social lives. You sell all the time. You sell when you walk into a networking event and want to impress potential business partners or prospective customers. You sell when you walk into a bar to attract someone you like. You sell when you tell a joke. You sell when you try to make a friend see your point of view or win an argument. Business is a game! An exciting life game most people refuse or fail to play because of misconceptions and fears they have toward certain aspects of Business.

Right now, I am selling you the idea that selling is a crucial skill to possess on all levels of life. People sell the entire time. You might not think of it this way, but all of us actually sell every single day. We sell ideas, points of view, hopes, favors, expectations, promises, in exchange of some form of reward. In a corporate setting, when on a job interview, you are selling yourself as the best candidate for a given position. Later, whether you work for a company, trying to walk your way up the ladder, you are still selling. You are selling people the idea that you deserve to be up there, instead of where you actually stand. When you want a pay rise, you are selling again! You are selling your boss the idea that, instead of your current salary you are worth X amount of money. These examples might sound commonplace but you spend your whole life selling, one way or another. In short, unless you learn and practice selling, you won't get what you want in Life and Business.

When I was a child my traditional idea of a sales person was that of an insurance agent, someone who knocks on people's doors, selling something they don't particularly fancy. Sales doesn't have to be hard. Selling a product you gave birth to and are proud of can be, in fact, a very enjoyable experience. It is essential to *learn to love* that process. When I started my first business I was not the most gifted sales person. I was priding myself in marketing and business development but less so in sales. This experience made me realize that there is a *conflict* between the ability to develop a product and the ability to *sell* that product. What I have found problematic as a strategy is that when people start a business they tend to spend most of their time working on the product. Even though it is a perfectly legitimate and noble thing to try to build the best possible product before throwing it to the market, this often happens to the detriment of actually getting the thing out there. Also, what is generally a noble motive—wanting to offer the best possible product—is often avoidance activity. At some point you need to get out there. When this finally happens, instead of transforming themselves into sales beasts, especially when they first launch it, many entrepreneurs sit back and relax. You would think why would they sit back and relax? Well, because they actually believe that having worked so hard to develop that product, sales will magically happen. They are convinced that the product's qualities are so obvious that it will become an instant best seller, with them having to make minimum efforts marketing and selling it.

My advice is this. Sell the product *first*. Yes. I am going to repeat this. *Sell the product first*. Sell the product before actually producing or marketing it. This is the best business advice I can offer to a startup. Like learning any new set of skills, developing and perfecting your sales skills requires a fair amount of practice and persistence. Before investing insane amounts of money to produce, market and advertise that phenomenal product, sell it first. As a new business, you have to prioritize product quality and brand identity. As a startup though, you cannot afford to do things the way big companies do. You simply cannot afford to come up with a great idea, design a product, develop it, then expect people to come and buy it. Don't forget that customers are risk-averse and always want to be able to trust the company making the products they buy, which is why you can build a great product and never make a single sale if customers don't trust your brand. If you wish to start your own business, become a professional coach, nutritionist, accountant, yoga instructor, mechanical engineer, high-tech innovator, or whatever it is you wish you do for a living, call somebody up and try to sell them something. That something doesn't even have to exist. Try to sell them a time machine! It is all about testing the sales potential of your product. In fact, if the nature of the business does not require you to invest heavily, I suggest that you should not risk any funds. You can minimize the risk and still reap great benefits out of an investment. If the business does not require you having to buy warehouse space and invest in physical property, sell your product first, then deliver it. It is precisely the moment somebody is ready to write a check to buy your product that you know you can throw money into this idea. So, here's my advice: don't invest any money in the business, other than the money you make out of that business.

If your business is about selling a service, "sell first" is the strategy to follow as minimal investment is normally required. It was exactly what I had in mind when I started my first business, a boutique consultancy offering services to wealthy Chinese students pursuing their academic studies at top institutions in the United States and Europe. Right from the beginning, I set myself the goal to finance the business *only* using funds coming from my first customers and projects. This worked. After successfully completing my first two projects I started throwing money into the business, using nothing but the funds coming from my first customers. I started by setting up a legal entity and invested in a good website, word-to-mouth marketing and brand building.

I still can't remember how many times I met admirably skillful, passion-driven people who were planning to set up a business. After listening to them carefully and being introduced to the specific qualities of the great service or product they would soon be throwing to the market I would ask them what their sales strategy was. Guess what. They didn't have any. They were all planning to *first* set up a legal business entity, rent office space, invest in a great website, print fancy business cards hire staff, and do all those things that costed them tons of money, without having attempted a single sale! Even worse, the funds used in start-ups often come from bank loans or money that has been borrowed from friends and family. People lose their life savings, go out of business, and ruin their lives every day making this mistake. Risk is an essential component of the business game. Something that you must embrace and enjoy as an entrepreneur. It is unnecessary risk that is harmful to your business, bank account and health.

Business Is Magic at Work

I have mainly experienced the world of business through being an entrepreneur in the incredibly dynamic and multicultural place that is South East Asia in this beginning of the 21st century. A very dynamic market, full of contradictions, challenges and tremendous business opportunities. China is a country I fell in love with very early on. It became a real love affair when I started learning the language and getting familiar with Asian culture, philosophy and local business practices. In prehistoric times it made sense to be a good hunter-gatherer. In Antiquity being a renowned military leader was a prestigious thing. In the Middle Ages knights were well-regarded. In the Age of Discovery it was cool to be an explorer in search of wealth and adventure. In the Italian Renaissance artists and polymaths like Da Vinci were in great demand. During the Industrial Revolution it was cool to be an inventor, while in the past century with the dawn of the Information Age it was pretty rewarding to be a technology innovator. By the same token, the 21st century is the century of the Enterprise. It is the right time to be in history for creative, value-adding risk takers. It is an age of synthesis that we are approaching. It is now time to incorporate and put into smart use the knowledge that has been built up throughout centuries of human strife and creativity. We are equipped with tools and technology our ancestors could never have imagined. There is a lot of expectation on our shoulders. And rightly so! We are about to move away from standard employment. We are about to transition to a project-based economy where people are encouraged to live on the go. I've always regarded entrepreneurship as adults' way to perpetuate teenage rebellion. Entrepreneurship is a revolutionary act in many ways. It's the power to dare. The power to risk. The power to venture into uncharted territory. The courage to break the rules, face complete uncertainty while enjoying the whole process. Entrepreneurship is the unshakeable belief that you can prove authorities, critics, skeptics–sometimes even the entire world!–wrong. Perhaps, it is also the ability to know when to close your ears to people whose advice leads you to safe harbors and open them back when there is something really useful to hear, something that will trigger you to further your entrepreneurial journey. Entrepreneurship is not a job. It is a way of life. To some people it is almost a religion.

Entrepreneurship is, in fact, more than the courage to deal with uncertainty and risk; it is the ability to thrive in these conditions. As I've already mentioned in the Leadership section, people are pattern-based. They naturally form habits, routines, and behavior patterns that they have a hard time to break later. In the United States, entrepreneurship is a well-established cultural habit. In fact, it is regarded as the very essence of the American national identity, that goes hand in hand with the optimistic and adventurous spirit of the American psyche. In many cultures, however, the idea of rejecting security to embrace a lifestyle of adventure and risk is still quite uncommon. Following an independent path and standing out from the crowd can result in complete exclusion by the crowd, that is, the social group. I regard entrepreneurship as the very essence of business, a major driver of the world economy, and a great game where the sky is the only limit.

A game for grown-ups who never lost their inner child and whose playfulness and naughty creativity cannot be buried under the skin of an adult. Having experienced work in large companies for a certain period made me realize that taking a different route would be in my best interest. I remember walking through one of Shanghai's largest business districts early in the morning, seeing hordes of people, much like an army of ants, walking their way to another office day and being prepared for an infinite number of such days to come. The sight of them made me panic and realize that this was the *exact* opposite of what I wanted to do in my life. It was back in my early days in China and at this point I was going through a very challenging period, facing lots of dilemmas and having to make firm life and career decisions. I cannot think of a life more miserable than spending endless days in a cubicle in exchange of safety and a monthly salary enough to cover your bills and afford annual summer holidays.

I preserve as vividly as I can in my memory the image of this crowd of people on their way to the cubicle and bring it to my mind every time I feel a bit tired or unmotivated. Being an entrepreneur is tough, but not quite so, especially if you think what the alternative is. Nobody has a monopoly on great ideas. Great ideas are countless. The same goes for great opportunities. They go hand in hand with great ideas and a bit of courage to follow uncharted routes. I believe that imagination and creativity are the natural condition, the default state of every healthy and alert mind. Ideas flow effortlessly every day in the minds of people brave enough to expose themselves to new challenges. It is through social interaction and exchange with other people that you will be able to receive those necessary stimuli that allow inspiration and creativity to take place. It is the way people drive their mind that makes all the difference. Do you let ideas fly away? Do you note them down and dedicate daily time to think them through and test their actual potential? Don't let these initial thoughts fly away. They are your bread and butter. Feed and grow them properly.

Business is magic. It's a tricky world. It requires the skills of a prestidigitator and the realism of a banker. It is the art of making people see things the way you see them. By extension, it is the art of making people buy your vision, products and services. It is also the art of creating impact, the ability to define trends and guide people's beliefs and lifestyle habits. In short, business is the art of expansion. The skill of leading people to advertise your ideas, brand, and products—for free. In this respect, business is about generating networks of supporters. I am not referring solely to social media followers but groups of people whose mind and heart have been profoundly affected by your message.

Pareto's Principle Applied in Life, Leadership and Business

It was back in 1906 when Vilfredo Pareto, an Italian economist came up with a mathematical formula to describe the unequal distribution of wealth in early 20th century Italy. He observed that 80 percent of the country's wealth was owned by around 20 percent of its people. This is nowadays known as the 80/20 formula or Pareto's Principle. In fact, it was in the late 1940s that Dr Joseph M. Juran, a quality management pioneer, attributed the 80/20 principle to Pareto, thus calling it "Pareto's Principle" and defining it as the rule of *the vital few and the trivial many*. Basically, Pareto's Principle is the observation that there is generally an uneven distribution in all things in life. The 80/20 formula describes the unbalanced distribution of benefit/loss and success/failure. To better illustrate this principle, here are a few areas of application:

- 20 percent of the input creates 80 percent of the result
- 20 percent of the customers create 80 percent of the company's profit
- 20 percent of the employees produce 80 percent of the work
- 80 percent of wealth is owned by 20 percent of the people
- 80 percent of sales come from 20 percent of a company's products
- 80 percent of value is achieved with 20 percent of effort

Studies in neuroscience are here to confirm Pareto's Principle. An intelligent brain is not a brain that works more. On the contrary, an intelligent brain is a brain that works less. This is called *neural efficiency*, a scientific term used to describe brain function as a way to measure intelligence. In short, being intelligent is not about complex thinking patterns, rather, it is about *solving a problem with minimal effort*. The neural efficiency theory argues that brighter individuals show lower brain activation than less bright individuals when working on cognitive tasks. When one thinks of a process as complex as human intelligence is, they must imagine that the brain is like an orchestra that is composed of different sections. The challenge is to discover how these sections interact, because as far as we know, there is no conductor! If the brain is an orchestra, then intelligence is music.

The neural efficiency hypothesis is in line with the 80/20 principle. Efficient people are well aware how uncannily accurate this principle is. Pareto's Principle is all about *creating more with less*. It is about creating the most value using the least resources. It is one of the greatest strategies used by the world's most effective people and organizations. In other terms, more effort does not equal more results, more work does not equal more rewards. What this formula is telling is this: Focus only on what is crucial. Ignore the rest. It is about working smarter, selectively, and more efficiently to save yourself time, effort and resources. Taking Pareto's Principle into the 21st century is the key to stand out of the crowd by creating a maximum of value using a minimum of resources. This principle alone, can offer uncontested advantages in the saturated, overworked era we live in.

What is exciting about this formula is that it is applicable in all areas of Life, Business and Leadership. It is a universal law that Pareto uncovered. The 80/20 formula is nothing but two parts of the same whole. It can either work 80/20 or 20/80. It's up to you. You can choose to be on the right side and make the most of your tangible and intangible assets, be it financial resources, time, effort, learning capacity, or skills development. The 80/20 formula is a key strategy to developing your business, leadership, and life skills by focusing on real income-generating tasks or whatever it is that brings real value to your life.

In sum:

1. Identify and invest most energy and resources in the critical few: the 20 percent of tasks, projects, and efforts producing 80 percent of the results.
2. If you are a company—especially if you are a small business or a start-up—focus on those products, services, and customers that bring you the most profit while minimizing or even eliminating the rest.
3. Make sure that a minority of carefully selected inputs leads to a majority of outputs.
4. Focus on those key activities that produce the majority of life satisfaction.
5. A minority of smart decisions will produce the majority of results in your projects, investments, and relationships.

Business Quotes

In the business world, everyone is paid in two coins: cash and experience. Take the experience first; the cash will come later.

—Harold Geneen

Business is the art of extracting money from another man's pocket without resorting to violence.

—Max Amsterdam

The secret of business is to know something nobody else knows.

—Aristotle Onassis

Business is a combination of war and sport.

—André Maurois

Time is the friend of the wonderful business, the enemy of the mediocre.

—Warren Buffett

Corporation: An ingenious device for obtaining profit without individual responsibility.

—Ambrose Bierce

Intellectual property has the shelf life of a banana.

—Bill Gates

I have found no greater satisfaction than achieving success through honest dealing and strict adherence to the view that, for you to gain, those you deal with should gain as well.

—Alan Greenspan

To succeed in business it is make others see things as you see them.

—Aristotle Onassis

I understand small business growth. I was one.

—George W. Bush

Successful enterprises are usually led by a proven chief executive who is a competent benevolent dictator.

—Richard Pratt

The salary of the chief executive of a large corporation is not a market reward for achievement. It is frequently in the nature of a warm personal gesture by the individual to himself.

—J.K. Galbraith

I don't pay good wages because I have a lot of money; I have a lot of money because I pay good wages.

—Robert Bosch

Professionalism is a frame of mind, not a paycheck.

—Cecil Castle

Our major obligation is not to mistake slogans for solutions.

—Edward R. Murrow

Theories are private property, but truth is common stock.

—Charles Caleb Colton

Let's be honest. There's not a business anywhere that is without problems. Business is complicated and imperfect. Every business everywhere is staffed with imperfect human beings and exists by providing a product or service to other imperfect human beings.

—Bob Parsons

The earth is the general and equal possession of all humanity and therefore cannot be the property of individuals.

—Leo Tolstoy

Justice is the insurance which we have on our lives and property.
Obedience is the premium which we pay for it.

—William Penn

Action

You are only as beautiful as your last action.

—Stephen Richards

Never mistake motion for action.

—Ernest Hemingway

You are what you do when it counts.

—John Steakly

Talk doesn't cook rice.

—Chinese Proverb

A real decision is measured by the fact that you've taken a new action.
If there's no action, you haven't truly decided.

—Tony Robbins

Either do something worth reading or do something worth writing.
—Benjamin Franklin

Understate and over deliver.

—Toby Bloomberg

Happiness is a state of activity.

—Aristotle

The smallest deed is better than the greatest intention.

—John Burroughs

The shortest answer is doing.

—Lord Herbert

The first step binds one to the second.

—French Proverb

Anyone can promise the stars. Only you can reach them.

—Dodinsky

Without consistent action, purpose and strategy are words of hope.

—Michael Kouly

Get involved. You don't want to look back on your life and realize that you successfully managed to stay out of it.

—Robert Brault

An idea not coupled with action will never get any bigger than the brain cell it occupied.

—Arnold H. Glasgow

Strong reason make strong actions.

—William Shakespeare

All know the way; few actually walk it.

—Bodhidharma

Some people want it to happen, some wish it could happen, others make it happen.

—Michael Jordan

The six W's: Work will win when wishing won't.

—Todd Blackledge

People may doubt what you say, but they will believe what you do.

—Lewis Cass

A vision without action is an hallucination.

—Japanese Proverb

Well done is better than well said.

—Benjamin Franklin

A promise is a cloud; fulfillment is rain.

—Arabian Proverb

The world is not dangerous because of those who do harm but because of those who look at it without doing anything.

—Albert Einstein

Think like a man of action. Act like a man of thought.

—Henri Bergson

Doing things is not the same as getting things done.

—Jared Silver

Do not be wise in words—be wise in deeds.

—Jewish Proverb

I do not believe in a fate that falls on men however they act; but I do believe in a fate that falls on man unless they act.

—G.K. Chesterton

My personal philosophy is not to undertake a project unless it is manifestly important and nearly impossible.

—Edwin Land, Inventor of the Polaroid camera in 1947.

We should be taught not to wait for inspiration to start a thing. Action always generates inspiration. Inspiration seldom generates action.

—Frank Tibolt

I have always thought the actions of men the best interpreters of their thoughts.

—John Locke

Nothing diminishes anxiety faster than action.
—Walter Anderson, The Confidence Course, 1997

Action is the antidote to despair.
—Joan Baez

The secret of getting ahead is getting started.
—Mark Twain

The vision must be followed by the venture. It is not enough to stare up the steps—we must step up the stairs.
—Vance Havner

What we think or what we know or what we believe is, in the end, of little consequence. The only consequence is what we do.
—John Ruskin

Trust only movement. Life happens at the level of events, not of words.
—Alfred Adler

Action is eloquence.
—William Shakespeare

Success will never be a big step in the future, success is a small step taken just now.
—Jonatan Mårtensson

Remember, people will judge you by your actions, not your intentions. You may have a heart of gold—but so does a hard-boiled egg.
—Author Unknown

Note to self: finding a cool quote and writing it in your journal is not a substitute for Getting. It. Done.
—Betsy Cañas Garmon

Do it, and then you will feel motivated to do it.
—Zig Ziglar

As I grow older I pay less attention to what men say. I just watch what they do.

—Andrew Carnegie

There are so many things that we wish we had done yesterday, so few that we feel like doing today.

—Mignon McLaughlin

Contemplation often makes life miserable. We should act more, think less, and stop watching ourselves live.

—Nicolas de Chamfort

The best way out of a problem is through it.

—Author Unknown

Action is the last resource of those who know not how to dream.

—Oscar Wilde

If we did all the things we are capable of doing, we would literally astonish ourselves.

—Thomas Edison

To get something done, a committee should consist of no more than three people, two of whom are absent.

—Robert Copeland

The first idea that the child must acquire, in order to be actively disciplined, is that of the difference between good and evil; and the task of the educator lies in seeing that the child does not confound good with immobility and evil with activity.

—Maria Montessori

What you allow, you encourage.

—Michael Josephson

We will have to repent in this generation not merely for the vitriolic words and actions of the bad people, but for the appalling silence of the good people.

—Martin Luther King, Jr.

God and the devil lose to a common enemy: inertia.

—Mignon McLaughlin, The Neurotic's Notebook, 1960

Career

People never realize how much work impacts their self-esteem and sense of purpose until they leave a job.

—Rob Payne

There are thousands and thousands of people out there leading lives of quiet, screaming desperation, where they work long, hard hours at jobs they hate to enable them to buy things they don't need to impress people they don't like.

—Nigel Marsh

If I had only known, I would have been a locksmith.

—Albert Einstein

Don't just let your business or your job make something for you; let it make something of you.

—Jim Rohn

Passion is the difference between having a job and having a career.

—Anonymous Author

Not 16 percent of the human race is, or ever has been, engaged in any kinds of activity at which they excel.

—Philip Mairet

If you want to achieve greatness, stop asking for permission.
I think the person who takes a job to in order to live – that is to say for
the money – has turned himself into a slave.

—Joseph Campbell

If you want to be successful in this world you need to follow your
passion, not a paycheck.
Be so good they can't ignore you.

—Steve Martin

Doing what you like is freedom, liking what you do is happiness.
The best days of those who enjoy what they do are better than the best
days of those who don't.

—Jim Rohn

I don't know anything about music. In my line you don't have to.

—Elvis Presley

My father taught me to always
The society which scorns excellence in plumbing as a humble activity
and tolerates shoddiness in philosophy because it is an exalted activity
will have neither good plumbing nor good philosophy…neither its
pipes nor its theories will hold water.

—John W. Gardner

When I was four I told my mother I wanted to be a rock star when
I grow up. She said: 'You can't do both'.

—Steven Tyler

It's no good running a pig farm for thirty years while saying: 'really
I was meant to be a ballet dancer'. By that time pigs will be your style.

—Quentin Crisp

If in one hundred years I am only known as the man who invented
Sherlock Holmes, then I will have considered my life a failure.

—Sir Arthur Conan Doyle

My choice early in life was either to be a piano player in a whorehouse or a politician. And to tell the truth, there's hardly any difference.

—Harry S. Truman

My mother has always been unhappy with what I do – she would rather I do something nice, like be a bricklayer.

—Mick Jagger

In order that people may be happy in their work, these three things are needed: They must be fit for it. They must not do too much of it. And they must have a sense of success in it.

—John Ruskin

We all live under the same sky but we do not all have the same horizon.

—Konrad Adenauer

The feeling of having taken a wrong turning in life was made worse by the fact that he could not, for the life of him, remember having taken any turnings at all.

—Charles Fernyhough

When a man is determined what can stop him? Cripple him and you have Sir Walter Scott. Put him in a prison cell and you have a John Bunyan. Bury him in the snows of Valley Forge and you have a George Washington. Have him born in abject poverty and you have a Lincoln. Put him in the grease pit of a locomotive round-house and you have a Walter P. Chrysler. Make him second fiddle in an obscure South African orchestra and you have a Toscanini. The hardships of life are sent not to be an unkind destiny to crush but to challenge.

—Sam E. Roberts

If you make a sale you can make a living. If you make an investment of time and good service in a customer, you can make a fortune.

—Jim Rohn

My father taught me to always do more than you get paid for as an investment in your future.

—Jim Rohn

It is never too late to be who you might have been.

—George Eliot

Make sure that the ladder you are climbing is not leaning against the wrong wall.

—Author Unknown

Taking jobs to build up your resume is the same thing as saving sex for old age.

—Warren Buffett

Competition

Your margin is my opportunity.

—Jeff Bezos

The healthiest competition occurs when average people win by putting above average effort.

—Colin Powell

You are not competition. You're just in my way.
I have been up against tough competition all my life. I wouldn't know how to get along without it.

—Walt Disney

Being underestimated is one of the biggest competitive advantages you can have. Embrace it.

—Author Unknown

Number one; cash is king…number two; communicate…number three; buy or bury the competition.

—Jack Welch

When you compete with yourself you become better. When you compete with others you become bitter.

—Author Unknown

The world is full of people who are grabbing and self-seeking. So, the rare individual who unselfishly tries to serve others has an enormous advantage. He has little competition.

—Dale Carnegie

Don't compare yourself with anyone in the world…If you do so, you are insulting yourself.

—Bill Gates

The best way to help the poor is not to become one of them.

—Lang Hancock

Everybody loves you until you become competition.

—Author Unknown

A flower does not think about competing to the flower next to it. It just blooms.

—Author Unknown

The essence of competitiveness is liberated when we make people believe that what they think and do is important – and then get out of their way while they do it.

—Jack Welch

They wanna see you do good but never better than them. Remember that.

—Author Unknown

Do your work with your whole heart, and you will succeed – there's so little competition.

—Elbert Hubbard

Competition brings out the best in products and the worst in people.

—Faqimi Fauzi

Competition is a by-product of productive work, not its goal. A creative man is motivated by the desire to achieve, not by the desire to beat others.

—Ayn Rand

Creativity

Creativity is the defeat of habit by originality.

—Arthur Koestler

You are lost the instant you know what the result will be.

—Juan Gris

Truth and reality in art do not arise until you no longer understand what you are doing.

—Henri Matisse

Some men see things as they are and ask why. Others dream things that never were and ask why not.

—George Bernard Shaw

Make it a practice to keep on the lookout for novel and interesting ideas that others have used successfully. Your idea has to be original only in its adaptation to the problem you are working on.

—Thomas Edison

Creative spirits always anticipate the course of events. They do not wait for the dawn of a new era. They resolutely begin the new era at the moment when they see that the old era is ended.

—Samuel McChord Crothers, "On the Evening of the New Day," The Atlantic Monthly, January 1919

In a world of innovation and creativity, words like crazy, weird and eccentric are compliments.

—Michael Kouly

What is originality? To see something that has no name as yet and hence cannot be mentioned although it stares us all in the face. The way men usually are, it takes a name to make things visible for them. Those with originality have for the most part also assign3ed names.

—Friedrich Nietzsche

Debt

Today, there are three kinds of people: the have's, the have-not's, and the have-not-paid-for-what-they-have's.

—Earl Wilson

Debt is the worst poverty.

—Thomas Fuller, Gnomologia, 1732

A man in debt is a man in chains.

—James Lendall Basford (1845–1915), c.1882

When a man is in love or in debt, someone else has the advantage.

—Bill Balance

Promises make debts, and debts make promises.

—Dutch Proverb

Credit buying is much like being drunk. The buzz happens immediately and gives you a lift.... The hangover comes the day after.

—Joyce Brothers

The only man who sticks closer to you in adversity than a friend is a creditor.

—Author Unknown

Before borrowing money from a friend, decide which you need most.

—American Proverb

Never spend your money before you have it.

—Thomas Jefferson

There are plenty of ways to get ahead. The first is so basic I'm almost embarrassed to say it: spend less than you earn.

—Paul Clitheroe

Enterprise

Entrepreneurship is living a few years of your life like most people won't, so that you can spend the rest of your life doing what most people can't.

—Author Unknown

Build your own dreams, or somebody else will hire you to build theirs.

—Farrah Gray

Be nice to geeks. You'll probably end up working for one.

—Bill Gates

Entrepreneurship is not a part-time job. It's not even a full-time job. It's a lifestyle.

—Carrie Layne

No enterprise is more likely to succeed than the one that is concealed from the enemy until it is ripe for execution.

—Niccolo Machiavelli

Entrepreneurs are simply those who understand that there is little difference between obstacle and opportunity and are able to turn both to their advantage.

—Niccolo Machiavelli

Everyone can tell you the risk. Only an entrepreneur can see the reward.

—Robert Kiyosaki

Excuses

No one ever excused his way to success.

—Dave Del Dotto

One of the most important tasks of a manager is to eliminate his people's excuses for failure.

—Robert Townsend

Justifying a fault doubles it.

—French Proverb

Don't do what you'll have to find an excuse for.

—Proverb

The only man who is really free is the one who can turn down an invitation to dinner without giving an excuse.

—Jules Renard

Excuses are the tools with which persons with no purpose in view build for themselves great monuments of nothing.

—Steven Grayhm

Pessimism is an excuse for not trying and a guarantee to a personal failure.

—Bill Clinton

If you don't want to do something, one excuse is as good as another.

—Yiddish Proverb

He that is good for making excuses is seldom good for anything else.

—Benjamin Franklin

Success is a tale of obstacles overcome, and for every obstacle overcome, an excuse not used.

—Robert Brault

Bad excuses are worse than none.

—Thomas Fuller

Difficulty is the excuse history never accepts.

—Edward R. Murrow

Bad men excuse their faults; good men abandon them.

—Author Unknown

He who excuses himself accuses himself.

—Gabriel Meurier

Sometimes I wish I had a terrible childhood, so that at least I'd have an excuse.

—Jimmy Fallon

We have forty million reasons for failure, but not a single excuse.

—Rudyard Kipling

Never ruin an apology with an excuse.

—Kimberly Johnson

Experience

Experience is not what happens to a man. It is what a man does with what happens to him.

—Aldous Leonard Huxley, Texts and Pretexts, 1932

Learn all you can from the mistakes of others. You won't have the time to make4 them all yourself.

—Alfred Sheinwold

Idealism is what precedes experience; cynicism is what follows.
—David T. Wolf

Experience is that marvelous thing that enables you to recognize a mistake when you make it again.
—Franklin P. Jones

Experience is the name everyone gives to his mistakes.
—Oscar Wilde, Lady Windemere's Fan, 1896

Fool me once, shame on you; fool me twice, shame on me.
—Chinese Proverb

Experience is the worst teacher. It always gives the test first and the instruction afterward.
—Benjamin Franklin

Experience is what you got by not having it when you need it.
—Author Unknown

There are many truths of which the full meaning cannot be realized until personal experience has brought it home.
—John Stuart Mill

Life can only be understood backward, but it must be lived forward.
—Søren Kierkegaard

No physician is really good before he has killed one or two patients.
—Hindu Proverb

God will not look you over for medals, degrees or diplomas, but for scars.
—Elbert Hubbard

A man begins cutting his wisdom teeth the first time he bites off more than he can chew.
—Herb Caen

If experience was so important, we'd never have had anyone walk on the moon.

—Doug Rader

Do you know the difference between education and experience? Education is when you read the fine print; experience is what you get when you don't.

—Pete Seeger

Experience is what causes a person to make new mistakes instead of old ones.

—Author Unknown

The experience I gained at age 21 would be useful if I were ever 21 again. But I'm 71 and new at it and keep making age 71 mistakes.

—Robert Brault

We have two lives—the one we learn with and the life we live after that.

—Bernard Malamud, The Natural

Information's pretty thin stuff unless mixed with experience.

—Clarence Day, The Crow's Nest

You must learn to make the whole world your school.

—Martin H. Fischer

If we could sell our experiences for what they cost us, we'd all be millionaires.

—Abigail Van Buren

Failure

Failure is an event, never a person.

—William D. Brown, Welcome Stress!

I don't know the key to success, but the key to failure is trying to please everybody.

—Bill Cosby

Never confuse a single defeat with a final defeat.

—F. Scott Fitzgerald

Nothing encourages creativity like the chance to fall flat on one's face.

—James D. Finley

There is no failure except in no longer trying.

—Elbert Hubbard

I don't believe in failure. It's not failure if you enjoyed the process.

—Oprah Winfrey

There are defeats more triumphant than victories.

—Michel de Montaigne

Failure is only the opportunity to begin again more intelligently.

—Henry Ford

Failure sometimes enlarges the spirit. You have to fall back upon humanity and God.

—Charles Horton Cooley

Failure is the condiment that gives success its flavor.

—Truman Capote

You always pass failure on your way to success.

—Mickey Rooney

There is no failure. Only feedback.

—Robert Allen

The men who try to do something and fail are infinitely better than those who try to do nothing and succeed.

—Lloyd Jones

Try again. Fail again. Fail better.

—Samuel Beckett

Dealing with failure is easy: Work hard to improve. Success is also easy to handle: you've solved the wrong problem. Work hard to improve.

—Alan J. Perlis

Adversity and failure are woven into the fabric of existence; without them, there can be neither test of mettle nor triumph of success.

—Dr. Idel Dreimer

People are not afraid of failure. It is the embarrassment of not succeeding that scares them most.

—Michael Kouly

You can fail at something you don't want, so might as well take a chance doing what you love.

—Jim Carrey

In victory, you deserve champagne, in defeat, you need it.

—Napoleon Bonaparte

My great concern is not whether you have failed, but whether you are content with your failure.

—Abraham Lincoln

Your most unhappy customers are your greatest source of learning.

—Bill Gates

Try as hard as we may for perfection, the net result of our labors is an amazing variety of imperfectness. We are surprised at our own versatility in being able to fail in so many different ways.

—Samuel McChord Crothers

Goals

The goal is the same: life itself, and the price is the same; life itself.

—James Agee

Goals are dreams with deadlines.

—Diana Scharf Hunt

A goal without a plan is just a wish.

—Antoine de Saint-Exupéry

Pick your impossibilities and accomplish them.
Don't be fooled by the calendar. There are only as many days in the year as you make use of.

—Charles Richards

What you get by achieving your goals is not as important as what you become by achieving your goals.

—Zig Ziglar

If you're bored with life, if you don't get up every morning with a burning desire to do things you don't have enough goals.

—Lou Holtz

Vision without action is a daydream. Action without vision is a nightmare.

—Japanese Proverb

One half of knowing what you want is knowing what you must give up before you get it.

—Sidney Howard

If your dreams are not scaring you, you are not dreaming big enough.

—Author Unknown

You must have long-range goals to keep you from being frustrated by short-range failures.

—Charles C. Noble

I am looking for a lot of men who have an infinite capacity to not know what can't be done.

—Henry Ford

The world is moving so fast these days that the man who says it can't be done is generally interrupted by someone doing it.

—Elbert Hubbard

Many are stubborn in pursuit of the path they have chosen, few in pursuit of the goal.

—Friedrich Wilhelm Nietzsche

If you focus on results, you will never change. If you focus on change, you will get results.

—Jack Dixon

Motivation is when your dreams put on work clothes.

—Author Unknown

We are kept from our goal not by obstacles but by a clear path to a lesser goal.

—Robert Brault

Visualize your long-term goals to paint your short-term action on the canvas of now.

—Terri Guillemets

A straight path never leads anywhere except to the objective.

—Andre Gide

Nothing interferes with my concentration. You could put on an orgy in my office and I wouldn't look up. Well, maybe once.

—Isaac Asimov

There is one quality more important than "know-how" and we cannot accuse the United States of any undue amount of it. This is "know-what" by which we determine not only how to accomplish our purposes, but what our purposes are to be.

—Norbert Wiener, The Human Use of Human Beings, 1954

Most people would succeed in small things if they were not troubled with great ambitions.

—Henry Wadsworth Longfellow, Drift-Wood

Know your limits, but never stop trying to exceed them.

—Author Unknown

As long as I have a want, I have a reason for living. Satisfaction is death.

—George Bernard Shaw

If you would hit the mark, you must aim a little above it; every arrow that flies feels the attraction of earth.

—Henry Wadsworth Longfellow

Arriving at one goal is the starting point to another.

—John Dewey

This is a story about four people named Everybody, Somebody, Anybody, and Nobody. There was an important job to be done and Everybody was sure that Somebody would do it. Anybody could have done it, but Nobody did it. Somebody got angry about that, because it was Everybody's job. Everybody thought Anybody could do it, but Nobody realized that Everybody wouldn't do it. It ended up that Everybody blamed Somebody when Nobody did what Anyone could have.

—Author Unknown

One may miss the mark by aiming too high as too low.

—Thomas Fuller

When people say to me: "How do you do so many things?" I often answer them, without meaning to be cruel: "How do you do so little?" It seems to me that people have vast potential. Most people can do extraordinary things if they have the confidence or take the risks. Yet most people don't. They sit in front of the telly and treat life as if it goes on forever.

—Philip Adams

Habits

We are what we repeatedly do. Excellence, then, is not an act, but a habit.

—Aristotle

The chains of habit are generally too small to be felt until they are too strong to be broken.

—Samuel Johnson

You will never change your life until you change something you do daily.

—John C. Maxwell

Motivation is what gets you started. Habit is what keeps you going.

—Jim Ryun

I think in terms of the day's resolutions, not the years'.

—Henry Moore

Men's natures are alike; it is their habits that separate them.

—Confucius, Analects

The fixity of a habit is generally in direct proportion to its absurdity.

—Marcel Proust

Habit is a second nature which prevents us from knowing the first, of which it has neither the cruelties nor the enchantments.
—Marcel Proust

We are sinners by nature, but much more so by practice.
—James Lendall Basford (1845–1915), "Human Life,"
Sparks from the Philosopher's Stone, 1882

To fall into a habit is to begin to cease to be.
—Miguel de Unamuno, The Tragic Sense of Life

Habits are safer than rules; you don't have to watch them. And you don't have to keep them, either. They keep you.
—Frank Crane

To change one's habits has a smell of death about it.
—Portuguese Proverb

Bad habits are easier to abandon today than tomorrow.
—Yiddish Proverb

Rigid, the skeleton of habit alone upholds the human frame.
—Virginia Woolf

Nothing is more desirable than to be released from an affliction, but nothing is more frightening than to be divested of a crutch.
—James Baldwin

The best way to break a bad habit is to drop it.
—Leo Aikman

Habit is overcome by habit.
—Thomas Kempis

The second half of a man's life is made up of nothing but the habits he has acquired during the first half.
—Feodor Dostoevski

A bad habit never disappears miraculously. It's an undo-it-yourself project.

—Abigail Van Buren (1918–2013)

I forgot that every little action of the common day makes or unmakes character, and that therefore what one has done in the secret chamber one has some day to cry aloud on the house-tops.

—Oscar Wilde

The unfortunate thing about this world is that good habits are so much easier to give up than bad ones.

—Somerset Maugham

The easier it is to do, the harder it is to change.

—Eng's Principle

Habit, if not resisted, soon becomes necessity.

—St. Augustine

Every grown-up man consists wholly of habits, although he is often unaware of it and even denies having any habits at all.

—Georges Gurdjieff

No monarch is so well obeyed as that whose name is Habit.

—James Lendall Basford (1845–1915), Sparks from the Philosopher's Stone, 1882

Nothing so needs reforming as other people's habits.

—Mark Twain

In most cases, misfortune is an acquired habit.

—James Lendall Basford (1845–1915), Seven Seventy Seven Sensations, 1897

If you don't watch out, putting on your unhappiness in the morning can become as instinctive as putting on your clothes.

—Robert Brault

Habit is thus the enormous flywheel of society, its most precious conservative agent. It alone is what keeps us all within the bounds of ordinance, and saves the children of fortune from the envious uprisings of the poor.

—William James, The Principles of Psychology

The strength of a man's virtue should not be measured by his special exertions, but by his habitual acts.

—Blaise Pascal, Pensées, 1670

Investment

If you buy things you do not need, soon you will have to sell things you need.

—Warren Buffett

Do not save what is left after spending, but spend what is left after saving.

—Warren Buffett

Never depend on single income. Make investment to create a second source.

—Warren Buffett

The first rule of any technology used in a business is that automation applied to an efficient operation will magnify the efficiency. The second is that automation applied to an inefficient operation will magnify the inefficiency.

—Bill Gates

Don't judge each day by the harvest you reap but by the seeds you plant.

—Robert Louis Stevenson

It is unfortunate we can't buy many business executives for what they are worth and sell them for what they think they are worth.

—Malcolm Forbes

To add value to others, one must first value others.

—John C. Maxwell

Don't educate your children to be rich. Educate them to be happy, so they know the value of things not their price.

—Author Unknown

There are so many men who can figure costs, and so few who can measure values.

—Author Unknown

You can fool all the people all the time if the advertising is right and the budget is big enough.

—Joseph E. Levine

Labor

Dreams don't work, unless you do.
Every job is a self-portrait of the person who does it. Autograph your work with excellence.

—Ted Key

If you want an apple pie from scratch, you must first create the universe.

—Carl Sagan

Work as if you own the company and soon you just might.

—Mike Dolan

If things seem under your control, you are not going fast enough.

—Mario Andretti

What you have become is the price you paid to get what you used to want.

—Mignon McLaughlin, The Neurotic's Notebook, 1960

My grandfather once told me that there are two kinds of people: those who work and those who take the credit. He told me to try to be in the first group; there was less competition there.

—Indira Gandhi

Too much attention to others' business often directs their attention to yours.

—James Lendall Basford (1845–1915), Sparks from the Philosopher's Stone, 1882

The trick to getting things done is to list things to do in doable order.

—Robert Brault

The cure for anything is salt water – sweat, tears, or the sea.

—Isaac Dinesen

God sells us all things at the price of labor.

—Leonardo da Vinci

Labor was the first price, the original purchase-money that was paid for all things. It was not by gold or by silver, but by labor, that all wealth of the world was originally purchased.

—Adam Smith

Without labor nothing prospers.

—Sophocles

Genius begins great works; labor alone finishes them.

—Joseph Joubert

Work isn't to make money; you work to justify life.

—Marc Chagall

Chop your own wood, and it will warm you twice.

—Old New England Saying

What the country needs is dirtier fingernails and cleaner minds.

—Will Rogers

A mind always employed is always happy. This is the true secret, the grand recipe, for felicity.

—Thomas Jefferson

Man is so made that he can only find relaxation from one kind of labor by taking up another.

—Anatole France

We are closer to the ants than to the butterflies. Very few people can endure much leisure.

—Gerald Brenan

Employment is nature's physician, and is essential to human happiness.

—Galen

When everything is finished, the mornings are sad.

—Antonio Porchia

Hard work, worry and whiskey are the friends of man.

—Martin H. Fischer

Learning

Be a student not a follower. Don't just go do what someone says. Take interest in what someone says, then debate it, ponder it, and consider it from all angles.

—Jim Rohn

I am learning all the time. The tombstone will be my diploma.

—Eartha Kitt

Live as if you were to die tomorrow. Learn as if you were to live forever.

—Mahatma Gandhi

I am always ready to learn although I do not always like being taught.
—Winston Churchill

Try to learn something about everything and everything about something.
—T.H. Huxley

Education is the kindling of a flame, not the filling of a vessel.
—Socrates

We need to focus more on learning with technology, not learning technology.
—George Couros

Learning is its own exceeding great reward.
—William Hazlitt

Anyone who stops learning is old, whether at twenty or eighty.
—Henry Ford

There is in Euripides some kind of learning that is always at the boiling point.
—Anne Carson, Grief Lessons: Four Plays by Euripides, 2006

Learning is a treasure that will follow its owner everywhere.
—Chinese Proverb

It's a mistake, when life hands you a tough lesson, to think that you can get back at life by not learning it.
—Robert Brault

Every act of conscious learning requires the willingness to suffer an injury to one's self-esteem. That is why young children, before they are aware of their own self-importance, learn so easily.
—Thomas Szasz

When the student is ready, the master appears.

—Buddhist Proverb

If we value the pursuit of knowledge, we must be free to follow wherever that search may lead us. The free mind is not a barking dog, to be tethered on a ten-foot chain.

—Adlai E. Stevenson Jr.

Learning without thought is labor lost.

—Confucius

Educating the mind without educating the heart is no education at all.

—Aristotle

Learning is the only thing the mind never exhausts, never fears and never regrets.

—Leonardo Da Vinci

No matter how one may think himself accomplished, when he sets out to learn a new language, science, or the bicycle, he has entered a new realm as truly as if he were a child newly born into the world.

—Frances Willard, How I Learned to Ride the Bicycle

The only real progress lies in learning to be wrong all alone.

—Albert Camus

People learn something every day, and a lot of times it's that what they learned the day before was wrong.

—Bill Vaughan

Learning is like rowing upstream: not to advance is to drop back.

—Chinese Proverb

You don't understand anything until you learn it more than one way.

—Marvin Minsky

Learning is like rowing upstream: not to advance is to drop back.
—Chinese Proverb

I have never met a man so ignorant that I couldn't learn something from him.
—Galileo Galilei

What we want is to see the child in pursuit of knowledge, and not knowledge in pursuit of the child.
—George Bernard Shaw

It is important that students bring a certain ragamuffin, barefoot irreverence to their studies; they are not here to worship what is known, but to question it.
—Jacob Bronowski

Children have to be educated, but they have also to be left to educate themselves.
—Abbé Dimnet, Art of Thinking, 1928

It's what you learn after you know it all that counts.
—Attributed to Harry S Truman

You learn something every day if you pay attention.
—Ray LeBlond

There are some things you learn best in calm, and some in storm.
—Willa Cather

Always walk through life as if you have something new to learn and you will.
—Vernon Howard

Education is indoctrination if you're white—subjugation if you're black.
—James Baldwin

Beware of the man who works hard to learn something, learns it, and finds himself no wiser than before.
—Kurt Vonnegut, Jr.

The man who is too old to learn was probably always too old to learn.

—Henry S. Haskins

There is nothing more notable in Socrates than that he found time, when he was an old man, to learn music and dancing, and thought it time well spent.

—Michel de Montaigne

We learn more by looking for the answer to a question and not finding it than we do from learning the answer itself.

—Lloyd Alexander

That is what learning is. You suddenly understand something you've understood all your life, but in a new way.

—Doris Lessing

I am what the librarians have made me with a little assistance from a professor of Greek and a few poets.

—Bernard Keble Sandwell

Learning is a lifetime process, but there comes a time when we must stop adding and start updating.

—Robert Brault

The best of my education has come from the public library... my tuition fee is a bus fare and once in a while, five cents a day for an overdue book. You don't need to know very much to start with, if you know the way to the public library.

—Lesley Conger

I will swear by a thing today, but I will have the courage to denounce it tomorrow, if needs be. The vows of ignorance are not binding upon enlightenment.

—Muriel Strode-Lieberman (1875–1964),
My Little Book of Life, 1912

Luck

The lucky person passes for a genius.

—Euripides

Ability is of little account without opportunity.

—Napoleon Bonaparte

Those who have succeeded at anything and don't mention luck are kidding themselves.

—Larry King

Name the greatest of all inventors. Accident.

—Mark Twain

It is the mark of an inexperienced man not to believe in luck.

—Joseph Conrad

Better an ounce of luck than a pound of gold.

—Yiddish Proverb

Luck is infatuated with the efficient.

—Persian Proverb

The only thing that overcomes hard luck is hard work.

—Harry Golden

There is a very easy way to return from a casino with a small fortune: go there with a large one.

—Jack Yelton

Luck is what you have left over after you give 100 percent.

—Langston Coleman

Whatever great advantages nature may give, it is not she alone, but fortune also that makes the hero.

—Francois de la Rochefoucauld

Luck never gives; it only lends.

—Swedish Proverb

Depend on the rabbit's foot if you will, but remember it didn't work for the rabbit.

—R.E. Shay

He that waits upon fortune is never sure of a dinner.

—Benjamin Franklin

It's hard to detect good luck – it looks so much like something you've earned.

—Frank A. Clark

The day you decide to do it is your lucky day.

—Japanese Proverb

Luck is when opportunity knocks and you answer.

—Author Unknown

Fortune brings in some boats that are not steered.

—William Shakespeare

Luck is being in the right place at the right time, but location and timing are top some extent under our control.

—Natasha Josefowitz

We must believe in luck. How else can we explain the success of those we don't like?

—Jean Cocteau

The only good luck many great men had was being born with the ability and determination to overcome bad luck.

—Channing Pollock

It is a great piece of skill to know how to guide your luck even while waiting for it.

—Baltasar Gracian

Good luck has its storms.

—George Lucas

Remember that sometimes not getting what you want is a wonderful stroke of luck.

—Dalai Lama

Luck visits a fool, but it never sits down with him.

—German Proverb

Some folk want their luck buttered.

—Thomas Hardy

Luck seeks those who flee and flees those who seek it.

—German Proverb

May your pockets be heavy and your heart be light. May good luck pursue you each morning and night.

—Irish Blessing

I've done the calculation and your chances of winning the lottery are identical whether you play or not.

—Fran Lebowitz

What we call luck is inner man internalized. We make things happen to us.

—Robertson Davies

Luck was a joke. Even good luck was bad luck with its hair combed.

—Stephen King

I am so unlucky that if I was to fall into a barrel of nipples I'd come out sucking my thumb.

—Freddie Star

Every dog has his day in luck.

—Japanese Proverb

Go and wake up your luck.

—Persian Saying

Mistakes

The only real mistake is the one from which we learn nothing.

—John Powell

Even if you fall on your face, you're still moving forward.

—Victor Kiam

While one person hesitates because he feels inferior, the other is busy making mistakes and becoming superior.

—Henry C. Link

Remember, if you're headed in the wrong direction, God allows U-turns!

—Allison Gappa Bottke

Making a different mistake every day is not only acceptable, it is the definition of progress.

—Robert Brault

The essence of success is that it is never necessary to think of a new idea oneself. It is far better to wait until somebody else does it, and then to copy him in every detail, except his mistakes.

—Aubrey Menen

Mistakes are part of the dues one pays for a full life.

—Sophia Loren

If a mistake is not a stepping stone, it is a mistake.

—Eli Siegel

Making mistakes simply means you are learning faster.
—Weston H. Agor

From the errors of others, a wise man corrects his own.
—Syrus

You must learn from the mistakes of others. You can't possibly live long enough to make them all yourself.
—Sam Levenson

Our blunders mostly come from letting our wishes interpret our duties.
—Author Unknown

If you shut your door to all errors truth will be shut out.
—Rabindranath Tagore

It is very easy to forgive others their mistakes; it takes more grit to forgive them for having witnessed your own.
—Jessamyn West

Truth will sooner come out of error than from confusion.
—Francis Bacon

Mistakes are the usual bridge between inexperience and wisdom.
—Phyllis Theroux

An expert is a man who has made all the mistakes which can be made in a very narrow field.
—Niels Bohr

A man of genius makes no mistakes. His errors are volitional and are the portals of discovery.
—James Joyce

The man who makes no mistakes does not usually make anything.
—Edward Phelps

You will do foolish things, but do them with enthusiasm.

—Colette

I never make stupid mistakes. Only very, very clever ones.

—John Peel

To go wrong is sometimes the surest way to go right. It is not always down to depths: it is down, sometimes, to heights. I got my first perspective of heaven from hell.

—Muriel Strode-Lieberman (1875–1964),
My Little Book of Life, 1912

Creativity is allowing yourself to make mistakes. Art is knowing which ones to keep.

—Scott Adams

Do not fear mistakes. There are none.

—Miles Davis

Money

He who has money can eat sherbet in hell.

—Lebanese Proverb

I'd like to live as a poor man with lots of money.

—Pablo Picasso

Lack of money is the root of all evil.

—George Bernard Shaw

There are people who have money and people who are rich.

—Coco Chanel

Money is neither my god nor my devil. It is a form of energy that tends to make us more of who we already are, whether it's greedy or loving.

—Dan Millman

After a certain point money is meaningless. It ceases to be the goal. The game is what counts.

—Aristotle Onassis

I don't need the money dear. I work for art.

—Maria Callas

It is better to have a permanent income than to be fascinating.

—Oscar Wilde

To suppose as we all suppose, that we could be rich and not behave as the rich behave, is like supposing that we could drink all day and stay sober.

—Logan Pearsall Smith

He that wants money, means, and content is without three good friends.

—William Shakespeare

Money is flat because it's meant to be piled up.

—Proverb

Money won't create success. The freedom to make it will.

—Nelson Mandela

If you have a gun you can rob a bank. If you have a bank you can rob everybody.

—Bill Maher

Money is human happiness in the abstract; and so the man who is no longer capable of enjoying such happiness in the concrete, sets his whole heart on money.

—Arthur Schopenhauer, Parerga and Paralipomena, 1851

Your friend lends and your enemy asks payment.

—Dutch Proverb

To get rich you have to be making money while you are asleep.

—David Bailey

It's a kind of spiritual snobbery that makes people think they can be happy without money.

—Albert Camus

Money isn't the most important thing in life, but it's reasonably close to oxygen on the "gotta have it" scale.

—Zig Ziglar

You must spend money to make money.

—Plautus

Do not value money for any more nor any less than its worth; it is a good servant but a bad master.

—Alexandre Dumas Jr., Camille, 1852

I wish I'd said it first, and I don't even know who did: The only problems that money can solve are money problems.

—Mignon McLaughlin

The little money I have—that is my wealth, but the things I have for which I would not take money, that is my treasure.

—Robert Brault

Money will buy you a pretty good dog, but it won't buy the wag of his tail.

—Henry Wheeler Shaw

The economy depends about as much on economists as the weather does on weather forecasters.

—Jean-Paul Kauffmann

Empty pockets never held anyone back. Only empty heads and empty hearts can do that.

—Norman Vincent Peale

People are living longer than ever before, a phenomenon undoubtedly made necessary by the 30-year mortgage.

—Doug Larson

We live by the Golden Rule. Those who have the gold make the rules.
—Buzzie Bavasi

Always live within your income, even if you have to borrow money to do so.

—Josh Billings

Money is much more exciting than anything it buys.
—Mignon McLaughlin, The Second Neurotic's Notebook, 1966

If women didn't exist, all the money in the world would have no meaning.

—Aristotle Onassis

Inflation is when you pay fifteen dollars for the ten-dollar haircut you used to get for five dollars when you had hair.

—Sam Ewing

It is natural that affluence should be followed by influence.
—Augustus William Hare and Julius Charles Hare, Guesses at Truth, by Two Brothers, 1827

Money and women. They're two of the strongest things in the world. The things you do for a woman you wouldn't do for anything else. Same with money.

—Satchel Paige

By the time I have money to burn, my fire will have burnt out.
—Author Unknown

A bank is a place that will lend you money if you can prove that you don't need it.

—Bob Hope

They deem me mad because I will not sell my days for gold; and I deem them mad because they think my days have a price.

—Khalil Gibran

If you think nobody cares if you're alive, try missing a couple of car payments.

—Earl Wilson

Always borrow money from a pessimist, he doesn't expect to be paid back.

—Author Unknown

Money is nothing more than arrogance on paper.

—Hunter Brinkmeier

Never spend your money before you have it.

—Thomas Jefferson

Budget: a mathematical confirmation of your suspicions.

—A.A. Latimer

They who are of the opinion that money will do everything, may very well be suspected to do everything for money.

—George Savile, Complete Works, 1912

My problem lies in reconciling my gross habits with my net income.

—Errol Flynn

Money can't buy happiness, but it can buy you the kind of misery you prefer.

—Author Unknown

A dollar picked up in the road is more satisfaction to you than the ninety and nine which you had to work for, and money won at faro or in stocks snuggles into your heart in the same way.

—Mark Twain

If money is your hope for independence you will never have it. The only real security that a man will have in this world is a reserve of knowledge, experience, and ability.

—Henry Ford

A little satisfies the poor, while the rich never cease their longings.
—James Lendall Basford (1845–1915), Sparks from the Philosopher's Stone, 1882

The "line of beauty" is a curve something like the letter S, but it attracts more attention when it has a parallel line drawn through it, thus—$.
—Mary Wilson Little, Reveries of a Paragrapher, 1897

Life shouldn't be printed on dollar bills.

—Clifford Odets

There's no money in poetry, but then there's no poetry in money, either.
—Robert Graves

It is an unfortunate human failing that a full pocketbook often groans more loudly than an empty stomach.

—Franklin Roosevelt

Whoever said money cannot buy happiness simply didn't know where to go shopping.

—Bo Derek

It frees you from doing things you dislike. Since I dislike doing nearly everything, money is handy.

—Groucho Marx

In the old days a man who saved money was a miser; nowadays he's a wonder.

—Author Unknown

One may see the small value God has for riches by the people He gives them to.

        —Alexander Pope, Thoughts on Various Subjects, 1727

When it is a question of money, everybody is of the same religion.

        —Voltaire

Money is like water: in sufficient volume, it erodes the bedrock of principle, and cuts its own channel.

        —Dr. Idel Dreimer

The waste of money cures itself, for soon there is no more to waste.

        —M.W. Harrison

When your outgo exceeds your income your upkeep is your downfall.

        —Author unknown, c.1945

A man is usually more careful of his money than of his principles.

—Oliver Wendell Holmes, Jr., speech, Boston, 1897 January 8th

You don't seem to realize that a poor person who is unhappy is in a better position than a rich person who is unhappy, because the poor person has hope. He thinks money would help.

        —Jean Kerr

If inflation continues to soar, you're going to have to work like a dog just to live like one.

        —George Gobel

Never call an accountant a credit to his profession; a good accountant is a debit to his profession.

        —Charles J.C. Lyall

The real measure of your wealth is how much you'd be worth if you lost all your money.

        —Author Unknown

The difference between necessities and luxuries is generally measured by the pocketbook.
> —Mary Wilson Little, Reveries of a Paragrapher, 1897

To be clever enough to get a great deal of money, one must be stupid enough to want it.
> —George Bernard Shaw

It is said that for money you can have everything, but you cannot. You can buy food, but not appetite; medicine but not health; knowledge but not wisdom; glitter but not beauty; fun but not joy; acquaintances, but not friends; servants, but not faithfulness; leisure but not peace. You can have the husk of everything for money, but not the kernel.
> —Arne Garborg

At the back of every great fortune lies a great crime.
> —Honoré de Balzac

The only thing money gives is the freedom of not worrying about money.
> —Johnny Carson

I have enough money to last me the rest of my life unless I buy something.
> —Jackie Mason

There are no pockets in a shroud.
> —Author Unknown

I'm so poor I can't even pay attention.
> —Ron Kittle, 1987

A full purse makes disagreeable men, and even knaves, tolerable in society.
> —James Lendall Basford (1845–1915), Sparks from the Philosopher's Stone, 1882

Sometimes I think that all mankind
exist but to be bought and sold:
The rich man's paramour is gold,
the poor man's goddess, gold, gold, gold.
            —Frederic Ridgely Torrence, The House of a Hundred Lights:
                          A Psalm of Experience After Reading
                                    a Couplet of Bidpai, 1899

Opportunities

Jumping at several small opportunities may get us there more quickly
than waiting for one big one to come along.

—Hugh Allen

I think I don't regret a single 'excess' of my responsive youth—I only
regret, in my chilled age, certain occasions and possibilities I didn't
embrace.

—Henry James

Opportunity is as scarce as oxygen; men fairly breathe it and do not
know it.

—Doc Sane

Every day is an opportunity to make a new happy ending.

—Author Unknown

While the optimist and pessimist argue whether the glass is half full or
half empty the opportunist walks in and drinks it.

—Author Unknown

It is often hard to distinguish between the hard knocks in life and
those of opportunity.

—Frederick Phillips

I was seldom able to see an opportunity until it had ceased to be one.
—Mark Twain

If opportunity doesn't knock, build a door.

—Milton Barle

A pessimist is one who makes difficulties of his opportunities and an optimist is one who makes opportunities of his difficulties.

—Harry Truman

What I do know is that if one wants to get a boat ride, one must be near the river.

—Anchee Min, Becoming Madame Mao

Opportunities do not come with their values stamped upon them.

—Maltbie Babcock

Don't wait for extraordinary opportunities. Seize common occasions and make them great.

—Orison Swett Marden

Opportunities fly by while we sit regretting the chances we have lost, and the happiness that comes to us we heed not, because of the happiness that is gone.

—Jerome K. Jerome, The Idle Thoughts of
an Idle Fellow, 1889

As you seek new opportunity, keep in mind that the sun does not usually reappear on the horizon where last seen.

—Robert Brault

Grasp your opportunities, no matter how poor your health; nothing is worse for your health than boredom.

—Mignon McLaughlin, The Second Neurotic's
Notebook, 1966

Nothing is so often irretrievably missed as a daily opportunity.

—Marie von Ebner-Eschenbach

Optimism-Pessimism

The average pencil is seven inches long, with just a half-inch eraser—in case you thought optimism was dead.

—Robert Brault

I invented my life by taking for granted that everything I did not like would have an opposite, which I would like.

—Coco Chanel

The usefulness of a cup is in its emptiness.

—Chinese Proverb

Of course I look at the glass half full. The only time I would look at it half empty is when I think about how good the first half tasted.

—Drew Deyoung

In the long run the pessimist may be proved right, but the optimist has a better time on the trip.

—Daniel L. Reardon

The man who is not dead still has a chance.

—Lebanese Proverb

I always like to look on the optimistic side of life, but I am realistic enough to know that life is a complex matter.

—Walt Disney

A pessimist is a man who thinks all women are bad. An optimist is a man who hopes they are.

—Chauncey Mitchell Depew

The best way to dispel negative thoughts is to require that they have a purpose.

—Robert Brault

When you show deep empathy toward others, their defensive energy goes down, and positive energy replaces it. That's when you can get more creative in solving problems.

—Stephen Covey

Being an optimist after you've got everything you want doesn't count.

—Kin Hubbard

An optimist is a person who starts a new diet on Thanksgiving Day.

—Irv Kupcinet

Pessimist: One who, when he has the choice of two evils, chooses both.

—Oscar Wilde

An optimist is the human personification of spring.

—Susan J. Bissonette

After 5000 years of recorded human history, you wonder 'What part of 2,000,000 sunrises doesn't a pessimist understand'?

—Robert Brault

A pessimist is one who makes difficulties of his opportunities and an optimist is one who makes opportunities of his difficulties.

—Harry Truman

The optimist proclaims that we live in the best of all possible worlds; and the pessimist fears this is true.

—James Branch Cabell, The Silver Stallion, 1926

Optimists are nostalgic about the future.

—Chicago Tribune

Both optimists and pessimists contribute to our society. The optimist invents the airplane and the pessimist the parachute.

—Gil Stern

Most people plan by disaster. They think of what can go wrong and then they master it.

—Richard Bandler

In optimism there is magic. In pessimism there is nothing.

—Abraham–Hicks

An optimist stays up until midnight to see the New Year in. A pessimist stays up to make sure the old year leaves.

—Bill Vaughan

A pessimist sees only the dark side of the clouds, and mopes; a philosopher sees both sides, and shrugs; an optimist doesn't see the clouds at all—he's walking on them.

—Leonard Louis Levinson

Optimism is the foundation of courage.

—Nicholas Murray Butler

The nice part about being a pessimist is that you are constantly being either proven right or pleasantly surprised.

—George F. Will, The Leveling Wind

People

Whenever two people meet there are six present. There is the man as he sees himself, each as the other person sees him, and each man as he really is.

—William James

You are the average of the five people you spend the most time with.

—Jim Rohn

Most people do not listen with the intent to understand. They listen with the intent to reply.

—Stephen R. Covey

Who is wise? He that learns from everyone. Who is powerful? He that governs his passions. Who is rich? He that is content. Who is that? Nobody.

—Benjamin Franklin

Every man is as Nature made him and sometimes a great deal worse.

—Miguel de Cervantes

It's a desperately vexatious thing that, after all one's reflections and quiet determinations, we should be ruled by moods that one can't calculate on beforehand.

—George Eliot

The Texan turned out to be good-natured, generous and likeable. In three days no one could stand him.

—Joseph Heller

He has all the virtues I dislike and none of the vices I admire.

—Winston Churchill

We don't really understand human nature unless you know why a child on a merry-go-round will wave at his parents every time around – and why the parents will always wave back.

—Bill Tammeus

Men can bear all things except good days.

—Dutch Proverb

People are like holidays. Do others see you as Christmas, or more like Tax Day?

—Terri Guillemets

If it has anything to do with honesty, compassion, appreciating the silence of a winter morning, remembering to listen when the leaves fall and believing in magic, then my parents were, and still are, hippies.

—Cecily Schmidt, "Common Threads," in Wild Child: Girlhoods in the Counterculture edited by Chelsea Cain, 1999

Strong people have strong weaknesses.

—Peter Drucker

Men would not live long in society, were they not the mutual dupes of each other.

—François VI de la Rochefoucault

Skill is fine and genius is splendid, but the right contacts are more valuable than either.

—Author Unknown

It is well to remember that the entire universe, with one rifling exception, is composed of others.

—John Andrew Holmes

Men rise from one ambition to another: first, they seek to secure themselves against attack, and then they attack others.

—Niccolo Machiavelli

Stay away from "still" people. Still broke, still complaining, still hating and still nowhere.

—Author Unknown

Let no man pull you low enough to hate him.

—Martin Luther King

When I'm out and about, people are annoying idiots. When I'm home alone, all mankind is loving and good.

—Terri Guillemets

Always remember that you are absolutely unique. Just like everyone else.

—Margaret Mead

Eventually you come to realize that most people aren't looking for a fight but for someone to surrender to.

—Robert Brault

A hundred men together are the hundredth part of a man.
—Antonio Porchia, Voces, 1943, translated from Spanish
by W.S. Merwin

The total history of almost anyone would shock almost everyone.
—Mignon McLaughlin, The Neurotic's Notebook, 1960

It is the greatest mistake to think that man is always one and the same. A man is never the same for long. He is continually changing. He seldom remains the same even for half an hour.
—G.I. Gurdjieff

If we had no faults of our own, we would not take so much pleasure in noticing those of others.
—François VI de la Rochefoucault

A small man can be just as exhausted as a great man.
—Arthur Miller

The real problem is in the hearts of and minds of men. It is not a problem of physics but of ethics. It is easier to denature plutonium than denature the evil from the spirit of man.
—Albert Einstein

History teaches us that men and nations behave wisely once they have exhausted all other alternatives.
—Abba Eban

Bad friends will prevent you from having good friends.
—Author Unknown

Any business with customers is in the "people" business.
—Help Scout

Men in general judge more by the sense of sight than by the sense of touch, because anyone can see but only a few can text by feeling. Everyone sees what you seem to be, few know what you really are, and those few do not dare take a stand against the general opinion.
—Niccolo Machiavelli

It is just as difficult to free a people that wants to remain servile as it is to enslave a people that wants to remain free.

—Niccolo Machiavelli

Planning

Make no small plans for they have no power to stir the soul.

—Niccolo Machiavelli

Action without planning is a nightmare.

—Japanese Proverb

If you don't design your own life plan, chance are you will fall into someone else's plan. And guess what they have planned for you? Not much.

—Jim Rohn

I find it fascinating that most people plan their vacations with better care than they plan their lives. Perhaps that is because escape is easier than change.

—Jim Rohn

The reason why most people face the future with apprehension instead of anticipation is because they don't have it well designed.

—Jim Rohn

Philosophy

Everything is vague to a degree you do not realize until you have tried to make it precise.

—Bertrand Russell

If the complexity of the universe demands, as explanation, an intelligent creator—then, by the same reasoning—so does the intelligent creator.

—Dr. Idel Dreimer

Procrastination

Procrastination is opportunity's assassin.

—Victor Kiam

What may be done at any time will be done at no time.

—Scottish Proverb

Procrastination is the thief of time.

—Edward Young

Only put off until tomorrow what you are willing to die having left undone.

—Pablo Picasso

There are a million ways to lose a work day, but not even a single way to get one back.

—Tom DeMarco and Timothy Lister

Putting off an easy thing makes it hard. Putting off a hard thing makes it impossible.

—George Claude Lorimer

Never put off until tomorrow what you can do the day after tomorrow.

—Mark Twain

Tomorrow is the only day in the year that appeals to a lazy man.

—Jimmy Lyons

One of the greatest labor-saving inventions of today is tomorrow.

—Vincent T. Foss

The two rules of procrastination: 1) Do it today. 2) Tomorrow will be today tomorrow.

—Author unknown

To think too long about doing a thing often becomes its undoing.

—Eva Young

Tomorrow is often the busiest day of the week.

—Spanish Proverb

Know the true value of time. Snatch, seize and enjoy every moment of it. No idleness, no laziness, no procrastination. Never put off till tomorrow what you can do today.

—Lord Chesterfield

Procrastination is the art of keeping up with yesterday.

—Don Marquis

You may delay, but time will not.

—Benjamin Franklin

Never do today what you can put off till tomorrow. Delay may give clearer light as to what is best to be done.

—Aaron Burr

If you wait, all that happens is that you get older.

—Larry McMurtry

Procrastination is something best put off until tomorrow.

—Gerald Vaughan

A year from now you may wish you had started today.

—Karen Lamb

The best way to get something done is to begin.

—Author Unknown

Nothing is so fatiguing as the eternal hanging on of an uncompleted task.

—William James, letter to Carl Stumpf, 1886

To always be intending to live a new life, but never find time to set about it—this is as if a man should put off eating and drinking from one day to another till he be starved and destroyed.

—Walter Scott

Procrastination is like masturbation. At first it feels good, but in the end you're only screwing yourself.

—Author unknown

If you want to make an easy job seem mighty hard, just keep putting off doing it.

—Olin Miller

It is an undoubted truth, that the less one has to do, the less time one finds to do it in.

—Earl of Chesterfield

You know you are getting old when it takes too much effort to procrastinate.

—Author Unknown

Things dreaded require double time to accomplish them.

—James Lendall Basford (1845–1915), Sparks from the Philosopher's Stone, 1882

There's nothing to match curling up with a good book when there's a repair job to be done around the house.

—Joe Ryan

I do my work at the same time each day—the last minute.

—Author Unknown

The problem with putting off things you've always wanted to do is that eventually you run out of always.

—Robert Brault

Expect an early death—it will keep you busier.

—Martin H.

The time to begin most things is ten years ago.
—Mignon McLaughlin, The Second Neurotic's Notebook, 1966
Fischer

It is a job that has never started that takes the longest to finish.

—J.R. Tolkien

If it weren't for the last minute, I wouldn't get anything done.

—Author Unknown

Anyone can do any amount of work, provided it isn't the work he is supposed to be doing at that moment.

—Robert Benchley

Progress

Progress is impossible without change and those who cannot change their minds they cannot change anything.

—George Bernard Shaw

Make the workmanship surpass the materials.

—Ovid

Progress far from consisting in change, depends on retentiveness. When experience is not retained, as among savages, infancy is perpetual. Those who cannot remember the past are condemned to repeat it. This is the condition of children and barbarians, in whom instinct has learned nothing from experience.

—George Santayana

Technological progress has merely provided us with more efficient means for going backwards.

—Aldous Huxley

Progress is not created by contended people.

—Frank Tyger

If you always do what you always did, you will always get what you always got.

—Albert Einstein

Progress imposes not only new possibilities for the future but new restrictions.
—Norbert Wiener, The Human Use of Human Beings, 1950

Stupidity does not give way to science, technology, modernity, progress; on the contrary, it progresses right along with progress.

—Milan Kundera

Emergencies have always been necessary to progress. It was darkness which produced the lam. It was fog that produced the compass. It was hunger that drove us to exploration. And it took a depression to show us the value of a job.

—Victor Hugo

Belief in progress is a doctrine of idlers and Belgians. It is the individual relying upon his neighbors to do his work.

—Charles Baudelaire

So long as all the increased wealth which modern progress brings goes but to build up great fortunes, to increase luxury and make sharper the contrast between the House of Have and the House of Want, progress is not real and cannot be permanent.
—Henry George, Progress and Poverty, 1879

If it keeps up, man will atrophy all his limbs but the push-button finger.

—Frank Lloyd Wright

Economic advance is not the same thing as human progress.

—John Clapham, 1920s

*All of the biggest technological inventions created by man – the air-
plane, the automobile, the computer – says little about his intelligence, but speaks volumes about his laziness.*

—Mark Kennedy

*Western society has accepted as unquestionable a technological imper-
ative that is quite as arbitrary as the most primitive taboo: not merely
the duty to foster invention and constantly to create technological
novelties, but equally the duty to surrender to these novelties uncondi-
tionally, just because they are offered, without respect to their human
consequences.*

—Lewis Mumford

Results

*Always look at the solution, not the problem. Learn to focus on what
will bring results.*

—Author Unknown

*People love chopping wood. In this activity one immediately sees
results.*

—Attributed to Albert Einstein

Success is a result, not a goal.

—Author Unknown

Results come over time not overnight.

—Author Unknown

*It is an immutable law in business that words are words, explanations
are explanations, promises are promises but only performance is reality.*

—Harold Geneen

If you want to have something you never had, then you have to do something you never done.
In all human affairs there are efforts, and there are results and the strength of the effort is the measure of the result.

—James Allen

However beautiful the strategy you should occasionally look at the results.
—Winston Churchill

You can have results. You can have excuses. However, you cannot have both.

—Stephen Luke

There's a difference between interest and commitment. When you are interested in doing something you do it only when it's convenient. When you are committed to something you accept no excuses. Only results.
—Kenneth Blanchard

Our life always expresses the result of our dominant thoughts.
—Kierkegaard

Forget about style. Worry about results.
Everything in your life is a reflection of the result of a choice you have made. If you want a different result, make a different choice.

—Nisan Panwar

Insanity: doing the same thing over and over again and expecting different results.

—Albert Einstein

Don't upset by the results you didn't from the work you didn't do.
—Author Unknown

Big results require big ambitions.

—James Champy

I've always believed that if you put in the work, the results will come.

—Michael Jordan

If you focus on results, you will never change. If you focus on change, you will get results.

—Jack Dixon

You may never know what results come from your actions, but if you do nothing, there will be no results.

—Mahatma Ghandi

Once you see results, it becomes an addiction.

—Author Unknown

Risk

What you risk reveals what you value.

—Jeannette Winterson

Nothing risqué, nothing gained.

—Alexander Woollcott

There is the risk you cannot afford to take; there is the risk you cannot afford not to take.

—Peter Drucker

The torment of precautions often exceeds the dangers to be avoided. It is sometimes better to abandon one's self to destiny.

—Napoleon Bonaparte

To dare is to lose one's footing momentarily. To not dare is to lose oneself.

—Søren Kierkegaard

It's a shallow life that doesn't give a person a few scars.

—Garrison Keillor

A moderate adventure is no adventure.

—Terri Guillemets

This nation was built by men who took risks—pioneers who were not afraid of the wilderness, business men who were not afraid of failure, scientists who were not afraid of the truth, thinkers who were not afraid of progress and dreamers who were not afraid of action.

—Brooks Atkinson

Take risks: if you win, you will be happy; if you lose, you will be wise.

—Author Unknown

You'll always miss 100% of the shots you don't take.

—Wayne Gretzky

Only those who dare to fail greatly can ever achieve greatly.

—Robert F. Kennedy

A general is a man who takes chances. Mostly he takes a fifty-fifty chance; if he happens to win three times in succession he is considered a great general.

—Enrico Fermi

One cannot refuse to eat just because there is a chance of being choked.

—Chinese Proverb

Nothing will ever be attempted, if all possible objections must be first overcome.

—Samuel Johnson, Rasselas, 1759

Death is not the biggest fear we have; our biggest fear is taking the risk to be alive – the risk to be alive and express what we really are.

—Don Miguel Ruiz

The knowledge of the world is only to be acquired in the world, and not in a closet.

—Lord Chesterfield

Behold the turtle. He makes progress only when he sticks his neck out.

—James Bryant Conant

Security is mostly a superstition. It does not exist in nature, nor do the children of men as a whole experience it. God Himself is not secure, having given man dominion over His works! Avoiding danger is no safer in the long run than outright exposure. The fearful are caught as often as the bold.

—Helen Keller

Only those who risk going too far can possibly find out how far they can go.

—T.S. Eliot

He that leaves nothing to chance will do few things ill, but he will do very few things.

—George Savile

The healthy being craves an occasional wildness, a jolt from normality, a sharpening of the edge of appetite, his own little festival of the Saturnalia, a brief excursion from his way of life.

—Robert MacIver

Prudence keeps life safe, but does not often make it happy.

—Samuel Johnson

If you are not willing to risk the unusual, you will have to settle for the ordinary.

—Jim Rohn

Never test the depth of a river with both feet.

—Warren Buffett

Every man has the right to risk his own life in order to preserve it. Has it ever been said that a man who throws himself out the window to escape from a fire is guilty of suicide?

—Jean-Jacques Rousseau

Yes, risk taking is inherently failure-prone. Otherwise, it would be called sure-thing-taking.

—Tim McMahon

Life's greatest dangers are often found in apparently small risks.

—James Lendall Basford

What great thing would you attempt if you knew you could not fail?

—Robert H. Schuller

Skills

You must either modify your dreams or magnify your skills.

—Jim Rohn

Knowledge is not skill. Knowledge plus ten thousand times is skill.

—Shinichi Suzuki

Learn to hide your need and show your skill.

—Jim Rohn

Success is a learnable skill.

—T. Harv Ekker

When love and skill work together, expect a masterpiece.

—John Ruskin

Don't wish it was easier; wish you were better. Don't wish for less problems; wish for more skills. Don't wish for fewer challenges; wish for more wisdom.

—Jim Rohn

Learning how to learn is one of the most important skills in life.

—Nourma F. Fauziyah

Repetition is the mother of skill.

—Anthony Robbins

Technical skills may teach you the job but soft skills can make you or break you as a manager.

—Author Unknown

Practice is just as valuable as a sale. The sale will make you a living; the skill will make you a fortune.

—Jim Rohn

Success

Follow your passion, and success will follow you.

—Terri Guillemets

Success is getting what you want; happiness is wanting what you get.

—Dale Carnegie

The toughest thing about success is that you've got to keep on being a success.

—Irving Berlin

Success is 99 percent failure.

—Soichiro Honda

Success and failure. We think of them as opposites, but they're really not. They're companions—the hero and the sidekick.

—Laurence Shames

Try not to become a man of success, but rather try to become a man of value.

—Albert Einstein

Success is blocked by concentrating on it and planning for it.... Success is shy—it won't come out while you're watching.

—Tennessee Williams

I dread success. To have succeeded is to have finished one's business on earth, like the male spider, who is killed by the female the moment he has succeeded in courtship. I like a state of continual becoming, with a goal in front and not behind.

—George Bernard Shaw

Pray that success will not come any faster than you are able to endure it.

—Elbert Hubbard

The closer one gets to the top, the more one finds there is no "top."

—Nancy Barcus

Success does not lie in results but in efforts. Being the best is not so important. Doing the best is all that matters.

—Author Unknown

Something in human nature causes us to start slacking off at our moment of greatest accomplishment. As you become successful, you will need a great deal of self-discipline not to lose your sense of balance, humility, and commitment.

—Ross Perot

Some people succeed because they are destined to, but most people succeed because they are determined to.

—Author Unknown

Winning is overrated. The only time it is really important is in surgery and war.

—Al McGuire

Unless a man undertakes more than he possibly can do, he will never all that he can. Henry Drummon Strength, will power, determination and a pinch of you. That's the cocktail for success.

—Adarshd

Judge your success by what you had to give up in order to get it.

—Author Unknown

How can they say my life is not a success? Have I not for more than sixty years got enough to eat and escaped being eaten?

—Logan Smith

Success is often the result of taking a misstep in the right direction.

—Al Bernstein

Work hard in silence, success will make the noise.

—Author Unknown

Eighty percent of success is showing up.

—Woody Allen

Sometimes I worry about being a success in a mediocre world.

—Lily Tomlin

I couldn't wait for success... so I went ahead without it.

—Jonathan Winters

Destiny has two ways of crushing us—by refusing our wishes and by fulfilling them.

—Henri Frederic Amiel

Time

One can make a day of any size.

—John Muir

The past is a foreign country. They do things differently there.

—L.P. Hartley

Each day is an opportunity to travel back into tomorrow's past and change it.

—Robert Brault

Time is a great teacher, but unfortunately it kills all its pupils.

—Hector Berlioz

Leave your past behind you. It's history. It's not reality.

—Author Unknown

The wise man does at once what the fool does finally.

—Niccolo Machiavelli

Waste your money and you're only out of money, but waste your time and you've lost a part of your life.

—Michael Leboeuf

You will never find time for anything. If you want time you must make it.

—Charles Buxton

What would be the use of immortality to a person who cannot use well a half an hour?

—Ralph Waldo Emerson

It is said that the present is pregnant with the future.

—Voltaire

There must be a tomorrow, because my life overflows today.

—Lois Chartrand

Begin doing what you want to do now. We have only this moment, sparkling like a star in our hand, and melting like a snowflake.

—Marie Ray

When one subtracts from life infancy (which is vegetation), sleep, eating and swilling, buttoning and unbuttoning—how much remains of downright existence? The summer of a dormouse.

—Lord Byron

I could stand on a busy corner, hat in hand, and beg people to throw me all their wasted hours.

—Bernard Berenson

I try to treat each evening and weekend as little slices of retirement because no one is guaranteed a lengthy one at the end of their career.

—Mike Hammar

Lost time is never found again.

—Benjamin Franklin

No man is rich enough to buy back his past.

—Oscar Wilde

The time you think you're missing misses you too.

—Terri Guillemets

Men talk of killing time, while time quietly kills them.

—Dion Boucicault

The more side roads you stop to explore, the less likely that life will pass you by.

—Robert Brault

There's never enough time to do all the nothing you want.

—Bill Watterson, Calvin and Hobbes

Those who make the worst use of their time are the first to complain of its shortness.

—Jean de La Bruyère

Regret for wasted time is more wasted time.

—Mason Cooley

The butterfly counts not months but moments, and has time enough.

—Rabindranath Tagore

If you were going to die soon and had only one phone call you could make, who would you call and what would you say? And why are you waiting?

—Stephen Levine

No man is quick enough to enjoy life to the full.

—Spanish Proverb

Who knows whether the gods will add tomorrow to the present hour?

—Horace

The future, according to some scientists, will be exactly like the past, only far more expensive.

—John Sladek

Later never exists.

—Author Unknown

The future has a way of arriving unannounced.

—George F. Will

There's time enough, but none to spare.

—Charles W. Chesnutt

Time, which changes people, does not alter the image we have retained of them.

—Marcel Proust

Don't wait for the Last Judgment. It happens every day.

—Albert Camus

Years, following years, steal something every day;
At last they steal us from ourselves away.

—Horace

The future is like heaven, everyone exalts it but no one wants to go there now.

—James Baldwin

The future is made of the same stuff as the present.

—Simone Weil

I never think of the future. It comes soon enough.

—Albert Einstein

I believe the future is only the past again, entered through another gate.

—Arthur Wing Pinero

Tomorrow is fresh, with no mistakes in it.

—L.M. Montgomery

We should all be concerned about the future because we will have to spend the rest of our lives there.

—Charles F. Kettering

A preoccupation with the future not only prevents us from seeing the present as it is but often prompts us to rearrange the past.

—Eric Hoffer

He who seeks to know the future is out of harmony with the present.

—James Lendall Basford

An aging man cannot rewrite his youth but a youth may rewrite his own future.

—Terri Guillemets

The clock talked loud. I threw it away, it scared me what it talked.
—Tillie Olsen, Tell Me a Riddle

Trust

Love is giving someone the ability to destroy you—but trusting them not to.

—Author unknown

A wedding anniversary is the celebration of love, trust, partnership, tolerance and tenacity. The order varies for any given year.

—Paul Sweeney

You can only trust yourself... and barely that.

—Paige Wilson

Put not your trust in money, but put your money in trust.
—Oliver Wendell Holmes

I trust everyone. I just don't trust the devil inside them.
—Troy Kennedy-Martin

You may be deceived if you trust too much, but you will live in torment unless you trust enough.

—Frank Crane

Few delights can equal the mere presence of one whom we trust utterly.
—George MacDonald

A skeptic is a person who would ask God for his ID card.
—Edgar A. Shoaff

Ultimately, there can be no complete healing until we have restored our primal trust in life.

—Georg Feuerstein

Never trust a man who speaks well of everybody.

—John Churton Collins

Unemployment

It's a recession when your neighbor loses his job; it's a depression when you lose your own.

—Harry S Truman

The trouble with unemployment is that the minute you wake up in the morning you're on the job.

—Slappy White

We believe that if men have the talent to invent new machines that put men out of work, they have the talent to put those men back to work.

—John F. Kennedy

Unemployment diminishes people. Leisure enlarges them.

—Mason Cooley

You take my life when you do take the means whereby I live.

—William Shakespeare

Cessation of work is not accompanied by cessation of expenses.

—Cato the Elder

The hardest work in the world is being out of work.

—Whitney Young

Unemployment is like a headache or a high temperature – unpleasant and exhausting but not carrying in itself any explanation of its cause.

—William Henry Beveridge

When we're unemployed, we're called lazy; when the whites are unemployed it's called a depression.

—Jesse Jackson

Hunger is not the worst feature of unemployment; idleness is.

—William E. Barrett

Wealth

Wealth is like sea-water; the more we drink, the thirstier we become.

—Arthur Schopenhauer

Men would live exceedingly quiet if these two words, mine and thine were taken away.

—Anaxagoras

It isn't necessary to be rich and famous to be happy. It's only necessary to be rich.

—Alan Alda

Life, liberty, and property do not exist because men have made laws. On the contrary, it was the fact that life, liberty, and property existed beforehand that caused men to make laws in the first place.

—Frederic Bastiat

Luxury... corrupts at once rich and poor, the rich by possession and the poor by covetousness.

—Rousseau, The Social Contract, 1762

Human prosperity never rests but always craves more, till blown up with pride it totters and falls. From the opulent mansions pointed at by all passers-by none warns it away, none cries, "Let no more riches enter!"

—Aeschylus

Someday I want to be rich. Some people get so rich they lose all respect for humanity. That's how rich I want to be.

—Rita Rudner

It is generally agreed, that few men are made better by affluence or exaltation.

—Samuel Johnson

I am what is mine. Personality is the original personal property.

—Norman Brown

Whenever there is a conflict between human rights and property rights, human rights must prevail.

—Abraham Lincoln

The things you own end up owning you. It's only after you lose everything that you're free to do anything.

—Author Unknown

When prosperity comes, do not use all of it.

—Confucius

We've got the most prosperous culture in human history and we've also got the biggest spiritual hole in human history.

—Mark Victor Hansen

As prosperity is promoted, thinking is demoted.

—Martin H. Fischer (1879–1962)

Few rich men own their property; the property owns them.

—Robert Ingersoll

By abolishing private property one takes away the human love of aggression.

—Sigmund Freud

(Con)Fusing Life, Leadership and Business

If you were truly you, who would you be?

—Danai Krokou

(Yes. This is my question to you! Can you take some time and answer it before you finish this book?)

Maya Angelou once said "If you are always trying to be normal, you will never know how amazing you can be." People have a hard time finding their direction in life and career. Life is complex. This complexity is reflected in all the statements you have read in this book. Each topic can be seen from countless angles. Making sense out of life is tough business. Society by its own perceptions and boundaries wants us to fit in a certain category. What happens though when your own definition of who you are or what you stand for does not match the definition society has bestowed upon you? Who wins then? Who defines you? Who has the last word? Whose truth is most likely to determine your future life and career? The answer is pretty simple. The definition that *you choose* to believe wins. Our worldviews, habits, goals, career paths and life choices depend on this very definition. Therefore, it's crucial that you get it right. Fulfillment is not a destination. It's a by-product of right choices. The result of aligning your goals with your natural talents and inclinations. People who don't have goals work for people who do.

Defining yourself outside of the realms of society is tough. It is hard to recognize when one's choices and direction are being influenced by others' definition of who they should be, what kind of career they should be pursuing, and what kind of existence they should be leading. Every single quote is a possible life stance. Have you decided on yours yet? Through reading *Power Quotes* you must have come across a number of statements that made you tick. Quotes that made you pause and reflect to what extent they do or could possibly apply to your specific life circumstances. These quotes are the ones you should be adding on your desktop wallpaper, your phone and calendar to keep yourself motivated every day or whenever you feel you need a generous amount of self-motivation. Pick a quote and make it your tagline for the day, week or month. Changing the world requires a change of perspective. Most importantly, changing the world requires that you change *your* illusions. Ultimately, your life is what you think you should be. That's what you are right now. You are what you thought you should be. Your thoughts are as important as your actions. We live in challenging, rapidly changing and delicate times. It is now more important than ever that our minds, our inner worlds expand at the same pace as the outer world. It is time for atonement. It is time for radical change. Embrace it. Lead it.

I believe that each one of us is equipped with the necessary tools to overcome our own limits. How early on in life these tools will be discovered and used depends on the particular circumstances one is born in and the amount of challenges they are willing to take in life. As a quote by an unknown author goes "If you do not dare to imagine and build a better life for yourself, you will have the life you deserve." I hope that the quotes you read inspired you and most importantly I hope that they shook you up enough. I also hope that you felt the urge to act. Don't wait. Don't procrastinate. Some quotes have resonated with you more than others. I do hope that you noted them down. Make them your personal mantra. Live by them and share them.

It is for the sake of clarity that I decided to divide this book into three main sections and treat each one of them separately. However, I would not have included these three apparently distinct areas of life in a same volume if no convergence was possible. Many topics of these three main areas certainly overlap but what is interesting to notice is their point of convergence, their area of fusion. It might sound evident that Life rules can be applied to Business and Leadership and this can function the other way around of course. People tend to separate different areas of their life. They regard work as a separate area. Their personal life being another. I am far from being a centenarian but what life has taught me so far is that all these three areas complement each other and function like communicating vessels. It has also taught me that focused efforts and smart work in *any one* of these areas—be it Life, Leadership, or Business—can produce results in *all* three of them.

I have encountered countless successful professionals who lead guilt-rotten lives because they invest all their waking time in their careers and feel that they cannot reap the benefits of this investment in other parts of their life. Be a multitude of people. That's what makes you unique as a professional, a friend, a lover, a parent. You don't have to perceive dedication to your career goals and ambitions as an enemy to your personal life. Mix them all. Combine all three areas of your life in a way that works best for you. Master the art of congruent living. Seduce people through your work, your mind, your character, your unique combination of skills and talents. Your personality, your very being is instilled in every bit of the work your produce. It is present in all the projects you get involved in. As a Buddhist proverb goes "To know and not to do...is not to know." It is now time that you get out there and live at the fullest, merging Life, Business and Leadership, mixing vocation and profession. This holistic approach to personal growth will help you invest time, energy, and effort in one area while reaping results in all three.

About the Author

Danai Krokou was born in Corfu, a Greek island in the Ionian Sea. She left her hometown at age 17 to study and work in numerous countries around the world. She is an international development consultant, Chinese market investment specialist, entrepreneur, and passionate polyglot. She studied in France, the United Kingdom, Spain, Denmark, and China. She holds three master's (MA, MSc) degrees. She majored in French Linguistics and Literature, in International Politics, and in Business. She is fluent in seven languages, including Mandarin Chinese. She started her first business at age 25 in Shanghai, China and is one of the youngest female entrepreneurs in Asia. She is the author of a series of business books aimed at Western SMEs and investors who seek to understand and ideally enter the Chinese market.

For more information visit: www.danaikrokou.com

Index

OTHER TITLES IN THE HUMAN RESOURCE MANAGEMENT AND ORGANIZATIONAL BEHAVIOR COLLECTION

- *Human Resources as Business Partner: How to Maximize the Value and Financial Contribution of HR* by Tony Miller
- *How to Manage Your Career: The Power of Mindset in Fostering Success* by Kelly Swingler
- *Infectious Innovation: Secrets of Transforming Employee Ideas into Dramatic Revenue Growth* by James Allan
- *HR Analytics and Innovations in Workforce Planning* By Tony Miller
- *Deconstructing Management Maxims, Volume I: A Critical Examination of Conventional Business Wisdom* by Kevin Wayne
- *Deconstructing Management Maxims, Volume II: A Critical Examination of Conventional Business Wisdom* by Kevin Wayne
- *The Real Me: Find and Express Your Authentic Self* by Mark Eyre
- *Across the Spectrum: What Color Are You?* by Stephen Elkins-Jarrett
- *The Human Resource Professional's Guide to Change Management: Practical Tools and Techniques to Enact Meaningful and Lasting Organizational Change* by Melanie J. Peacock
- *Tough Calls: How to Move Beyond Indecision and Good Intentions* by Linda D. Henman
- *21st Century Skills for Non-Profit Managers: A Practical Guide on Leadership and Management* by Don Macdonald
- *Agile Human Resources: Creating a Sustainable Future for the HR Profession* by Kelly Swingler

Announcing the Business Expert Press Digital Library

Concise e-books business students need for classroom and research

This book can also be purchased in an e-book collection by your library as

- a one-time purchase,
- that is owned forever,
- allows for simultaneous readers,
- has no restrictions on printing, and
- can be downloaded as PDFs from within the library community.

Our digital library collections are a great solution to beat the rising cost of textbooks. E-books can be loaded into their course management systems or onto students' e-book readers.
The **Business Expert Press** digital libraries are very affordable, with no obligation to buy in future years. For more information, please visit **www.businessexpertpress.com/librarians**. To set up a trial in the United States, please email **sales@businessexpertpress.com**.